advancing learning, changing lives

Edexcel GCE History

Henry VIII: Authority, Nation and Religion 1509–1540

Alastair Armstrong

Series editors: Martin Collier   Rosemary Rees

Unit 2 Student Book

A PEARSON COMPANY

Heinemann is an imprint of Pearson Education Limited, a company incorporated in England and Wales, having its registered office at Edinburgh Gate, Harlow, Essex, CM20 2JE. Registered company number: 872828

www.heinemann.co.uk

Heinemann is a registered trademark of Pearson Education Limited

Text © Alastair Armstrong 2008

First published 2008

12 11 10 09
10 9 8 7 6 5 4 3

British Library Cataloguing in Publication Data is available from the British Library on request.

ISBN 978 0 435 30810 0

Edited by Florence Production Ltd, Stoodleigh, Devon
Designed by Florence Production Ltd, Stoodleigh, Devon
Typeset by Florence Production Ltd, Stoodleigh, Devon
Produced by Florence Production Ltd, Stoodleigh, Devon
Cover design by Siu Hang Wong
Picture research by Zooid Pictures
Printed in China (CTPS/03)

Acknowledgements
The author and publisher would like to thank the following individuals and organisations for permission to reproduce photographs:

© Visual Arts Library (London)/Alamy p. iv; © Paris, Bibliothèque Nationale/akg-images p. 14; © Ashmolean Museum, University of Oxford, UK/Bridgeman Art Library p. 36; © Visual Arts Library (London)/Alamy p. 79

Every effort has been made to contact copyright holders of material reproduced in this book. Any omissions will be rectified in subsequent printings if notice is given to the publishers.

Dedication
For Harry and Oliver.

Contents

Introduction

The image opposite comes from the title page of the Great Bible – the first authorised edition of the Bible in English, published in April 1539. The title page shows Henry dispensing the Word of God, like Christ himself. On his left is Thomas Cromwell, his leading minister, and on his right is Thomas Cranmer, Archbishop of Canterbury. The Word of God is passed down to the king's subjects who cry out 'God save the King'.

Up to this point the Bible had only been published in Latin. When the first edition of the Great Bible appeared an injunction was published by Thomas Cromwell stating that a copy of it should be set up in every parish church in the country. By the end of Henry VIII's reign there was a copy of the Bible in English in 9,000 parish churches. The publication of this Bible tells us a great deal about the religious and political changes that took place during Henry's reign.

In many ways this title page, drawn by Hans Holbein, was a piece of sixteenth-century propaganda. In 1534 Henry had replaced the Pope as head of the Church in England, and Holbein's work reinforced Henry's royal supremacy. He, not the Pope, dispenses the Word of God. Moreover his nobles, clergy and subjects rejoice in Henry's position proclaiming 'vivat rex' and 'God save the king!' The translation of the Bible into English also confirmed the national identity of the Church as one free from papal laws. Now English priests could preach the Word of God in English, and confirm Henry's authority at the same time. What makes this Bible so extraordinary is that for the first twenty years of Henry's reign it would have been very dangerous to publish, read or purchase an English Bible. Indeed one of the first men to translate the Bible into English, William Tyndale, had been tried for heresy in Antwerp and burned at the stake in 1536. His last words were reported to have been 'Lord! Open the King of England's eyes'. Three years later Henry's eyes were opened but it would be wrong to see Henry as a radical religious reformer just because he cut English ties with Rome. Henry's personal circumstances and the future of the Tudor dynasty go a long way to explaining his need to break with Rome. Yet that decision to establish an English Church changed the religious and political make up of Britain for ever.

Opposite: The title page of *The Great Bible*, published in 1539.

The break with Rome and the Royal Supremacy

1509 – Henry VIII becomes king

1515 – Thomas Wolsey, Archbishop of York, is made Lord Chancellor of England and Cardinal

1517 – The Protestant Reformation begins; Martin Luther nails his '95 Theses' against the Catholic practice of selling indulgences on the church door at Wittenberg

1521 – Henry VIII receives the title 'Defender of the Faith' from Pope Leo X for his opposition to Luther

1529 – Henry VIII dismisses Lord Chancellor Thomas Wolsey for failing to obtain the Pope's consent to his divorce from Catherine of Aragon; Sir Thomas More appointed Lord Chancellor; Henry VIII summons the 'Reformation Parliament' and begins to cut the ties with the Roman Catholic Church

1533 – Henry VIII marries Anne Boleyn and is excommunicated by Pope Clement VII; Thomas Cranmer appointed Archbishop of Canterbury

1534 – Act of Supremacy: Henry VIII declared Supreme Head of the Church of England

1535 – Sir Thomas More is beheaded in the Tower of London for failing to take the Oath of Supremacy

1536 – Anne Boleyn is beheaded; Henry VIII marries Jane Seymour; dissolution of monasteries in England begins under the direction of Thomas Cromwell, completed in 1539.

1537 – Jane Seymour dies after the birth of a son, the future Edward VI

1540 – Henry VIII marries Anne of Cleves following negotiations by Thomas Cromwell; Henry divorces Anne of Cleves and marries Catherine Howard; Thomas Cromwell executed on charge of treason

Tasks

1 Do some research on the three key figures we have mentioned in this introduction:

- Henry VIII
- Thomas Cromwell
- Thomas Cranmer.

Write up a mini biography for each man in which you fill in the missing details.

- Name:
- Date of Birth:
- Title:
- Family:
- Known for:
- Milestones:
- Death:

The Tudor dynasty

Key questions

- What was the legacy left by Henry VII on his death to his son Henry VIII?
- How far did the accession of Henry VIII in 1509 mark a new era in English kingship?

Timeline

1485	Henry VII became King after defeating Richard III at the Battle of Bosworth
1491	Henry VIII born at Greenwich Palace
1501	Arthur, Prince of Wales and Catherine of Aragon married
1502	Arthur died
1503	Julius II grants dispensation for Henry and Catherine's betrothal
1509	21 April, Henry VII died 11 June, Henry VIII marries Catherine of Aragon 23 June, Henry VIII's coronation
1510	March, Truce with France renewed August, Empson and Dudley executed
1512	February, War with France and Scotland Wolsey comes to prominence.

We will unite the white rose and the red:
Smile, heaven, upon this fair conjunction,
That long hath frowned upon their enmity!

Now civil wounds are stopped, peace lives again:
That she may long live here, God say Amen!

William Shakespeare, *Richard III*, v. iv. 32–4, 53–4

Questions

1 What is meant by Shakespeare's line *We will unite the white rose and the red*?
2 What are the *civil wounds* referred to by Shakespeare?
3 The play was written partly for the pleasure of Queen Elizabeth I (daughter of Henry VIII). How might this affect its reliability as a historical source?

These words were written by England's most famous playwright, William Shakespeare, in 1592–93. In this play Shakespeare examines Richard of Gloucester's rise and fall as King Richard III, and leaves us in 1485 after the Battle of Bosworth. In that battle Richard loses his horse and is killed by the Earl of Richmond, who is declared King Henry VII, the agent of a new order in England. The Tudor dynasty had begun.

SKILLS BUILDER

Throughout this chapter you will find out about Henry VII and Henry VIII, setting the scene for your study of Henry VIII. You will be asked to plan out an answer to the following question:

How far did Henry VIII's reign begin a new era in Tudor kingship?

To help you plan this answer, as you read through the chapter make notes on the following topics for each King:

- his character
- how he controlled factions
- his foreign policy.

Who was Henry VII?

- Accession: 1485, having defeated Richard III at the Battle of Bosworth.
- Claim to throne: weak blood claim through his mother Margaret Beaufort. Her great grandfather was John of Gaunt whose marriage to Catherine Swynford had been legitimised only on condition that no descendants should use it to claim the throne.
- Childhood: Henry spent his younger years in exile, in Brittany, with his uncle, Jasper Tudor, after the Lancastrian defeat in 1471.
- Achievements: on becoming King he initiated a number of policies designed to consolidate his right to rule and secure the Tudor dynasty, e.g. marriage to Elizabeth of York. Survived several high-profile rebellions from the **White Rose Party** and was able to pass on the Crown to his second son, Henry VIII, in 1509.
- Reputation: careful, conscientious and spendthrift ruler. Closer scrutiny reveals he was willing to spend money on his court, and grand banquets, processions and jousts were commonplace.
- Foreign policy: avoided war and generally unadventurous, apart from one expedition to France in 1492.
- Domestic policy: centred on swelling the Crown coffers and keeping the nobility in check.
- Controlling the aristocracy: aristocrats were kept in line through a system of **bonds and recognisances** that threatened financial ruin for any noble that proved to be disloyal.
- Family: Henry's later years were marked by tragedy as his eldest son, Arthur, died in 1502 and his wife Elizabeth followed him to the grave a year later. Arthur had been married to Catherine of Aragon for five months in a match designed to seal an Anglo-Spanish alliance. Papal dispensation was received in 1503 for Catherine to marry Henry VIII, but this wedding would not take place until after Henry VII's death.

Definitions

White Rose Party

Relatives of the Yorkist line replaced by Henry VII in 1485 were known as the White Rose Party. The Tudors were the last remaining branch of the House of Lancaster, which was descended from Edward III's fourth son, John of Gaunt. The House of York was descended from Edward III's third son, Lionel.

Bonds and recognisances

These were contracts between the nobility and the Crown in which the aristocracy promised to remain loyal to the King. If a noble breached that bond of good behaviour he would face a large fine. A particularly disruptive noble may have to find other leading men to sign surety bonds on his behalf, and therefore a whole network of bonds and recognisances might emerge.

Source A

After 1502 Henry VII began to treat his people with more harshness and severity than had been his custom, in order to ensure they remained more thoroughly and entirely in obedience to him. The people themselves had another explanation for his action, for they considered they were suffering not on account of their own sins but on account of the greed of their monarch. It is not indeed clear whether at the start it was greed; but afterwards greed did indeed become apparent, so irresolute, vacillating and corrupted are all human purposes.

Polydore Vergil, *Anglica Historia*, 1555

SKILLS BUILDER

In evaluating a historical source you need to look very carefully at the author and the date of the source. The *Anglica Historia* was a history of England, first published in 1535. It ends with the death of Henry VII. Do you think it is likely that Vergil would have written the above account during Henry VII's reign?

Take it further

Find out more about Polydore Vergil.

Definitions

The Wars of the Roses (1455–85)

A series of civil wars in England, which started during the weak monarchy of Henry VI; named from the emblems of the two rival branches of the House of Plantagenet, York (white rose) and Lancaster (red rose).

Agrarian society

A society and economy that is based on farming and working the land.

Henry VII's kingdom

- At the start of the sixteenth century England was recovering from thirty years of civil war between the Houses of Lancaster and York known as **the Wars of the Roses**. The result of this war was a decrease in the authority of the Crown.

- The Crown had changed hands six times from the time of Henry VI's mental breakdown in 1453 to Henry VII's victory over Richard III at Bosworth in 1485.

- By 1500 the population of England was still recovering after the Black Death (1348–49). There were approximately 2.5 million people living in England in 1500. England's only city of any size or stature was London. Outside London the largest towns were Norwich, Bristol, Exeter, York and Coventry but none had a population of over 12,000. By continental standards England had few towns of any size.

- England was an **agrarian society**; 90 per cent of the population lived in the countryside. England's main exports throughout the Tudor period were wool and cloth. The gradual rise in population throughout the sixteenth century created an increase in demand for cereals and this in turn led to a growth in agricultural prices, as demand often outstripped supply. Pressure on land, unemployment, inflation and food shortages were all problems faced by Tudor governments throughout the sixteenth century.

- Parliament consisted of a House of Lords and a House of Commons. The Lords was made up of secular peers and ecclesiastical leaders.

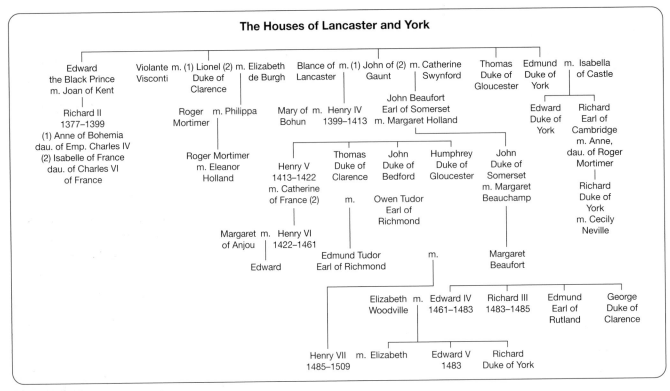

1.1 The families of York and Lancaster.

Definitions

Privy Council

Inner cabinet consisting of the King's leading ministers. It has been argued that this more formal advisory body developed in the reign of Henry VIII under Thomas Cromwell.

Humanism

An intellectual movement based on the study of the classical world. Renaissance humanists aimed to revive classical culture and relate the literature and languages of Greek and Latin to modern life.

The Commons housed leading representatives of county communities. The King could summon and dismiss parliament at will and parliamentary sessions were usually short. Parliament's two main functions were to grant taxation and ratify legislation. It played little part in policy making. Instead, for advice, the King would turn to the **Privy Council**, which was made up of leading nobles and churchmen.

- Law and order in the localities was generally upheld by regional magnates. Justices of the Peace were appointed to ensure that the royal will was carried out. Their number increased under Henry VII but they remained unpaid and not entirely effective. Outlying border areas on the borders of Scotland and Wales were notoriously lawless.

- Religiously the inhabitants of England were bound together in their loyalty towards the Catholic Church, and Christian rites and sacraments were central to people's lives.

- Culturally England was something of a backwater at the start of the sixteenth century. It had only two universities, Oxford and Cambridge, and the influence of **humanism** arrived late.

What was Henry VII's legacy to his son?

Keeping the nobility in check

Henry VII was wary of the English nobility. Over the course of the fifteenth century, the nobility had grown in power. The Wars of the Roses demonstrated the power of key nobles such as Richard Neville, the Earl of

Warwick, who was influential in the deposition of both Henry VI and Edward IV. Henry VII was determined to restore the authority of the Crown and keep the nobility in line. In reality he was fortunate that many leading noble lines had died out and he himself had few blood relatives. At the same time he was careful not to create too many new peers and imposed a strict system of bonds and recognisances on the aristocracy of England (see page 2). Henry VII established the **Council Learned in the Law** to oversee the administration of bonds and recognisances. By the end of Henry VII's reign the Council Learned was deeply unpopular, but Henry VIII unquestionably benefited from this restoration of royal authority.

Was Henry VII's policy towards the nobility a success?

> **Definition**
>
> **Council Learned in the Law**
>
> Established in 1495, the Council Learned in the Law was so called because its members were all legally trained. The role of this council was to defend the King's position as a feudal landlord and make sure that he received all the financial dues owed to him.

Source B

Bacon has a story of how, to the great rejoicing of the whole court, Henry VII's pet monkey tore up the notebook in which the King had recorded the characters and demeanours of those about him. This trivial incident, whether or not it actually occurred, encapsulates the essence and the fragility of Henry's rule. It perhaps also suggests a certain superficiality of achievement despite all the auguries of change: an impermanence, a fragility caused in part by the tensions that Henry VII himself caused in binding and dividing the ruling elites.

M Condon, Ruling Elites in the Reign of Henry VII in
C D Ross (ed.) *Patronage, Pedigree and Power
in the late Medieval England*, 1979

Source C

Out of sixty-two peerage families in existence between 1485 and 1509, a total of forty-six or forty-seven were for some part of Henry's reign at the King's mercy. Seven were under attainder, thirty-six gave bonds and recognisances, and three more were fined. Only sixteen remained free of financial threats. A situation arose in which a majority of the peerage were legally and financially in the King's power and at his mercy. The system was so extensive that it must have created an atmosphere of chronic watchfulness, suspicion and fear.

J.R. Lander, *Bonds, Coercion and Fear;
Henry VII and the Peerage*, 1971

SKILLS BUILDER

1 Make a list of points on which these sources all agree.

2 What can you learn from these sources about how successful Henry VII was in keeping the nobles in check?

Securing the dynasty

Henry VII united the Houses of Lancaster and York through his marriage to Elizabeth of York. Furthermore he withstood several attempts to challenge his crown. Yorkist opponents created pretenders to the throne, such as Lambert Simnel and Perkin Warbeck.

- Lambert Simnel was made out to be Edward, Earl of Warwick, who had a better claim to the throne than Henry VII. The real Warwick was in the tower, but this did not prevent Yorkist sympathisers at home and abroad rallying around Simnel and using him as a figurehead to try to knock the new Tudor monarch off the throne. As a result, in 1487 Henry VII had to defeat a Yorkist army at Stoke in order to maintain his throne.

Questions

1 Do you agree that Henry VII's main achievement was actually remaining in power and securing the Tudor line? Explain your answer.

2 What might have happened had the young Henry (future Henry VIII) died?

- Between 1491–99 Henry VII faced the Warbeck conspiracy in which leading Yorkists proclaimed another relatively obscure figure to be Richard of York, second son of Edward IV. Warbeck received support from Ireland, the Holy Roman Emperor **Maximilian** and **James IV** of Scotland (see page 64) among others before he was finally captured and executed in 1499. These Yorkist plots go to show just how fragile Henry VII's throne was in the years 1485–1500.

- Even after the Warbeck conspiracy was over, there remained dangerous Yorkist claimants such as Edmund de la Pole, Earl of Suffolk, and his brother Richard. By the end of his reign Henry had imprisoned Suffolk but Richard remained at large on the continent. Thus, Henry had done much to secure the Tudor dynasty and stave off Yorkist threats. Henry VIII would finish off the purge of the Pole family in the 1530s but he can be grateful to his father for his relatively calm and unchallenged accession to the throne in 1509.

Source D

Henry VII's problem of security was not solved with the deaths of Warbeck and of Warwick in 1499. Not until 1506 could he feel that so far as Yorkist claimants were concerned he had little to fear. But by then his dynastic hopes had come to rest solely upon his surviving son Henry.

S.B. Chrimes, *Henry VII*, 1972

Foreign affairs and diplomacy

Henry VII avoided foreign conflict where possible because warfare was expensive and England's resources were relatively meagre compared to the rest of Europe. Added to this was the fact that Henry VII had his work cut out securing his own throne, and he could not afford to spend the time or money carrying out foreign adventures. Although Henry VII did launch an invasion of France in 1491, it was relatively half-hearted and designed to achieve three things:

1 save face over the loss of Breton independence

2 attain a sizeable pension from the French King

3 a promise that France would not support Yorkist rebels.

In this Henry VII was successful, but for the most part his foreign policy revolved around diplomacy and the creation of marriage alliances. Most significant was the marriage treaty with Spain in 1489 that eventually resulted in the wedding of **Catherine of Aragon** (see page 83) to **Prince Arthur** (see page 85), eldest son of Henry VII.

However, the death of Prince Arthur in 1502, after only five months of marriage, endangered the Anglo-Spanish alliance. In 1503 Catherine was betrothed to the 12-year-old Prince Henry, the only surviving male heir to the English throne. The necessary dispensation for the marriage between Henry and his brother's widow was received from Pope Julius II in 1503 although the marriage itself did not take place for another six years. Catherine remained in England during this period although it was far from certain at times whether the marriage would actually take place, as Henry VII and her father Ferdinand of Spain continued to use her as a diplomatic pawn.

Therefore, in 1509, Henry VIII had cause to be grateful to his father on several counts:

- the Crown's finances were in good health
- the localities were by and large under control
- the authority of the Crown had been restored
- a ready-made marriage alliance with Spain awaited.

Contemporary views of Henry VII

Source E

He [Henry VII] likes to be spoken about and looked up to by the whole world. In this he fails because he is not a great man. Although he claims many virtues, his love of money is too great. He spends all the time he is not in public or in his Council in writing his accounts of his expenses with his own hand.

The Spanish Ambassador writes home to Ferdinand and Isabella in 1489

Source F

Henry VII's politic wisdom in governance was singular, his wit always quick and ready, his reason pithy and substantial, his memory fresh and holding, his experience notable, his counsels fortunate and taken by wise deliberation, his speech gracious in diverse languages, his person godly and amiable, his natural complexion of the purest mixture, his issue fair and in good number; leagues and confederacies he had with all Christian princes, his mighty power was dreaded everywhere, not only within his realm but without also; his people were to him in as humble subjection as ever they were to king.

Henry VII's funeral oration delivered by John Fisher, Bishop of Rochester, 1509

SKILLS BUILDER

1 Why do sources E and F differ in their outlook on Henry VII? Think carefully here about the role of an ambassador in the sixteenth century as well as the purpose of a funeral oration.

2 Having read through the information about Henry VII's reign, create a summary of the strengths, weaknesses, opportunities and threats that you think Henry VIII inherited in 1509.

Definition

Chivalry

A medieval code relating to the forms and conventions of aristocratic warrior lifestyle. The chivalric spirit was reinvented during the Renaissance as a means of projecting the power and grandeur of sixteenth-century monarchs.

How can we tell that Henry VIII was going to rule differently from his father?

Foreign policy

It was clear from the start that Henry VIII would rule differently from his father. Henry was not interested in paperwork and administration. Instead he dreamed of re-asserting England's traditional claim to the Crown of France. Henry wanted to replicate the glories of previous warrior kings such as Edward III and **Henry V** (see page 12), and in the process project an image of strong, personal Renaissance kingship on the rest of Europe. He believed that it was his **chivalric** duty to wage war on France and he was unwilling to listen to councillors who advised him to continue with Henry VII's cautious policies.

Men such as **William Warham** (Archbishop of Canterbury and Lord Chancellor) and Richard Fox (Lord Privy Seal) were adamant that war was expensive and fruitless. Although Henry was rather tricked by them into signing a peace settlement with **Louis XII**, King of France, in 1510, it was not long before plans were afoot for an invasion of France in 1512. He was supported in this aggressive policy by an old soldier, **Thomas Howard**, the Earl of Surrey, and by his new wife Catherine of Aragon who was eager to promote her father's interests. Although the young, exuberant and bellicose Henry VIII did not want to replicate the foreign policy of his father, it became clear to him that England's resources simply could not support a sustained period of warfare and that more pragmatic decisions had to be taken.

Biography

William Warham (1450–1532)

Archbishop of Canterbury and Lord Chancellor from 1504. In 1509 he crowned Henry VIII and Catherine of Aragon, but Warham represented the cautious policies of the old regime, from which Henry VIII was eager to disassociate himself. In 1515 Warham resigned to be replaced by Thomas Wolsey.

Biography

Louis XII (1462–1515)

King of France from 1498, and known as the *Father of the People*. In 1514 he married Henry VIII's sister, Mary Tudor. His reign was devoted to the Italian Wars, foreign adventures that proved costly and fruitless.

Biography

Thomas Howard, 2nd Duke of Norfolk, Earl of Surrey (1443–1524)

Fought against Henry VII at Bosworth, and imprisoned for three years as a result. Howard was released in 1489 and given a chance to prove his loyalty to the new regime. A fine soldier, his finest hour was possibly his crushing victory over James IV at Flodden in 1513. Norfolk never saw eye-to-eye with Wolsey.

Personnel

Source G

Henry VII's style of management left no room for faction; Henry VIII, on the other hand with his fluctuations, enthusiasms and irregular handling of business, gave it an open invitation to flourish . . . Indeed it seems clear that it was the mounting dispute over religion, and the King's failure to come down firmly on either side, that screwed faction to such a pitch of intensity by the later years of Henry VIII's reign.

D. Starkey, *The Reign of Henry VIII: Personalities and Politics*, 1985

Question

How does David Starkey compare the two Kings?

SKILLS BUILDER

1 Look up the word faction in a dictionary and write your own definition.

2 What reasons does Starkey give in support of the view that faction would be more of a problem for Henry VIII than it had been for Henry VII?

Naturally, Henry VIII inherited his father's councillors, but some of these figures were deeply unpopular as a consequence of Henry VII's hard line on the nobility. In particular Richard Empson and Edmund Dudley had courted antagonism through their work on the Council Learned in the Law, the body that enforced the system of bonds and recognisances. In 1509 Empson and Dudley were arrested on fictitious charges of treason because it was impossible to prove that they had acted against royal instructions. Attempts to **attaint** them in parliament failed, but one year later they were executed anyway. Henry had immediately displayed his ruthlessness in ordering these executions.

The actual evidence against Empson and Dudley was thin on the ground, but their executions marked the beginning of a new era. Henry did little to cancel existing bonds but the show trial and executions of two hated figures gained him favourable publicity and immediate popularity.

At first it was inevitable that the Council would be dominated by Henry VII's men, but they were ageing and this was certainly a time when a new rising star might emerge. The key to advancement in Henry's court was gaining his trust and that was achieved through effective and loyal service to the Crown. In 1510 Thomas Wolsey was appointed as Royal Almoner, and from there he would rise to become the leading cleric and layman in the land.

Definitions

Attaint

To convict someone of treason.

Papal dispensation

An exemption from an obligation of canon law given by the papacy.

Marriage

Within a few weeks of becoming King, Henry married Catherine of Aragon on 11 June 1509. Catherine had of course been previously married to Henry's brother Arthur, but on his death in 1502 negotiations had immediately begun for a second marriage to Henry VII's remaining son and heir Henry. A **papal dispensation** was received for the marriage to go ahead. Yet the wedding did not take place immediately, nor did Henry VII allow Catherine to return home to Spain. Instead she led a fairly miserable existence for seven years while Henry VII used her as a diplomatic tool in his negotiations with Ferdinand of Spain. In that time Catherine was essentially penniless and unsure of her future.

On the death of Henry VII, the new King wasted no time in marrying Catherine. In doing so he was seen to be righting the injustices of Catherine's treatment at the hands of his father while at the same time cementing the Anglo-Spanish alliance in readiness for an invasion of France.

The Renaissance King

In May 1509 **Thomas More** wrote to Desiderus Erasmus about the new, young King:

> Our King does not wish for gold or gems or precious stones, but virtue, glory and immortality.

It can certainly be argued that there was a genuine feeling throughout England that Henry VIII's reign marked a shift away from the old, cautious policies of the past towards a new bright future.

More went on to compose a poem for Henry's coronation that stated:

> This day is the end of our slavery, the fount of our liberty, the end of our sadness, the beginning of joy.

Henry's age and character genuinely brought about an excitement and anticipation of a long and glorious reign. Indeed, this new dawn coincided with a general feeling of intellectual and cultural rejuvenation across Europe known as **the Renaissance**. Monarchs were expected to extol Renaissance values and live up to their billing as God's representative on Earth. A sixteenth-century monarch would be expected to be:

- Able to dictate policy to his ministers and representative institutions such as parliament.
- Capable of maintaining law and order. The royal will would be carried out by the King's subjects without hesitation. Taxation and loans would be collected without delay. The nobility would raise armies for the King in time of war and show loyalty to the Crown.

Exam tip

Watch out for contemporary descriptions of the new King. It was always likely that courtiers and ministers were likely to flatter the young prince, as their advancement depended upon his patronage and support. Moreover, Sir Thomas More was merely following the literary conventions of the age in heralding the accession of a new King.

- A good servant of the Church. The Church was a pillar of monarchical authority, reinforcing the King's right to rule over his subjects. It was the King's duty to ensure that heresy did not take hold in his kingdom and to turn back the advances of the heathen foe in Europe.

- Able to project his majesty and power on a wider stage by conducting continental wars. Victory in battle and the acquisition of foreign lands was seen as one of the key hallmarks of a Renaissance prince.

- Able to reflect his strength at home through the splendour of the royal court. Art, architecture and dress would all play a part in emphasising the position and power of the Crown. The King should be a patron of the arts and be able to attract great men to his court. Their intellect and achievements would reflect well on his kingship.

Conclusion: out with the old and in with the new?

Source H

Wonder it were to write, of the lamentation that was made, for this Prince, Henry VII amongst his servants and other of the wisest sort, and no joy that was made for his death by such as were troubled by rigour of his law. Yet the toward hope, which in all points appeared in the young king, Henry VIII, did both repair and comfort the heavy hearts of them which had lost so wise and sage a prince: and also did put out of the minds such as were relieved by the said King's death, all their old grudge and rancour and confirmed their new joy by the new grant of his pardon.

Edward Hall, *The Union of the Two Noble and Illustre Families of Lancaster and York*, 1548

Source I

His Majesty, Henry VIII, is 29 years old and extremely handsome. Nature could not have done more for him. He is much handsomer than the King of France; very fair and his whole frame admirably proportioned. On hearing that Francis I wore a beard he allowed his own to grow, and as it is reddish, he now has a beard which looks like gold. He is very accomplished, a good musician, composes well, is a most capital horseman, speaks good Latin, French and Spanish. He is very religious . . . He is very fond of hunting, and never takes this diversion without tiring eight or ten horses. He is extremely fond of tennis, at which it is the prettiest thing to see him play, his fair skin glowing through a shirt of the finest texture.

The Venetian Ambassador, Sebastian Guistiniani, writes of Henry VIII in 1519

SKILLS BUILDER

1 Edward Hall was a contemporary historian. How does that affect what he writes?

2 What might you say about the tone of Guistiniani's account of Henry? What words in his account support your ideas? How can you explain the tone that he uses?

Biographies

King Arthur (Sixth century)

Semi-mythical King of the Britons who united the British tribes against the invading Saxons. The legend of Arthur grew over time thanks to writers such as Geoffrey of Monmouth in the twelfth century.

Henry V (1387–1422)

English King from 1413. On 25 October 1415 he won a great victory over the French at Agincourt. Two years later he invaded France once again, and by the end of 1418 Normandy was under English rule. In 1420 he concluded the Peace of Troyes under which Henry was recognized as regent and heir of France.

Although the dawning of the sixteenth century did mark a new age in European history, many of the criteria listed above would have applied to medieval monarchs also. Henry VII had done little to prepare his son for kingship, but Henry VIII was very aware of his chivalric duties. He had been brought up in the royal court, and tutored in glorious deeds of days gone by, principally the heroism and valour of **King Arthur** and the Knights of the Round Table. From a young age Henry played out the deeds of that mythical King in jousting tournaments. Glory on the battlefield was an essential component of the chivalric code, and Henry dreamed of following in the footsteps of **Henry V** who claimed the Crown of France after the Battle of Agincourt in 1415.

Henry's accession to the throne in 1509 also roughly coincided with the emergence of two other leading players on the European scene. In France, Francis I became King in 1515 while Charles of Burgundy had claimed the thrones of Spain and the Holy Roman Empire by 1519. Both were as equally thrusting and ambitious as Henry, and both had more material resources at their disposal. Francis and Charles would fight out the Habsburg–Valois Wars in Italy, while Henry looked to take advantage of any military or political weakness from either side but particularly France. Henry could not compete with these two powers although he remained determined to promote England's cause abroad.

SKILLS BUILDER

Use the information you have been gathering throughout this chapter to plan out an answer to the following question:

How far did Henry VIII's reign begin a new era in Tudor kingship?

In order to assess the extent to which a new era began, you will have to examine the key aspects of Henry VII's policies and his character. Use the following bullet points to structure your paragraphs, and include information about both Henry VII and Henry VIII in each paragraph. Also include evidence from the sources you have looked at in this chapter.

- character
- control of faction
- foreign policy
- conclusion.

Add to this plan throughout your study of Henry VIII and continue to construct it as you proceed.

KNOWLEDGE FOCUS

- Henry VII left a relatively sound financial and political legacy to his son Henry VIII.

- Perhaps Henry VII's greatest achievement was holding onto the Crown and securing the Tudor dynasty.

- Henry VII became increasingly unpopular in the last years of his reign and people welcomed a change of ruler.

- The young, handsome and adventurous Henry VIII was very different in character and outlook from his old, wisened father.

- The year 1509 is often seen as a watershed mark in English history because it not only witnesses the accession of Henry VIII but perhaps also a new style of modern Renaissance kingship.

- Historians have been keen to play down the idea that this new style of modern kingship emerged, as Henry VIII continued to rely upon many of the medieval mechanisms of monarchy.

SKILLS FOCUS

- In evaluating source material, you need to be able to put the document that you are studying into its historical context. This is where your own knowledge becomes important – not to describe events but to give you the ability to understand the tone and purpose of the author.

- In writing any extended response make sure you have a quick and effective plan before you commit your ideas to paper.

Key questions

- How important was the Church in the everyday lives of the people?
- How far was the English Church in need of reform?
- Who opposed the Catholic Church in England before the Reformation?

Questions

1 What is happening in this picture?
2 What does it tell us about the importance of religion in sixteenth-century English society?

2.1 Parishioners from an English village gather round the priest at Mass.

The pre-Reformation Church in England

Henry VIII's reign was notable for a number of reasons, including the establishment of royal control over the Church and the break with Rome. Essentially the foundations of an Anglican Church were laid in Henry's reign. This was a radical change to the fabric of the Church although Henry's own religious outlook remained very conservative, making it difficult at times to see what direction the Henrician Church was taking. To the rest of Catholic Europe, Henry's actions were heretical and England was no longer part of the universal Church, because it no longer looked to the Pope as its spiritual head.

At roughly the same time, the early **Reformation** in Europe was taking shape under reformers such as Martin Luther (see pages 22–3). More radical reformers hoped that the break with Rome would only be the start of Henry's reforms and that England might adopt a more Protestant stance, but they were to be disappointed.

All through the Henrician Reformation the actual doctrine of the Church remained essentially Catholic although there were moderate reformers in England, some of whom held high political office, who wanted to push the Church on towards Protestantism. Henry remained orthodox in his views to the end, but there is little doubt that the destruction of some Catholic rites and practices, not least the authority of Rome, paved the way for future Protestant reform. Yet while it is relatively easy to chart the progression of the Henrician Reformation through parliament, it is harder to gauge the popular reaction to events. In this light it is crucial to have some understanding of the Church on the eve of the Reformation.

Protestant historians such as **John Foxe** were eager to portray a pre-Reformation Catholic Church riddled with corruption and ready to collapse. These historians emphasise high levels of popular dissatisfaction with the Church, which manifested itself in rampant **anti-clericalism**. On the back of dissatisfaction with the Catholic Church, Henry's supremacy was welcomed and there was popular support for further, more radical reforms after papal authority had been removed.

However, this line of argument has been shown to be outdated and false. Through the study of churchwarden's accounts, wills and parish registers we can see that for the majority of people in England the Catholic Church continued to play a central role in their lives. The Church was crucial both in a spiritual and social sense.

Definitions

The Reformation

Ideological and doctrinal challenge to the Catholic Church that emerged in the early sixteenth century. Martin Luther in Germany is often seen as the beginning of the Reformation. Catholic historians argue that a Catholic Reformation, reforming the traditional Church from within, predated Luther's attack on the rites and practices of Roman Catholicism.

Erastian Kingship

A belief that the Church should be subordinate to the State.

Anti-clericalism

Criticism of the practices and morality of the Catholic clergy.

Biography

John Foxe (1516–87)

English martyrologist and Protestant, he was forced into exile during the reign of Mary I. Most famous for his *Book of Martyrs*, which details a history of English Protestant martyrs from the fourteenth century to his own day.

Questions

1 Why does Scarisbrick see wills as a particularly important source of evidence for historians studying the Church in England before the Reformation?

2 What would John Foxe make of Scarisbrick's argument?

Definitions

Salvation

God's act of saving man from sin and conferring eternal happiness upon him through admission to Heaven.

Sacrament

A religious ceremony regarded as an outward and visible sign of an inward and spiritual grace.

Mass

Central act of worship for Christians called the Mass (Catholics), Holy Communion or Lord's Supper (Protestants). Based on the example of Jesus Christ at the Last Supper, when he identified the bread that he broke and the wine that he poured with his body and blood.

Source A

Up to the very moment when the traditional medieval religious institutions and practices were swept away, English layfolk were pouring money and gifts in kind into them. Wills are a source which, quite rightly, have attracted plenty of attention recently – because so many survive and because . . . quite humble folk as well as those at the top wrote them . . . they show a society committed to the old religion until the moment when it was supplanted.

J.J. Scarisbrick, *The Reformation and the English People*, 1984

Why was the Catholic Church so important in the lives of the ordinary people?

Catholicism was the sole Christian religion of western Europe and all Catholics were expected to attend Church. The Christian community was defined by its membership of the Catholic Church. **Salvation** could only be found through following the teachings of the Church. Spiritually the people followed the seven **sacraments**:

- Baptism
- Confirmation
- Marriage
- Ordination
- Penance (see page 17)
- Extreme unction
- the Eucharist (see below).

Of these the Eucharist was the most important to the common man or woman.

The Mass and the Eucharist

Mass was heard every Sunday and on Holy Days. Mass was said in Latin by a priest, and at its heart lay the Eucharist. In the sixteenth century people believed that when they attended the parish Mass they were witnessing a re-enactment of Christ's sacrifice, and that the bread and the wine were transformed into the body and blood of Christ. The priest was central to the service as a channel of divine grace – when he held the consecrated bread above his head, the faithful believed that they were gazing upon Christ's return to Earth. This doctrine concerning the transformation of the elements of the bread and the wine into the body and blood of Christ was known as **transubstantiation** (see page 17).

The Mass was in many ways about participation, and the miracle of the Mass bound the faithful together. Yet while the congregation would say their own personal prayers and feel the solidarity of Christian worship, they celebrated apart from the priest. The priest stood at the high altar, whispering the words of the rite in Latin. The Eucharist was usually only taken by the priest before the priestly blessing was offered. The people received communion only once a year at Easter, and then only the bread. The congregation was separated from the priest by the rood screen and could not hear nor understand his words in Latin. However, it should not be assumed that this in any way devalued the experience for the common man. The Mass was celebrated on Sundays and Holy Days without fail, and it was the focus of popular spirituality.

Penance

Confession and **penance** were required to absolve oneself of sin and receive the Eucharist. People also believed that to die in a state of sin was to risk eternal damnation in the next world. Unsurprisingly no Catholics wanted to die suddenly before they had confessed of their sins. If one died in a state of minor sin it was believed that one would have to enter **Purgatory** where sins were painfully cleansed before one could enter Heaven. The length of time spent in Purgatory depended upon the nature and number of one's sins, so Catholics performed penance while on Earth. To shorten the amount of time that the souls of loved ones might have to spend in Purgatory, people could purchase indulgences or pay for masses for the dead to be said in their name. Lay guilds or **confraternities** were also established to say prayers for the dead. The faithful even prayed for all Christian souls on All Souls' Day.

The community

Above all else the late medieval Church was about participation and action. The Church was very much a focal point of the local community. The religious calendar dictated people's lives. Christmas and Easter were obviously the two key religious festivals, but numerous holy days and saints' days were also observed. Religious plays, performed in English, were popular and served to instruct as well as entertain.

Saints

Saints were viewed as powerful intercessors between God and Man. Everyone venerated the Virgin Mary, but other saints were also adopted by communities and individuals to protect against misfortune, death and destruction. Specific saints had specific powers, such as St Sebastian who protected against plague. For this reason images and statues of saints were venerated and candles lit before them.

The cult of saints spawned an upsurge in the quantity and quality of religious art. Many people chose to go on pilgrimages to holy shrines in the hope that they might gain Grace and advance their entry into Heaven. Popular sites in England included the Shrine of Our Lady of Walsingham in Norfolk. It was believed that miracles were performed here as a means of revealing divine power to the faithful.

Definitions

Transubstantiation

Transubstantiation is the change of the substance of bread and wine into the Body and Blood of Christ occurring in the Eucharist according to the teaching of the Roman Catholic Church.

Penance

To reinforce repentance for sin through prayer, confession, fasting and good works.

Purgatory

A place of punishment where those who have died with some sins unforgiven must go until they have done sufficient penance. Once they have endured their punishment, they are permitted to enter heaven.

Confraternities

Lay associations formed to pray for the souls of the dead.

Source B

And here out of our records I shall mention some of the images and relics to which the pilgrimages of those times brought devotion and offerings such as the milk of our Lady, the bell of St Guthlac and the belt of St Thomas of Lancaster, the coals that roasted St Lawrence, the ear of St Malchus and the blood of Jesus Christ brought from Jerusalem to Gloucestershire, being kept for many ages. This last has brought many great offerings to it from remote places, but was proved to be the blood of a duck, every week renewed by the priests. Besides which it is possible to see an image of St John of Osulston who was said to have shut up the Devil in a boot.

From Lord Herbert of Cherbury's *Life and Reign of King Henry VIII*, published in 1649

Source C

My body is to be buried in the palace near the chapel that I caused to be made in the south aisle of St Magnus' Church.

For tithes forgotten: 3s 4d.

For masses to be said in the church for my soul, my wife's soul and all Christian souls, every month for one year after my death: £6.

Every Friday for a year after my death 3s 4d to be given to prisoners in Newgate one Friday, those in Ludgate the next Friday. The very best canvas for shirts and smocks for the poor people in Bedfordshire. £100 towards the making of an altar table.

The will of Richard Berne, London 1525

Donations

The common people showed their devotion and loyalty to the Church through bequests in wills to parish churches as well as monetary donations for the upkeep and rebuilding of local churches. Professor Andrew Pettegree, a modern historian, writes that in Suffolk during the fifteenth century, 'something approaching 50 per cent of parish churches were substantially remodelled, as citizens poured the new wealth generated by a successful wool trade into their religious lives'.

Lay confraternities were popular as people grouped together to say prayers for the souls of dead relatives in order to speed their passage through purgatory. Another modern historian, Susan Brigden states that there were 176 such confraternities in London alone in the fifteenth century. Therefore the picture that has been constructed here is of a population with a deep and unquestioning commitment to the Catholic faith.

How far was the Church in need of reform?

Source D

These are [. . .] ravenous wolves [. . .], devouring their flock. The goodliest lordships, manors, lands and territories are theirs. Besides this, they take a tenth part of everyone's wages, a tenth part of [all goods] produced, and even every tenth egg from poor widows. And what do these greedy, idle, holy thieves do with all these yearly exactions they take from the people? Nothing but suck all rule, power, authority and obedience from you [Henry VIII] to themselves!

From Simon Fish's *A Supplication for the Beggars*, published in 1529

Source E

People always hear Mass on Sunday and give generously to the Church and to the poor. There is not a parish church in the kingdom that does not have crucifixes, candlesticks and cups of silver, as well as many other ornaments worthy of a cathedral.

From a description by an Italian visitor to England in 1500

Source F

It is from stupidity and the darkness of ignorance that there arises a great and deplorable evil throughout the whole Church of God. Everywhere through town and countryside there exists a crop of oafish and boorish priests, some of whom are engaged on ignoble and servile tasks, while others abandon themselves to tavern haunting, swilling and drunkenness. Some cannot get along without their wenches; others pursue their amusement in dice and gambling all day long. There are some who waste their time in hunting and hawking, and so spend a life which is utterly and wholly idle and irreligious even to advanced old age.

From an extract from a sermon preached by William Melton, Chancellor of York Minster, in 1510

Source G

The Church was full of weaknesses and abuses; reforms had been talked about for a very long time. The parish clergy were often ill-educated and ignorant, unable to understand and sometimes even to read the Latin of the services; often too, they were wretchedly poor. Coming from the same class as their flocks, they could rarely command the respect that a better education or a slightly higher standard of living would have produced. The higher clergy were wealthy and worldly and resented by their own inferiors; many of them practised those abuses against which pope after pope, and council after council, had issued their edicts.

G.R. Elton, *England under the Tudors*, 1955

Questions

1 What problems do Sources D–G suggest existed within the English Church on the eve of the Reformation?
2 Why were Church services in Latin? What difference would it have made were those services in English?

What were the causes of dissatisfaction with the Catholic Church?

Uneducated priests

Some parish priests were uneducated and therefore unable to deliver the traditional services to their lay flock. They could not understand the significance of the Mass and were unable to recite basic parts of the liturgy such as the Lord's Prayer.

Clerical abuses

At a higher level, some bishops were accused of serious breaches of Church discipline. Humanist reformers such as Thomas More and John Colet drew attention to common clerical abuses such as:

* simony – to purchase a clerical office from a leading cleric or prince
* pluralism – to hold more than one clerical office at the same time, usually for material benefit
* non residence – bishops who did not reside in their diocese but still collected tax
* nepotism – donating a clerical post to a member of one's family
* sexual misconduct – ignoring clerical vows of celibacy.

Mini case study: Thomas Wolsey

Thomas Wolsey, Lord Chancellor from 1515 and Henry's chief minister until 1529, hardly set a fine example in this respect. Wolsey was Archbishop of York, while holding several other bishoprics at the same time and serving the King in high political office into the bargain! Wolsey also used his position in the Church to secure benefices for his illegitimate son, Thomas Winter. The enormous wealth that Wolsey amassed in the process made him an obvious target for anti-clerical sentiment, especially after he lost Henry's trust in 1528. Indeed in 1529 an anti-clerical common lawyer called Simon Fish wrote a tract entitled *A Supplication for the Beggars* (see Source D on page 18). It was a vicious and satirical attack on the corruption of the clergy. Bishops were accused of exploiting the wealth of ordinary lay folk in order to fund their lavish lifestyles.

Monks and nuns

Bishops and priests are collectively referred to as the secular clergy, whereas monks and nuns are regular clergy. Monks and nuns lived in their own communities and did not interact with the ordinary people as much as the secular clergy. They devoted their lives to God through prayer and contemplation.

In 1509 there were roughly 800 **religious houses** in England. Many, especially in the north of England, continued to play an important part in the local community in terms of education and caring for the poor and needy as well as saying prayers for the souls of the dead. Yet, some houses were in a state of disrepair with numbers dwindling and moral standards dropping. Some abbots had grown extremely wealthy from land rents and were effectively living the lives of country gentry.

Benefit of the clergy

A privilege of the Church that aroused anti-clerical sentiments at the beginning of the sixteenth century was benefit of the clergy. This allowed for members of the clergy who had committed serious crimes to escape trial in secular courts. Such a system of immunity was open to abuse and miscarriages of justice.

Definition

Religious houses

Places of worship and work for religious orders such as Augustines or Benedictines. Includes monasteries, abbeys, friaries and convents.

Mini case study: Richard Hunne

One particular incident, which occurred in London in 1514, demonstrated the anger that benefit of the clergy provoked among the laity. Richard Hunne was a well-off London merchant who challenged the Church authorities over the exorbitant mortuary fees he had been forced to pay in order to bury his infant son. In response the Church drew up charges of heresy against Hunne and had him arrested. While awaiting trial, Hunne was found hanged in his cell. The officials of the bishop of London claimed that Hunne had committed suicide whereas Hunne's supporters were convinced that he had been murdered. To make matters worse, the Church found Hunne guilty of heresy posthumously and confiscated his property as a result. The bishop of London's chancellor was implicated in the affair and although the matter was investigated by the King's Council, no one was held to account for Hunne's death. The case caused uproar in London and heightened anti-clerical feelings in the capital. The Hunne Affair, as it became known, epitomised for many Londoners the corruption of the Church and stoked the flames of anti-clerical sentiment for several years.

Conclusion

Source H

Such, then, in bald outline was the situation of the English clergy during the early decades of the sixteenth century. Their power and influence in society was more apparent than real. They were beginning to lose their once effortless intellectual ascendancy. They stood in no favourable posture to wage any conflict against the growing pretensions of the laity and of the State. Their leaders lacked inspiration, unity and loyalty to the supranational concept of Christendom. While the Papacy as yet needed to reform itself before it could inaugurate reform within the national churches, our English Church remained too full of conflicting interests, too complacent in its conservative and legalist routines to reform itself.

A.G. Dickens, *The English Reformation*, 1964

Source I

Late medieval Catholicism exerted an enormously strong, diverse and vigorous hold over the imagination and the loyalty of the people up to the very moment of Reformation. Traditional religion had about it no particular marks of exhaustion or decay, and indeed in a whole host of ways, from the multiplication of vernacular religious books to adaptations within the national and religious cult of saints, was showing itself well able to meet new needs and new conditions . . . when all is said and done the Reformation was a violent disruption, not the natural fulfilment, of most of what was vigorous in late medieval piety and religious practice.

Eamon Duffy, *The Stripping of the Altars*, 1992

SKILLS BUILDER

1 Make a note of what Dickens and Duffy say about the state of late medieval Catholicism. How do they disagree?

2 With such conflicting opinions, how do we know which historian to trust? Can they both be right?

3 Look at Source J. Where does Whiting stand on this debate?

Source J

In the south east, it is true, there are signs of a partial weakness of Catholic enthusiasm before the Reformation; here the Dickens/Elton model has a measure of validity. Outside this region, however, devotion generally remained strong: in most parts of England it is the Haigh/Scarisbrick model that seems the more applicable.

R. Whiting, *The Blind Devotion of the People: Popular Religion in the English Reformation*, 1989

There were some grounds for complaints against the Church, but anti-clerical feelings were not widespread. Yes, anti-clericalism was probably greater in the south-east than in the rest of England and discontent with the Church was periodically heightened by affairs such as the Hunne episode in London. Yet the majority of priests were properly trained, and the number of university graduates entering the clergy continued to rise at the beginning of the sixteenth century.

Some high-profile bishops such as Wolsey may not have set the best of examples to the rest of the beneficed clergy, but there were many others such as Archbishop John Morton (Archbishop of Canterbury 1486–1500) who had dedicated themselves to positive, internal reform. Other bishops such as Bishop Longland of Lincoln (1521–47) despised the practices of non-residence and absenteeism and did their best to ensure that the clergy under their jurisdiction served their flock effectively.

Many of the abuses had been around for centuries and there is no evidence that the English Church was on the brink of collapse. It also has to be remembered that Henry himself appeared to have no real problems with the standards of the clergy. He was content to use anti-clerical sentiments and radical bishops as a means of crushing the legal powers of the English Church and establishing himself at its head in place of the Pope, but he did not challenge the fundamental doctrines and practices of the Catholic Church.

SKILLS BUILDER

1 Split up into two groups:

- One group should compile evidence from pages 18–21 to support the view that the pre-Reformation Church was in need of reform.

- The other group should gather material from pages 15–18 to support the view that people were satisfied with the Church.

Write down your main points clearly. Then stage a debate about the condition of the Church. At the end, note down the ideas of the other group so that you have a balanced argument.

2 Was it possible for either side to win that debate outright and prove the other wrong?

3 What has this exercise taught you about using historical evidence?

Definition

Indulgences

Indulgences were pieces of paper signed by the Pope that could be purchased by the laity. The recipient of an indulgence was cleansed of sin, and often indulgences were purchased for dead relatives in order to save their souls in purgatory. Luther condemned indulgences because he believed that only faith could ensure salvation.

The Reformation in Europe and Lutheranism

Martin Luther (1483–1546) was a leading German reformer and the most prominent religious figure in the early Reformation. He initiated the Reformation in Germany when he posted his *95 Theses* in Wittenberg in 1517 that criticised the sale of **indulgences**. Luther was excommunicated by Pope Leo X in 1520, but escaped prosecution as a heretic through his powerful supporters in Saxony, not least the Elector Frederick the Wise. Luther faced **Charles V** (see page 87) at Worms in 1521 where the reformer refused to recant his views.

In 1525 the peasants of Germany rose up in revolution against their noble masters. Many of them used Luther's ideas as a rallying cry for violence and murder. Luther was deeply upset that his ideas of spiritual equality were being misinterpreted and he denounced the peasants and reiterated his support for the **princes**. Increasingly, the Lutheran Reformation in Germany was organised and supported by the nobility. In 1555 at the religious peace of Augsburg, Lutheranism was legally recognised. However, Luther's stubbornness prevented any unity with other Protestant groups such as the **Zwinglians**.

Impact of Lutheranism in England

Although Lutheran literature was smuggled into England, Lutheranism had little impact outside Germany. In 1521 Thomas More helped Henry VIII pen a robust defence of Catholic orthodoxy in the *Assertio Septem Sacramentorum*, or a *Defence of the Seven Sacraments*, and it earned him the title of Defender of the Faith from the papacy. Henry was consistently anti-Lutheran, and those who read Luther's works or preached his ideas were in danger of being tried as a heretic and burned. Although Henry's later fear of diplomatic isolation in Europe in the 1530s prompted him to entertain thoughts of a Lutheran alliance, it would be fair to say that he never embraced Luther's doctrine. That said, some important figures such as **Thomas Cranmer** (see page 92), Archbishop of Canterbury, and **Thomas Cromwell** (see page 92), **Vice Gerent in Spirituals**, probably secretly harboured Lutheran ideas and did their utmost to push reform in that direction without being suspected of actually being Lutheran.

Henry himself was attracted to some elements of radical thought, particularly that which endorsed his imperial kingship and headship of both Church and State. For example, an English Lutheran in exile, named William Tyndale, about whom more is written below, wrote a work entitled *Obedience of a Christian Man* in 1528 that called on the King to use his divinely appointed position to head the Church and lead reform. Such endorsements of Henry's supremacy were one reason why more radical figures were able to fill important political and religious posts in Henry's reign.

Cambridge University appears to have been a hotbed of radicalism, and it was in that city that evangelicals such as **Robert Barnes** (see page 138) met at the White Horse Tavern to discuss Lutheran doctrine. Both Barnes and Cromwell would be executed in 1540 for their religious views, but not before they had done much to advance key elements of the reformed cause such as the vernacular Bible.

Definitions

Princes

Leading nobles who ruled over the 400 or so semi-autonomous states in the Holy Roman Empire. From 1530 an increasing number supported Luther.

Zwinglians

Followers of the Swiss reformer Zwingli. Zwinglians were more radical than Lutherans in that they believed that the Eucharist was a purely symbolic ritual, whereas Lutherans believed that the real presence of Christ still entered the bread and the wine. Luther and Zwingli fell out over this point in 1529 at the Colloquy of Marburg.

Vice Gerent in Spirituals

This was the title given by Henry VIII to Thomas Cromwell. It allowed Cromwell to make policy on religious as well as secular matters.

Papal primacy

The concept that the Pope was spiritual head of the Catholic Church with no superior on Earth.

Papal infallibility

The Pope was the sole authority on matters of doctrine. He was always right on doctrinal issues and could not be wrong.

What was Lutheranism?

2.2 Martin Luther's doctrine.

Justification by faith alone:
People were sinners and could not make themselves perfect before God through good works on Earth. Salvation would be found in faith

Luther's doctrine encapsulated three main ideas:

Sola Scriptua:
Luther believed that all doctrine had to be grounded in scripture. He called for a regeneration of spiritual life based on the Word of God. Luther himself translated the New Testament into German in 1521, as well as composing countless hymns and sermons in the vernacular. Luther's belief in the authority of scripture led to his denial of **papal infalibility** and the esistence of only two sacraments

Priesthood of all believers:
People should forge a closer personal relationship with God. Clerical hierarchy was unnecessary and **papal primacy** unfounded in scripture. Each person could act as his or her own priest and read the Word of God for him or herself. Ministers were required to preach and teach, but they were not superior to everyone else

Take it further

Find out more about Martin Luther. Draw up a timeline showing the major events of his life. Make sure that you include the following key events: the posting of the *95 Theses*, the Bull Exsurge Domine, the Diet of Worms, the Peasants Revolt and the Colloquy of Marburg. Explain the significance of each of these events to the Reformation.

Mini case study: William Tyndale

Perhaps the most active and outspoken Lutheran in England was William Tyndale. Tyndale not only led a vicious attack on the standards of the clergy but he also endorsed Luther's ideas on salvation. Tyndale was forced to flee England to the continent where he met Luther personally and began work on an accurate translation of the Bible into English. Tyndale's translation of the New Testament in English was published in 1525, and this was his most important contribution to the Reformation in England, as numerous copies were smuggled illegally into the country. Just over a decade later in 1538 Henry and Cromwell authorised the circulation of the English Bible across every parish. The Old Testament translation had been carried out by John Rogers and Miles Coverdale but the New Testament was entirely Tyndale's work. He was not there to see the occasion as he was burned as a heretic in Antwerp in 1536.

Who opposed the Catholic Church in England before the Reformation?

The humanists

One group of intellectuals who advocated reform of the Church were the humanists. Humanists were conservative in that they did not propose new doctrines or a new way of worshipping but rather they called for an improvement in the intellectual and moral standards of the clergy. Christian humanism was part of a wider movement originating from the Italian Renaissance, and included key thinkers such as **Erasmus**.

The humanists believed that a return to the original scriptures was necessary because subsequent editions of the Latin **Vulgate** had been mistranslated. Erasmus translated the New Testament into Greek in 1516, and his corrections undermined the Vulgate and further fuelled the movement for a revitalised Church. As well as translations of the Vulgate, ancient texts and scriptures were studied, criticised and in some instances re-translated.

Some historians argue that Erasmus laid the intellectual foundations for Luther in that many Protestant reformers used his Greek New Testament as the basis for later vernacular translations. Certainly both Luther and Erasmus viewed the Word of God as a key instrument of worship, but whereas Luther used scripture to denounce papal authority, Erasmus used it as a means to encourage reform from within.

Christian humanists aimed to revitalise the Church and improve standards of literacy and understanding among the clergy. Erasmus visited England on several occasions and met both John Colet (Dean of St Pauls') and Thomas More. All three were like-minded in their approach to reform from within the structures of the Church.

Colet used his position as Dean of St Paul's to launch scathing attacks on the abuses of the Church, reinforcing his idea that holiness could only be achieved through an understanding of the Scriptures. His fiery preaching brought him into conflict with the ecclesiastical authorities, most notably the Bishop of London himself.

However, the impact of the humanists on the ordinary people was minimal and there is no reason to believe that the common man was particularly bothered about some of the high-profile corruption within the Church so long as it did not affect their everyday worship.

The Lollards

There was a small minority of radicals within England who went a step further than the humanists in challenging papal authority and the doctrine of the Catholic Church.

> **Biography**
>
> **Erasmus**
>
> The foremost Christian humanist in Europe. He published a number of satirical works such as *In Praise of Folly* (1509), criticising the immorality and worldliness of the clergy. He also championed a revival in classical learning.

> **Definition**
>
> **The Vulgate**
>
> The Latin version of the Bible.

The Lollards were followers of a fourteenth-century theologian called John Wyclif. Wyclif's programme for reform included a Bible in English, the closure of monasteries and the secularisation of Church property. He also attacked papal and priestly powers, arguing that all men should be equal as subjects under the Crown. His views, which were regarded as heretical, appear to predate many of the ideas put forward by the sixteenth-century Protestant reformers.

Wyclif's followers were forced underground by persecution in the fifteenth century, and it remains difficult to gauge their numerical strength on the eve of the Reformation. Certainly Lollard communities existed in southern England, but they were relatively few in number and appear to have done little to advance radical ideas during the Henrician Reformation.

Source K

What evidence can be found of contact between the Lollard groups and early Lutheranism? How often did the Lutheran book agents, who were active in England from the late 1520s, find backers in people with established Lollard affinities? Considering the secret character of these transactions, it is surprising how many instances of them can be produced. The chief vehicle of early Lutheranism was Tyndale's New Testament of 1526 which, printed in Antwerp, was soon finding eager buyers among the native dissenters . . . In various parts of East Anglia and south eastern England, even in the North at Halifax, a strongly Puritan or dissenting tradition seems to show continuity of growth from local mid Tudor radicalism based mainly on Lollardy.

A.G. Dickens, *The English Reformation*, 1964

Source L

Some of the historians who have followed through the insights of Dickens and Elton have now abandoned the conventional interpretation of the English Reformation, an interpretation which came to appear archetypally whiggish . . . The task of the historian is the explanation of events: he tries to show why things turned out as they did. Since the eventual outcome of the Reformation was a more or less Protestant England, too often the history of the English Reformation has been written as the origins of English Protestantism: we have been given a history of the progressives and the victors in which those men, ideas and issues seen as leading towards the final Reformation result are linked together in a one sided account of change.

C. Haigh, *The English Reformation Revised*, 1987

Questions

1 What importance does Dickens attach to the Lollardy movement?
2 What was the significance of an English Bible?
3 What problems does Haigh have with historians such as Dickens?
4 Write your own definition of Whig history.

Historiography

The pre-Reformation Church and the Henrician Reformation

There are three main historical arguments to bear in mind as we approach our study of the Henrician Reformation.

1 The state of the Church in England on the eve of the Reformation is a contentious issue among historians.

- Traditional historians have viewed the pre-Reformation Church as a corrupt and unpopular institution that buckled easily and quickly under the pressure exerted upon it by Henry VIII.
- Revisionist historians argue that the pre-Reformation Church in England was in relatively good health. There were isolated examples of

corruption and abuse but on the whole the laity were devoted and loyal to the Catholic Church.

2 The motives for religious change are also a source for debate among historians studying Henry's reign.

- One school of thought argues that the Henrician Reformation was entirely an act of state. Henry's religious policies were imposed upon the population, with parliament merely acting as a 'rubber stamp' for them. Historians who subscribe to these ideas describe religious change during Henry's reign as *a Reformation from above*.

- An alternative school exists which states that there was a popular reception for Henry's policies and that a groundswell of Protestant support emerged throughout Henry's reign as a consequence of the religious change. Historians from this school talk of *a Reformation from below.*

3 The pace of religious change is also an area over which Tudor historians have disagreed for some time.

- On the one hand we have those historians who argue that the Henrician Reformation did little to change the everyday worship of the people, and that Catholic orthodoxy remained at the heart of English lay spiritual beliefs. The Reformation was a slow process and the Protestantisation of the people did not begin to happen until the reign of Elizabeth I.

- On the other hand we have those historians who argue that the Reformation in England happened quickly and that Protestantism had made real progress by the death of **Edward VI** (see page 141) in 1553.

One should not necessarily see these arguments as separate entities. Each line of argument has a potential knock-on effect on the next issue. For example, a historian who sees a pre-Reformation Church in decay is likely also to see a relatively quick Reformation supported from below. On the other hand another school of historians might see a relatively healthy Church that comes under attack from above with little lay support and therefore change occurs very slowly.

SKILLS BUILDER

1 Go through all the historians in this chapter and try to match them to the schools of thought outlined above.

2 Now you have found out about Henry VIII's religious policies, add a new paragraph to the essay plan you began in Unit 1 (page 12).

KNOWLEDGE FOCUS

- The pre-Reformation Church in England was in need of reform because ordinary priests were poorly paid and ill-educated while important bishops often abused their position to gather great wealth.

- One must not over state the decrepit condition of the Church. Ecclesiastical abuses were often high profile and attracted great attention but they were also limited in number. There were lots of good priests and bishops in England who were doing their job well.

- Levels of anti-clericalism were higher in the south than in the north.

- Ordinary people appeared largely satisfied with the Church.

- The Catholic Church in England will come under serious attack from Henry VIII between 1530–40, but this will be for political as much as religious reasons.

SKILLS FOCUS

- You need to understand that historians sometimes fundamentally disagree on the same issue. In no way does this undermine the study of history, as long as each group of historians can provide credible evidence to support his/her views.

- It should also be remembered that historians tend to focus their research on one particular area of the country and therefore regional variations may account for differences of opinion.

3 The structure of government: the role of Wolsey

Key questions

- How did Wolsey rise to power under Henry VIII?
- How did Wolsey maintain his position?
- Why did Wolsey fall from power in 1529?

Timeline

1473	Wolsey born in Ipswich
1498	Ordained as a priest
1502	Chaplain to Archbishop Deane of Canterbury
1507	Appointed chaplain to Henry VII
1509	Appointed Dean of Lincoln and Royal Almoner
1510	Appointed a royal councillor
1513	Organises Henry VIII's successful expedition to France Appointed Bishop of Tournai
1514	Appointed Bishop of Lincoln and Archbishop of York
1515	Created a Cardinal by Pope Leo X and made Lord Chancellor by Henry VIII
1518	Appointed *Legate a Latere* and Bishop of Bath and Wells Diplomatic success of Treaty of London
1520	Organises meeting between Henry VIII and Francis I at Field of the Cloth of Gold
1521	Treaty of Bruges with Charles V against France
1524	Appointed Bishop of Durham (exchanged for Bath and Wells)
1525	Failure of Amicable Grant and widespread unrest as a result
1526–27	Diplomatic revolution sees Wolsey ally with France against Charles
1527–29	Failed attempts to resolve the Great Matter with cooperation of Rome
1529	Bishop of Winchester (exchanged for Durham); resigns as Lord Chancellor
1530	Dies at Leicester Abbey.

Wolsey's last words on his deathbed in 1530

If I had served God as diligently as I have done the King, he would not have given me over in my grey hairs.

Questions

1 What do these words suggest about Wolsey's career?
2 How do we know that Wolsey uttered these words?

Source A

Why come ye not to court?
To which court?
To the King's court, or Hampton Court?
For Hampton Court is the finer . . .

John Skelton, *Why come ye not to court?*, 1522

John Skelton's infamous words hint at the importance of a man who would serve Henry VIII as chief minister for fifteen years. Thomas Wolsey (1473–1530) remains one of the most intriguing and colourful characters of the Tudor court. His political importance as the King's main adviser and personal servant is indisputable and the fact that he served Henry for so long suggests that the King was more than satisfied with Wolsey's efforts.

Yet Skelton's words also highlight one of the traditional reasons cited for Wolsey's unpopularity and ultimate downfall, namely the lavish nature of his court combined with his political pre-eminence. Wolsey built palaces such as Hampton Court and York Palace (now the Palace of Westminster). Such was his importance that many contemporaries and indeed historians believed that *he* held real power at court, not Henry VIII. Wolsey's monopoly of political power gained him the title of *Alter Rex*, or second King and, as Skelton suggests, Wolsey's wealth was greater and his household more lavish than that of the King himself.

How did Wolsey rise to power under Henry VIII?

Wolsey's rise to political pre-eminence under Henry VIII was down to a combination of luck and skill. Undoubtedly he was able and ambitious, but he was also fortunate in that many of the important ministers from Henry VII's reign were ageing and ready to settle for a quieter life, leaving Wolsey free to win the new King's favour and trust.

Source B

The choice of a ruler's ministers is a very important matter; whether they are good or not depends on the ruler's shrewdness.

Machiavelli,
The Prince, 1513

That said, Wolsey possessed a fine mind highlighted by the fact that he gained his first degree from Oxford at the age of only fifteen. From there he went on to take holy orders in 1498 and his first post was as chaplain to Henry Deane, the Archbishop of Canterbury. Sir Richard Nanfan, deputy lieutenant of Calais, brought him to the attention of Henry VII, who appointed him as a chaplain in 1507. Therefore Wolsey came to notice during the last years of Henry VII's reign when he went on to serve Bishop Foxe of Winchester. He was employed on small diplomatic missions to the Netherlands and Scotland, where he stood out as an efficient administrator. Yet it was Henry VII's death in 1509 that gave Wolsey a chance to really shine.

The new regime brought with it a vibrant new feeling of hope and optimism characterised by the immediate and popular arrests of Henry VII's hated ministers Empson and Dudley (see page 9). Henry VIII was seventeen years old, muscular, athletic and able. He soon grew tired of the old councillors from Henry VII's reign who surrounded him in 1509, viewing them as his father's men rather than his own. They appeared cautious and unwilling to act decisively, keen to follow the same old policies that had characterised the reign of Henry VII. Wolsey was given the chance to prove his worth and he took it.

Definitions

Royal Almoner

A royal official whose task it is to distribute the king's alms (charity).

Royal Council

The king's main advisory body, made up of the most important political figures in the land.

In 1509 Wolsey became **Royal Almoner**, a post that automatically made him a member of the **Royal Council**. This was crucial because the success of a minister in sixteenth-century England depended upon winning the trust of the King and serving him personally. Regular access to the King in person combined with the opportunity to shine were key aspects of ministerial success and Wolsey had both at the beginning of Henry VIII's reign.

In 1509 Henry VIII was young, politically inexperienced and more interested in sporting pursuits such as hunting. Henry was largely disinterested in mundane, administrative matters of state. His energetic almoner was more than willing to take on such routine bureaucratic tasks and in the process make himself indispensable to Henry VIII. Wolsey worked exceptionally hard over the course of 1512–13 in organising the expeditionary force to invade France. He ensured that the logistics of this complex campaign ran smoothly, allowing an English army of over 12,000 to set sail for Gascony.

Henry VIII had found someone who could get things done quickly and efficiently. Wolsey showed remarkable skill and energy in carrying out the King's will. It was of course inevitable that in the process Wolsey would cross other key political figures in his bid to get things done quickly and efficiently. Throughout 1512 and 1513 Wolsey was ruthless in sidelining anyone who tried to disrupt his plans or objectives. Henry did not care because he had found someone both willing and capable.

Over the next years Wolsey was rewarded with multiple offices and titles:
- in 1514 he became Bishop of Tournai and of Lincoln;
- later that year he was made Archbishop of York;
- in September 1515 he became a Cardinal;
- later in 1515 Henry appointed him Lord Chancellor, the top political position in the royal government.

The year 1515 was a key turning point for Wolsey because now he actually held the senior office of state, making it very difficult for other nobles to challenge his decisions. Moreover, in being made a Cardinal Wolsey also bolstered his power over the Church, although William Warham remained Archbishop of Canterbury and technically the most powerful churchman in England. However, that changed in 1518 when Wolsey was appointed *Legate a latere* by the Pope giving him the authority to reform the Church and **appoint to benefices**. By 1518 Wolsey was the most powerful man in England.

Was Wolsey's rise down to luck or skill?

Wolsey's luck

Wolsey had been the right man for Henry at the right time and in this respect he was fortunate. Henry VIII grew tired of the inner council made up of his father's men and was on the lookout for someone who could represent his interests and carry out the everyday paperwork of state. Wolsey was that man. He was also willing and able to carry out duties that he knew the King could not be bothered with.

Definitions

Legate a latere

A personal representative of the Pope, deputed for important diplomatic missions on the papacy's behalf.

Appoint to benefices

Wolsey now had the authority, through Rome, to make clerical appointments in England.

Source C

Soon the council of the early years vanished. Surrey – now as victor of Flodden, restored to the Howard dukedom of Norfolk – was too old to fight the upstart (Wolsey), and his son was as yet too young to do so. In 1515 Warham resigned the chancellorship and Wolsey stepped into his shoes; in 1516 Fox retired from the privy seal to devote himself to his episcopal duties at Winchester, and Wolsey obtained the office for Thomas Ruthal, a faithful follower. From 1515 to 1529 Wolsey was not only the King's chief minister, he was virtually his only one.

G.R. Elton, *England under the Tudors*, 1955

Wolsey's skill

Source D

Everytime Wolsey wished to obtain something from Henry he introduced the matter casually in to his conversation; then he brought out some small present or other, a beautifully fashioned dish, for example or a jewel or ring or gifts of that sort, and while the King was admiring the gift intently, Wolsey would adroitly bring forward the project on which his mind was fixed.

Polydore Vergil, *Anglica Historia*, published 1555

Source E

The King conceived a most loving disposition towards him, especially as he was most earnest and readiest among all the council to advance the King's mere will and pleasure. The King . . . called him near unto him, and esteemed him so highly that his estimation and favour put all other ancient councillors out of the accustomed favour.

Wolsey was an opportunist. He was able to adapt his views and ideas to fit those of the King. Wolsey had initially opposed the idea of war with France but on hearing of Henry's enthusiasm for such a campaign Wolsey emphatically changed his mind and threw himself into the organisation of readying troops and supplies. In this respect Wolsey was a skilful political operator who ensured that his own personal ambition also tied in with the needs and wishes of his master.

George Cavendish, *Thomas Wolsey, late Cardinal, his Life and Death*, written 1554

SKILLS BUILDER

1 Does Elton imply that it was luck alone that allowed Wolsey to rise to power? If not, what else does he suggest might have contributed?

2 Why and in what ways do Sources D and E differ in their opinions on how Wolsey gained influence with the King?

Exam tip

Comparison questions require you to examine the content and the context of the source. The content is straightforward. Look at the ways in which the sources agree and disagree on Wolsey's nature and relationship with the King. The context of the source requires you to look at the author of the source and when it was written. Only by doing this can you understand why a particular view of Wolsey was taken. Use information from pages 39–40 to help you with the above question.

How did Wolsey maintain power in the period 1515–29?

Wolsey's maintenance of power as Henry's chief minister for fifteen years was based upon three key principles:

1 political relationship with Henry VIII
2 wealth
3 ruthlessness.

Wolsey's political relationship with Henry

As we have seen, one of the crucial elements of Wolsey's rise to power was the way in which he gained the trust of the King. After the perceived success of the French invasion in 1513 Henry trusted Wolsey unequivocally. Wolsey for his part recognised that as long as he continued to serve the King loyally and efficiently, his position was secure.

Traditional historiography views Wolsey as the *Alter Rex*, the second king. This interpretation suggests that Wolsey held real power at court, and almost resigns Henry to a passive role within government. Such an interpretation sees Wolsey as the master and Henry as the puppet.

Source F

Ye are so puffed with pride	You are so puffed up with pride
That no man nay abyde	That no man can like you
Your high and lordely lokes	Your arrogant and lordly looks
Ye caste up then your bokes	You then take upon your books
And vertu is forgotten . . .	And virtue is forgotten.
Ye boost, ye face, ye crake,	You boast and taunt and laugh
And upon you take	And take it upon yourself
To rule Kynge and Kayser.	To rule over King and Emperor
And yf ye may have layser,	And if you have your way
Ye wyll brynge all to nought.	You will bring it all to nothing
And that is all your thought.	And that is what you want.

John Skelton, *Collyn Clout*, 1522

SKILLS BUILDER

1 How would you describe the tone of Skelton's poem?
2 Select the key phrases which demonstrate the point that Wolsey made policy at the Tudor court.

Yet this view has been challenged by recent historians, who argue that the relationship between Henry and Wolsey was one of political partnership. Henry may have been willing to give Wolsey space and latitude in the early years when the King's attentions were turned to hunting and feasting, but even here the King always made the final decision on key issues. Henry was content to allow Wolsey to get on with mundane matters of State, but major decisions concerning foreign policy or important domestic affairs could not be made independently by the King's Cardinal.

Source G

By conventional standards Henry allowed his servants a remarkable degree of latitude. But he always retained the right to have the last word; therefore he was the ultimate arbiter of policy. For much of the twentieth century it has been claimed that Wolsey and Cromwell enjoyed prime ministerial ascendancy during Henry's reign, but this paradigm is borrowed from an understanding of Victorian politics. In Tudor terms it is anachronistic and misleading. Henry's ministers advised the King and controlled the implementation of Crown policy once a strategy had been conceived. But, since the King might intervene or change his mind at will, policy might waver, collapse or undergo revision at any moment in the interests of European diplomacy or domestic expediency. It is scarcely surprising that under so volatile a system Wolsey and Cromwell became the victims less of their own mistakes than of their master's egoism.

John Guy, Henry VIII and his Ministers, in *History Today*, December 1995

SKILLS BUILDER

1 Define the term anachronistic.

2 How does Guy's assessment of Wolsey differ from that of Skelton?

Henry and Wolsey did not always see eye-to-eye as one would expect from a political partnership that lasted for fifteen years, and it would not be true to say that Henry knew or approved of every decision that Wolsey made. Yet only rarely between 1515 and 1529 did Henry and Wolsey disagree.

Examples of disagreement include:

- the occasion in 1522 when Wolsey proposed a surprise attack on the French navy but Henry thought the plan foolhardy

- in 1528 the two men fell out over a seemingly trivial matter involving the appointment of an abbess to the nunnery at Wilton in Wiltshire. Wolsey ignored Henry's instructions regarding who should get the post and was forced to make a grovelling apology to his master.

Henry was no fool, nor was he easily manipulated. The very fact that Wolsey remained his chief minister for fifteen years demonstrates that Henry was very much his own man. Wolsey's wealth and power created inevitable resentment among other nobles and councillors, but Henry never yielded to criticism of his leading minister because Wolsey served him loyally and effectively. One can begin to see cracks appearing in the relationship from 1525 over the **Amicable Grant crisis** (see pages 44–5), but it was not until the failure of Wolsey to secure an annulment of Henry's marriage to Catherine of Aragon that the Cardinal was dismissed from his post.

Wolsey's wealth

Wolsey's enormous wealth served to further his political power and create both awe and envy among other courtiers. Although many nobles resented Wolsey's success, especially as he was of **low birth**, they were unable to do much about it as long as Wolsey held the trust of the King.

Wolsey's court was magnificent, and one which the historian David Starkey describes as *quasi royal*. This highlights our point that Wolsey used the trappings of political success to set himself up as the most important man in the country save for the King. Other nobles and councillors could be in no doubt as to Wolsey's pre-eminence in the Henrician government if they visited Hampton Court. Wolsey's household numbered 500, which was the same as Henry's, while the furnishings and clothes on display were the rival of any royal court.

Foreign envoys were treated to magnificent banquets and celebrations, and it is little wonder that many contemporary reports of Wolsey's authority in England come from foreign ambassadors who had witnessed such grandeur. Whenever Wolsey left his palace he did so as a churchman on his mule but in the midst of a large and lavishly decked out cavalcade of servants and guards.

Wolsey had the largest disposable income in England, and he was probably ten times richer than his nearest political rival. His income came from a variety of sources:

- Multiple bishoprics such as York, Tournai, Bath and Wells, Durham, and Winchester contributed around half of Wolsey's income. Wolsey also became Abbot of St Albans in 1525, which was the richest monastery in England.

- A large amount came from the fees that Wolsey charged in his ecclesiastical courts as well as monetary gifts that he received from clients and patrons.

Through the building of palaces such as Hampton Court and the establishment of Cardinal College, Oxford, Wolsey further enhanced his leading position in Henry's government and promoted himself as a man of great importance.

Definitions

Amicable Grant crisis

Wolsey's attempts to raise a non-parliamentary tax in 1525 in order to raise war funds for Henry VIII. His monetary demands came on top of the loans of 1522 and the subsidy of 1523. It was too much for the laity and Wolsey's Amicable Grant caused a serious rebellion in Suffolk and East Anglia.

Low birth

Thomas Wolsey was born in about 1473, son of a butcher and cattle dealer from Ipswich. His low birth was often used as a source of ammunition against him by courtiers who were jealous of the heights that Wolsey reached in Henry's government and the wealth that he attained in the process. Put simply, leading nobles regarded Wolsey as something of a social upstart.

3.1 A contemporary sketch of Hampton Court.

Source H

Above all, the sight of his daily procession to Westminster Hall, dressed in crimson satin robes and jewelled shoes, surrounded by a glittering retinue of noblemen and servants, preceded by the great seal, cardinal's hat, crosses and silver pillars which were the symbols his authority, epitomized his magnificence.

S.J. Gunn and P.G. Lindley, *Cardinal Wolsey – church, state and art*, 1991

Wolsey's ruthlessness

Wolsey's perceived ruthlessness has been much exaggerated. He inevitably courted envy and criticism from contemporary figures at court. His monopoly of power for fifteen years produced attacks on his character and policies. Allegations of misleading the King, misreporting events and deliberately alienating noble rivals were common. Polydore Vergil (see page 40) was supposedly imprisoned on Wolsey's command in 1515 for failing to gain Papal approval for Wolsey's appointment as a Cardinal. More significantly Wolsey was rumoured to have had a part in the execution of the Duke of Buckingham in 1521. Servants such as Richard Pace were sent abroad, actions that other courtiers perceived as the ruthless alienation of political rivals. Much of this criticism has to be seen for what it is, namely the sounding-off of frustrated and jealous nobles. Most of the evidence suggests that Wolsey did consult other nobles on the important matters of the day and did not deliberately ostracise political opponents. Yet what frustrated others at court was the fact that policy had clearly been decided upon between Henry and Wolsey in private before being presented to the council. The political partnership between King and Cardinal operated on mutual trust and respect. The King respected Wolsey because he achieved things and carried out the King's wishes efficiently. Other councillors could hardly criticise Wolsey's policies because they were the King's policies.

Mini case study: The Execution of Buckingham, 1521

Edward Stafford, third Duke of Buckingham, was executed in 1521 for treason. Buckingham was descended from Edward III's youngest son, and as such was sympathetic to the White Rose Party. Henry was rightfully suspicious of him, and prevented Buckingham from taking up the great hereditary office of constable of England. Buckingham resented having to serve the King and was displeased with his lot under the new regime. Buckingham regularly flouted laws against **retaining** and was deliberately provocative in expressing his lineage. Henry was insecure at this stage as he had only his daughter, Mary, to succeed him.

In November 1519 Buckingham allegedly made the threat that he would kill Henry VIII as his father had been prepared to kill Richard III. This charge was brought against him later in 1521 after Buckingham had sought a licence to visit his lordships in Wales with 400 armed men. Buckingham was ordered to London, where he was tried and executed for treason. Many have seen Wolsey as a key figure in bringing about Buckingham's downfall, using the affair as further evidence of Wolsey's fierce anti-noble mentality.

Yet as John Guy points out, Wolsey actually tried to steer Buckingham away from danger in 1519, and Stafford could only have himself to blame for his repeated indiscretions. Essentially, Buckingham had paid with his life for his refusal to serve the King faithfully and loyally. The evidence used to bring him down may have been suspect, but Buckingham's execution served as a warning shot to other would-be malcontents.

Definition

Retaining

When a noble keeps a private army that owes loyalty first to him and then to the King.

SKILLS BUILDER

1 Assess the claim made by the Venetian ambassador in 1519 that Wolsey ruled both the King and the entire Kingdom.

Divide into two groups.

- One group should take the traditional line that Wolsey made policy in the period 1515–29. Think carefully about the evidence that you are going to select in order to reinforce your points. Use the relevant sources in this chapter to further your argument.

- The other group should take the revisionist line that ultimately Henry was in charge and that Wolsey merely advised him on what course of action to take. Again, think about your evidence selection and plan to build in to your argument some of the sources.

Once you have presented and debated the key points write up a measured and balanced conclusion to this question in which you consider both sides of the argument.

2 Here are the lines of argument taken by some contemporaries, as well as some leading historians on the Tudor period. Who do you agree with? Why?

a) To many contemporaries such as Vergil, Hall and Skelton as well as the Venetian ambassador, Sebastian Giustinian, Wolsey was indeed the other King, a man capable of making key decisions without first consulting the King. This model therefore views a very strong minister imposing policy on a very weak King.

b) More recently, historians such as Peter Gwyn have seen Wolsey as a man of some ability entrusted with authority during a complex period of Tudor politics by the King. Yet Wolsey's authority was never total. He relied upon the trust and goodwill of the King who always retained ultimate control of affairs.

c) Other historians such as John Guy tread a similar path in viewing the Henry/Wolsey relationship as something of a political partnership. The King entrusted authority to his chief minister and expected his bidding to be carried out. Henry may not have known everything that Wolsey carried out but nor did he want to. Henry revelled in the glory of Wolsey's achievements, such as the Treaty of London in 1518, although he was also willing to condemn Wolsey when things started to go wrong.

d) Finally, historians such as Eric Ives take this argument one step further in acknowledging Henry's centrality in the decision-making process, but at the same time viewing the King as vulnerable to the forces of faction at certain times. Ives argues that at times pressure was brought to bear on Henry by courtiers. For much of the period 1515–29, it was Wolsey who had the King's ear and therefore he was able at times to put ideas into Henry's mind while at the same time allowing the King to believe that he had formulated that idea. Contrary to Gwyn, Ives views an aristocratic faction as playing an important part in Wolsey's downfall in 1529.

Thomas Wolsey – a study in character assassination?

The next key question that we are going to consider is: 'To what extent was Wolsey the most disappointing man who ever held great power in England?'

This question revolves around the *disappointing man* quotation from G.R. Elton made in the 1950s, and in many ways Professor Elton summarises the traditional view of Cardinal Wolsey held until the 1970s. Elton goes on to write 'all his [Wolsey's] doings were attended by folly, arrogance, false aims and final failure'.

Elton is joined in his condemnation of Wolsey by fellow scholars, J.J. Scarisbrick and A.G. Dickens, both of whom wrote on Henry VIII's reign in the 1960s. Scarisbrick writes that Wolsey 'has had terrible judgement passed against him for having squandered power that was greedily amassed, for having mishandled, violated, corrupted or neglected most of what was in his charge' (1968).

Dickens states that 'Wolsey's personal arrogance, his enormous wealth and splendid ostentation were resented' (1964).

Reassessing Wolsey

There has since been somewhat of a reassessment of Wolsey's achievements, peaking with Peter Gwyn's work, *The King's Cardinal*, published in 1990. Gwyn writes that Wolsey 'had not set out to antagonize the nobility, or in any way harm its interests, except when they directly conflicted with those of the Crown and common weal'.

Any assessment of Wolsey's character or achievements is bound to be problematic given the nature of the source material that is available. There is little in the way of a private archive available for Wolsey, few letters and no diary entries, so it is difficult to gauge events from his own personal perspective. We must therefore rely upon contemporary opinions of Wolsey and that is where we encounter problems because both Wolsey's enemies and friends had reason to offer their interpretations of the facts rather than the facts themselves. Enemies mock Wolsey whereas friends admire him, but both do so for their own reasons. We are now going to look at the four most prominent and important contemporary commentators on Wolsey, and remember that much of what has been subsequently written on Wolsey by historians is based upon the writings of these men.

George Cavendish

Source I

Wolsey took upon him therefore to disburden the King of so weighty a charge and troublesome business, putting the King in comfort that he should not need to spare any time from his pleasure for any business that should necessarily happen in the council. So long as Wolsey was there, and had the King's authority and commandment, he doubted not to see all things sufficiently provided for and perfected. He would first make the King aware of all such matters as should pass through the councillor's hands, before he would proceed to the finishing or determining the same. And he would fulfil and follow the King's mind and pleasure to the uttermost, wherewith the King was wonderfully pleased . . .

George Cavendish, *Life and Death of Cardinal Wolsey*, 1544

Cavendish was Wolsey's household servant and first biographer. Cavendish wrote his *Life and Death of Cardinal Wolsey* some thirty years after Wolsey's death. Given the proximity of a gentleman usher to his master we might expect Cavendish's account to be trustworthy. Yet Cavendish did not enter Wolsey's household until 1522, fully seven years after Wolsey was appointed Lord Chancellor. More significantly, Cavendish was not privy to Wolsey's political life, only his personal one. Therefore, although he can tell us that Wolsey wore a piece of the true cross on a chain around his neck and a hair shirt he cannot tell us much about Wolsey's policy making. Cavendish sheds little light on the Great Matter, and is predictably sympathetic to his master's cause. Where Cavendish does come in particularly useful is after Wolsey had been stripped of his titles in 1528 and cast into the political wilderness by Henry. Cavendish was with Wolsey right up to his death in November 1530 and offers us a personal insight into the Cardinal's final year.

Polydore Vergil

Vergil was an Italian humanist who arrived at the court of Henry VII in 1502 to act as deputy collector of the Peter's Pence. He soon gained a reputation as a fine scholar and Henry VII commissioned him to write a history of England. Vergil's *Anglica Historia* was first published in 1535 but did not include anything on Henry VIII's reign at that point. A subsequent edition, published in 1555, took England's history up to 1537 and therefore covered Wolsey's career. Vergil's analysis of Wolsey's role in Henrician affairs was not favourable. Yet Vergil had an ongoing personal feud with Wolsey that unquestionably shaped his subsequent writings. Vergil had been a former favourite of Henry VII but felt slightly aggrieved by the new King's patronage of other Italian humanists at court such as Andrea Ammonio. Vergil was convinced that Wolsey favoured Ammonio to the detriment of his own chances of advancement. Perhaps out of spite, Vergil did little to enhance Wolsey's hopes of attaining a cardinal's hat through his rude letters back to Rome, and on hearing of this correspondence Wolsey even condemned Vergil to a spell in the Tower in 1515. It was therefore inevitable that Vergil would not write kindly of Wolsey in his *Anglica Historia*.

Edward Hall

Hall was another contemporary historian and wrote *The Union of the Two Noble and Illustre Families of Lancastre and York*, published in 1548. Hall was not close to Wolsey and held no personal grudge against him, which immediately puts him ahead of Vergil in the reliability stakes. Yet Hall's political and religious stance is very clear in his work and it is equally transparent that he stood for very different ideals from Wolsey. Hall was typical of London's professional classes in his anti-clerical views. He was very supportive of the break with Rome and saw Wolsey as the epitome of clerical vice and corruption. Like many other London merchants and lawyers he was a **francophobe** and looked down on Wolsey's alliance with the French in the late 1520s. Again, Hall is a relatively unfriendly source on Wolsey but one that is down in print and tempting for historians to call upon in an assessment of the Cardinal's achievements.

Source J

Wolsey, with his arrogance and ambition, raised against himself the hatred of the whole people and, in his hostility towards nobles and common folk, procured their great irritation at his vainglory.

Polydore Vergil,
Anglica Historia, 1555

Source K

The poor men perceived that he [Wolsey] punished the rich, then they complained without number, and brought many an honest man to trouble and vexation.

Edward Hall, *The Union of the Two Noble and illustre Families of Lancastre and York*, 1548

Definition

Francophobe

A person who dislikes the French.

John Skelton

Skelton was Henry VII's poet laureate and tutor to the future Henry VIII. Skelton mercilessly mocks Wolsey in poems such as *Speke, Parrot* and *Why come ye nat to Courte?*.

Yet Skelton penned his verses in order to attain the patronage of the King and wealthy London citizens. Skelton was aiming to attain fame and fortune through his work and he knew that his audience would approve of the subject of his jibes. 'Speke, Parrot' was written to attract royal favour at a time when Henry was losing faith in his minister. There was a long history of English satirical writing and in many ways Skelton was merely following in the footsteps of others such as John Lydgate who penned the 'Fall of Princes'. Once again we must be careful in taking Skelton's work at face value, as he moulded his material to suit current concerns and play upon any flaws or mishaps that occurred.

Source L

So rygorous revelying,
In a prelate specially;
So bold and so bragging,
And was so baselye borne;
So lordlye of hys lokes,
And so dysdayneslye;
So fatte a magott,
Bred of a flesh-flye

John Skelton,
Speke, Parrot, 1522

SKILLS BUILDER

Read Sources I–L by the contemporary commentators. In what ways does the material reflect the point of view and situation of the author? You might find it useful to complete a table like the one below to record your ideas.

	What each writer says about Wolsey	Why they might have written what they did – think about their situation and/or position
Source I: George Cavendish Source J: Polydore Vergil Source K: Edward Hall Source L: John Skelton		

How successful were Wolsey's domestic policies?

Many historians argue that Wolsey's focus was on foreign affairs and that he could have done more to reform government at home. Yet most contemporaries were content with things as they were. They did not expect Wolsey to bring about radical change in the systems of government.

The key to good government in the sixteenth century was maintaining law and order and upholding the power of the Crown and Church. Domestic achievements were never going to raise the status and prestige of the Crown as much as those on the foreign stage, and as long as Henry craved foreign glory, Wolsey made that his focus.

Yet, at the same time, efficient tax collection was necessary for conducting adventurous foreign policies and a stable domestic government was vital for diplomatic success. Moreover, given Wolsey's natural vitality and energy it was likely that he would want to involve himself in all matters of government. Indeed, that can be seen as one of his key failings in that the King's Cardinal took on a huge amount of domestic administration leading

Definitions

Court of Star Chamber

A royal law court that could be used by the King's subjects to get justice.

Civil law

A system of law having its origin in Roman law, as opposed to common law or canon law.

Common law

The system of laws originated and developed in England and based on court decisions, on the doctrines implicit in those decisions, and on customs and usages rather than on codified written laws.

Benefice

A clerical position.

Question

What was the potential problem of Wolsey favouring the poor?

to a backlog of cases in the **Court of Star Chamber** and unfinished plans for reform.

Justice

Following Wolsey's appointment as Lord Chancellor in 1515 he was active in both the Court of Chancery and the Court of Star Chamber. The historian John Guy has highlighted Wolsey's impact in legal reform and commended his attempts to bring greater justice to the system. Wolsey presided over many cases in person, with the centre of his legal activities lying in Star Chamber.

Wolsey's success can be attributed to the fact that anyone was able to bring their case before him in Star Chamber, regardless of their wealth or social status. Star Chamber dealt with over 120 cases each year under Wolsey, compared with around twelve cases per year in the reign of Henry VII. It appears that Wolsey genuinely wanted to see impartial justice delivered in his courts and there is little doubt that he enjoyed championing the cause of poorer litigants against richer and stronger ones. Wolsey also promoted **civil law** over **common law** in the Court of Star Chamber and frequently used his courts to overturn common law verdicts.

Source M

Wolsey had the reputation of being extremely just: he favours the people exceedingly, and especially the poor: hearing their suits and seeking to despatch them instantly.

Venetian Ambassador Guistiniani in 1515

Civil law was seen as more progressive and just in that it laid an emphasis on natural justice rather than on precedent when decisions were being made. Common law was seen as outdated and often unjust as one party might win on a legal technicality based on past precedents. Therefore Wolsey's achievements in the law hinge on his pursuit of justice for all, and the endorsement of a progressive legal system. Of course there were times when Wolsey used the courts to further his own position and carry out personal vendettas against enemies. An often-cited example of this is Wolsey's treatment of Sir Amyas Paulet.

On entering his first **benefice**, Wolsey had been put in the stocks by Paulet in a bid to teach the young man a lesson about humility and good grace. Wolsey never forgot his humiliation at the hands of Paulet and used his position as Lord Chancellor to have his revenge. Sir Amyas had to wait in daily attendance at Wolsey's court for five years under threat of confiscation of all his property if he left London.

There is also no doubt that Wolsey created further resentment through his work in Star Chamber, especially among those nobles who were targeted for abusing their aristocratic privileges. In 1515 the Earl of Northumberland was sent to Fleet Prison and in 1516 Lord Burgavenny was accused of illegal retaining. Perhaps Wolsey also saw the law as a means of bringing his social superiors down to size.

Finally, it should be pointed out that Wolsey's achievements in the law did not outlast him. He used the existing machinery of the law to carry out his work and failed to carry out any lasting institutional reform. He may well have been active and energetic in his role as Lord Chancellor but it is also true that there was an enormous backlog of cases to be heard in Star Chamber by 1529 and much of the administration there was chaotic.

Enclosure

The historians Scarisbrick and Peter Gwyn both place much emphasis upon the legal actions that Wolsey took against those nobles who enclosed land illegally. Enclosure involved fencing-off common land for profitable sheep rearing, and this action was thought to be responsible for rural depopulation and poverty. Three statutes had been passed against enclosure before Wolsey became Lord Chancellor, but had been largely ignored. Wolsey went to work on enclosure in 1517, launching a national inquiry into enclosed land. Many of those brought to court were ordered to rebuild houses that had been destroyed and return land to arable farming.

Once more we can see Wolsey's drive and determination in bringing great men to justice, and to challenge the power of the aristocracy. At the same time one might question the long-term practical results of Wolsey's activities. Enclosure continued to take place and rural poverty continued to climb. Wolsey's actions furthered his unpopularity with the ruling classes. Indeed in a parliamentary session of 1523 Wolsey was forced to accept all existing enclosures demonstrating that he was not always able to exert his political power over the nobility.

Finances

> **Question**
>
> Why do you think it was difficult to bring people to court in sixteenth-century England?

> **Source N**
>
> When embarking upon the enclosure inquiry of 1517, Wolsey wanted to do something for the common weal, and to that end some 260 people are known to have been brought to court. This in itself is remarkable, when one remembers how rarely anyone appeared in court
>
> Peter Gwyn, *The King's Cardinal*, 1990

> **Source O**
>
> The ability to tax efficiently is a valid index of the strength of an early modern regime. Henrician government was so successful in this respect that it created a system of taxation which for its sophistication and attention to the principles of distributive justice was several centuries ahead of its time. To this achievement Wolsey made the greatest contribution. For the first time since 1334 the Crown was levying taxation which accurately reflected the true wealth of taxpayers.
>
> John Guy, *Tudor England*, 1988

> **Source P**
>
> Wolsey's greatest weakness lay in the realm of finance . . . he was a bad financier because he could neither make do with the existing revenue nor effectively increase it. He had little understanding of economic facts . . . Wolsey's taxation made enemies of many whose hostility could be dangerous.
>
> G.R. Elton, *England under the Tudors*, 1955

> **Questions**
>
> 1 Explain in your own words what is meant by levying taxation which accurately reflected the true wealth of taxpayers.
> 2 Make a note of how Guy and Elton differ on their view of Wolsey's abilities as a financier. Why do you think they might hold different viewpoints?

Definition

Fifteenths and tenths

The standard form of taxation in England paid by towns and boroughs to the Crown.

Wolsey's greatest achievement in financial policy was to replace the traditional **fifteenths and tenths** with a system that accurately reflected the true wealth of taxpayers across England. In doing this Wolsey rejected the fixed rates of the fifteenths and tenths with a more flexible and realistic subsidy, based on the ability to pay. Commissioners were despatched to the localities to supervise assessments of wealth while graduated rates of tax were established that placed a greater financial burden on the very rich.

The subsidy and fifteenths and tenths continued to exist together, but it was clearly the subsidy that Wolsey favoured because it raised more money and it was more progressive. Between 1513 and 1516 the subsidy raised £170,000 while fifteenths and tenths raised £90,000. From 1513 to 1529, Wolsey raised:

- £325,000 in parliamentary subsidies
- £118,000 from fifteenths and tenths
- loans totalling £250,000.

However, money caused Wolsey problems both in his dealings with Henry VIII and parliament. In 1523 Wolsey demanded over £800,000 in taxation from parliament on top of the loans that were still being collected from 1522, which amounted to £260,000. Wolsey's manner with parliament was forthright and although he did obtain some extra money, he was forced to settle for much less than he had wanted.

Wolsey also had to accept concessions on enclosure (see page 43) and it is clear that the parliamentary session did not pass harmoniously. It was also clear that Wolsey's fiscal policies were causing much resentment among the ruling classes. This can be seen by the increasingly late payments that characterised the years 1523–25, as Wolsey looked to anticipate payments of the subsidy from taxpayers, thus accounting for money that the Crown did not yet have.

The Amicable Grant, 1525

Matters came to a head in February 1525, after the French army had been annihilated at the Battle of Pavia. Henry VIII saw this defeat as an opportunity to invade France, especially as the French King, Francis I, was held captive by Charles V. However, the coffers were empty, so Wolsey demanded a non-parliamentary tax called the Amicable Grant. The new demand would target both clergy and laity based on a sliding scale, but coming so soon after the forced loans and parliamentary tax of the previous three years, the Amicable Grant met with violent displeasure.

The results were a refusal to pay and rebellion across Suffolk and East Anglia. Ten thousand men marched on Lavenham, an important cloth-making centre in Suffolk, highlighting the scale of this tax rebellion. The hostility was not initiated by nobles, indeed the Dukes of Norfolk and Suffolk did their bit to restore order. Yet the spontaneous nature of the uprising was evidence of the unpopularity of Wolsey's policies.

The Amicable Grant was abandoned in May 1525, and no further taxation was attempted by Wolsey. To many historians the Amicable Grant marks the beginning of the end for Wolsey, the point at which Henry began to doubt the talents of his leading minister. Henry denied all knowledge of the Amicable Grant and Wolsey's opponents began to sense the vulnerability of the King's Cardinal. English foreign policy subsequently turned full circle as a result of the abandonment of the French invasion. Wolsey switched from an alliance with Charles V to a French alliance, which proved both unpopular and ultimately disastrous in the context of the King's Great Matter.

How far did Wolsey deliberately monopolise political power?

Source Q

Anyone could see that Wolsey had tried to do the impossible, to rule as King when he was not the king, to ignore the legal and constitutional traditions of England and substitute them for his own self-confident judgement, to do a highly professional job in a very amateur manner. He had lasted so long because in two things he was not amateur at all; he knew how to promote himself, and for most of the time he knew how to keep Henry satisfied.

G.R. Elton, *England under the Tudors*, 1955

Source R

Wolsey's workload was staggering, but he was able both physically and mentally to take it in his stride. That he had these qualities should come as no surprise. Why it might is because there has been a tendency to hide Giustinian's man of vast ability under the glitz and razzmatazz of Renaissance politics, in the process turning Wolsey into some kind of strutting peacock devoted only to self glorification and self indulgence. The truth is much more sober . . . it is right to start with the fact that Wolsey was a man of enormous ability, for it provides the simple answers to the question why he became the King's leading minister.

Peter Gwyn, *The King's Cardinal*, 1990

SKILLS BUILDER

1 What does Elton suggest about Wolsey's relationship with Henry?
2 How far does Gwyn support Elton's argument?

As Lord Chancellor, Wolsey was the head of the country's secular legal system, while as Archbishop of York and then as Cardinal he was also England's most prominent churchman. Although there was nothing unusual in a man of the Church holding political power in the sixteenth century, it would bring Wolsey problems in his domestic administration.

Parliament met only twice during Wolsey's ascendancy, and it is generally perceived that Wolsey did not trust its members. The role of parliament in sixteenth-century England was to pass laws and grant taxes. Wolsey believed that parliament was a potential source of trouble for the government and therefore himself.

It is easy to see why historians argue that Wolsey deliberately sidelined parliament in a bid to pursue his policies unopposed. Wolsey only used parliament when he had to, and by that stage he had caused such resentment among the members of parliament that they were reluctant to give him what he wanted.

That said, parliament was not at the heart of Tudor government. Indeed its powers were very limited and it was seen as an institution to carry out the wishes of the King. Policy was devised in the King's household, at Court. Here, administrative affairs were overseen by the Council, made up of leading nobles and churchmen, while the Chamber saw to the King's most intimate needs and was made up of his most trusted friends.

David Starkey argues that the Privy Chamber, as it became known in the 1490s, was the heartbeat of Tudor government as those trusted confidantes who served on it had daily access to the King. The Gentlemen of the Privy Chamber were usually thrusting, young ambitious men who wished to serve their King and further their careers. These were men such as Nicholas Carew and Sir Edward Guilford. Therefore the royal palaces at Westminster, Greenwich and Eltham became the places for such young men to win the favour of the King.

It has been argued that Wolsey saw such men as political rivals and purposefully initiated a purge of the Privy Chamber in 1519, expelling these rising stars and ensuring that they were given mundane jobs away from court. Certainly the make up of the Privy Chamber changed in 1519 and the Venetian ambassador was moved to write that, 'within the last few days his majesty has made a very great change in the court here, dismissing four of his chief lords in waiting who enjoyed extreme authority in this kingdom'.

Yet Gwyn believes that these men were not completely ostracised from court, that they all picked up important posts which did not hamper their career prospects and that Wolsey was not so paranoid as to believe that such minions were a threat to his political pre-eminence. He writes that 'Wolsey did not control royal patronage, did not surround himself with yes men, nor was he hated by everybody.' Still many others believe that such actions continued to build resentment against Wolsey, which would come to a head in 1529 when the King's Cardinal lost the trust of his master.

The wars of 1522–25 continued to keep young nobles away from Court, and on their return Wolsey secured the **Eltham Ordinances** through which the number of **Gentlemen of the Bedchamber** was reduced from twelve to six. Gwyn again defends Wolsey on the grounds that such a reduction was a necessary cost-cutting exercise, and that fewer numbers would increase the efficiency of administration within the King's household. Yet given the circumstances, and the subsequent disinterest paid to the Eltham Ordinances by Wolsey in terms of a reforming measure, it would appear

Definitions

Eltham Ordinances

A royal edict of 1526 that cut the number in the royal household.

Gentlemen of the Bedchamber

Henry's personal attendants and advisors.

that by this stage Wolsey was intent on destroying the power base of those he perceived as rivals for the King's favour.

Conclusion

Faction was an inevitable part of any European court, but the sheer monopolisation of political power by Wolsey for fifteen years meant that latent faction was not really in evidence. One can be sure that Wolsey guarded his position and status fiercely and made sure that he was well informed of any political manoeuvring by ambitious young men. The extent to which Wolsey purposefully isolated these nobles has been keenly debated but it is indisputable that power rested on the will of the King. As we have established already, Wolsey's pre-eminence could last only as long as Henry saw fit. As long as Henry believed that Wolsey was serving his interests effectively, the Cardinal was effectively untouchable. What Wolsey did in terms of building up his wealth and adding to his titles and positions merely confirmed his status. It must be remembered that Henry made Wolsey and Henry had the capacity to break him also.

Key text: *The King's Cardinal*, by Peter Gwyn

Published in 1990, Gwyn's work attempts to rehabilitate Wolsey's reputation in history. Gwyn views Wolsey as a loyal servant of the Crown who did not go out of his way to antagonise nobles nor ruthlessly monopolise power at the expense of other courtiers. Gwyn believes that Wolsey served the King diligently and effectively until circumstances conspired against him in 1529. Some historians criticised Gwyn for taking a rather rosy view of Wolsey's political dealings.

Did Wolsey carry out any meaningful reform of the Church?

What was the impact of the Hunne Affair?

The 1515 parliamentary session was dominated by the Hunne Affair (see page 20), and the anti-clerical backlash from this controversy impacted upon Wolsey. Richard Hunne was a prosperous London merchant, who had challenged the Church through the law courts over the high rate of mortuary fees that he had been forced to pay on the death of his infant son. In response the Church had allegedly trumped up charges of heresy against Hunne and he was imprisoned while awaiting trial. Hunne was subsequently found dead in custody and his demise caused uproar in the City of London. The case fuelled anti-clericalism in London, as the Church was accused of making up charges of heresy, murdering a well-to-do merchant and then convicting him of all charges after his death in order to seize his property. The case is widely cited by historians as evidence of widespread dissatisfaction with the Church, and subsequently one of the reasons why Catholicism crumbled under Henry's later attacks.

Taking it further

Polydore Vergil's description of Wolsey

Soon he began to use a golden seat, a golden cushion, a golden cloth on his table, and when he went on foot, he had his hat – the symbol of the cardinal's rank – carried before him by a servant, and raised aloft like a holy idol, and he had it put upon the very altar in the king's chapel during divine service.

Find another description or an image of Wolsey that you think best portrays the cardinal's pomp and vanity.

Definition

Probate courts

Ecclesiastical courts dealing with wills left by the laity that often included monetary donations to the Church.

In reality this was not the case and many remained loyal and devoted to the Catholic Church. However, within the confines of London the Hunne Affair was notorious and it did nothing to convince Wolsey that parliament was a force for good.

At the same time a friar named Henry Standish attacked the legal precedent of benefit of the clergy. Benefit of the clergy allowed members of the clergy to have any criminal cases heard in ecclesiastical courts rather than secular courts where it was assumed that they would gain a more lenient hearing. Not only that, but benefit of the clergy had been widely abused over the course of the late-medieval period, to the point that any educated and literate man might be able to claim immunity from secular trial. An Act of 1512 restricted benefit of the clergy and in the 1515 session the principle was once more raised, adding further to the anti-clerical atmosphere. The Act was not renewed but Wolsey had to swear to Henry personally that royal authority held sway over ecclesiastical power.

The anti-clericalism of 1515 perhaps explains why the next parliament did not meet until 1523. Only Wolsey's desperate need for money to fund Henry's foreign policy explains why parliament met in 1523 and, as we have seen, Wolsey was forced to compromise his policy against enclosure in order to get extra cash (see page 43).

Ecclesiastical extravagance

There is no hiding from the fact that Wolsey's exploitation of his ecclesiastical positions did bring him incomparable wealth in England. His appointment as *Legate a latere* merely enhanced his ecclesiastical authority and allowed him to establish his own **probate courts** through which his income was increased still further. Wolsey's wealth was there for all to see and unquestionably created jealousy and resentment.

Wolsey's pomp and magnificence opened him up to criticism and a certain amount of ridicule from contemporary satirists such as Skelton. Still, given the authority vested in him by the Pope as *Legate a latere* Wolsey was in a strong position to reform the Church, which as we have seen in the parliamentary session of 1515 was coming in for some criticism.

Pluralism, nepotism and absenteeism

Wolsey's reputation as a churchman has been widely criticised. He has been held up by subsequent Protestant historians as the embodiment of all that was wrong with the Catholic Church. It is undeniable that Wolsey held bishoprics in plurality (by 1529 he held the archbishopric of York, bishopric of Winchester and the abbey of St Albans) and used ecclesiastical patronage to support his illegitimate son, Thomas Winter. He also never actually visited his sees of Lincoln, Bath and Wells, and Durham. Indeed he only went to York after his fall from grace.

Yet as the historian S.J. Gunn points out, senior churchmen across Europe indulged in simony, nepotism and pluralism, and these abuses were nothing new. In many ways they were viewed as part of the post and did not attract the level of contemporary criticism that we might think they would.

However, all of this adds fuel to the idea that Wolsey was only interested in exploiting the Church for his own personal financial gain. Wolsey did hold an **Ecclesiastical Council** in 1518 at York that discussed ways of improving the conduct and work of the provincial clergy. Yet the York Convocation said nothing new and could be seen merely as a means by which Wolsey could impress the Pope in light of his upcoming appointment as *legate*. As John Guy points out, 'it is hard to rate Wolsey's ecclesiastical policy as anything much beyond the level of good intentions'.

Monastic reform

Wolsey initiated legatine **visitations** of monastic houses in England, and his proposals for reform among the religious orders were constructive and positive. The visitors to some monastic houses reported that not all abbots and monks were observing the prescribed monastic lifestyle that they had sworn to, and as a result some were replaced, while statutes for the Benedictines and Augustinians were drawn up. By the end of his career Wolsey was proposing the creation of thirteen new **episcopal see**s based on dissolved monasteries to bring English dioceses into line with population change. Still such achievements were modest and not without opposition.

Many, such as Archbishop Warham, objected to the heavy handed way in which Wolsey tried to carry out reform. Moreover, Wolsey's additional dissolution of thirty religious houses to pay for the building of Cardinal College, Oxford, and Ipswich School upset defenders of the monastic way. Wolsey's promotion of education and humanism may sound worthy but again the principal reason behind the endowment of these two colleges was to further Wolsey's own reputation and standing within the Tudor court.

Pope or King?

Both the Pope and Henry hoped that they would benefit financially from Wolsey's appointment as papal legate. Despite being appointed *Legate a latere* in 1524 Wolsey did not deliver a subsidy to Rome, but he did succeed in taxing the clergy at a rate that was even greater than the avaricious Henry VII. Therefore, although there was an apparent conflict of interests between Pope and King, it was evident that Wolsey never forgot that Henry was his real master. Ultimately Henry expected Wolsey to be able to use his legatine influence in Rome to solve his Great Matter and, when circumstances turned against Wolsey, Henry turned on the Cardinal.

Definitions

Ecclesiastical Council

A meeting of leading bishops to discuss the condition of the Church.

Visitation

Inspection of a church or religious house by Crown commissioners.

Episcopal see

A bishopric or the specific area over which a bishop has authority.

Conclusion: did Wolsey weaken the English Church?

The extent to which Wolsey actually weakened the Church has been much debated. Certainly his personal conduct is not impressive but, as we have established, his actions were not unusual at the time. To his credit Wolsey shielded the Church from monarchical attack in the period 1515–29. Over the issue of benefit of the clergy, Wolsey had tried to defend clerical privileges as best he could, and used his political position to assure Henry that the royal prerogative was not being undermined by appeals to Roman canons.

Yet at the same time Wolsey weakened the Church through his intensely centralising policies in all aspects of ecclesiastical affairs. Wolsey was personally involved in all important Church matters but he was first and foremost Henry's servant. Essentially Henry could use Wolsey as a loyal and effective civil servant in charge of the Church. Wolsey served to increase royal control over the Church and weakened its sense of independence at the same time. No one could foresee the events of the 1530s that lay ahead and the establishment of the Royal Supremacy, but it is tempting to argue that the Church was unable to withstand the attack it came under from Henry in the 1530s as a consequence of Wolsey's legatine legacy.

SKILLS BUILDER

1 Using the sources and information in this unit, complete a table like the one below to organise your ideas about Wolsey's domestic policies.

	Wolsey's policies	Evidence	Success or failure?
Church Nobility/Councillors Finance Justice Enclosure			

Sorting your ideas in this way will help you when you come to answer questions on Wolsey.

2 Below is an example of a b) type question on Wolsey's domestic policies. Make some notes on what you would include in your answer to this question. Then write your answer.

Question (b)

Use Sources T, U and V and your own knowledge.

Do you accept the view in Source V that Wolsey's domestic policies were disappointing? (40 marks)

Source T

Thus Wolsey, with his arrogance and ambition aroused against himself the hatred of the whole country, and by his hostility towards the nobility and the common people, caused him the greatest irritation through his vainglory. He was indeed detested by everyone, because he assumed that he could undertake nearly all the offices of state by himself.

From Polydore Vergil, *Anglica Historia*, 1534

Source U

He alone transacts as much business as that which occupies all the magistrates, offices and councils of Venice, both civil and criminal. He is thoughtful and has the reputation of being extremely just. He favours the people exceedingly, and especially the poor; hearing their cases and seeking to despatch them instantly. He also makes the lawyers plead without charge for all paupers.

From a report by the Venetian ambassador, Guistiniani

Source V

Any conclusion on Wolsey seems to carry an air of disappointment. His capacity for detailed hard work together with his creativity promised more than was delivered . . . By twentieth century standards his achievements seem limited but there is a danger of judging by anachronistic standards. We expect change and improvement where the sixteenth century sought stability and security-objectives that are not necessarily achieved by change. It is also easy to forget that ultimate responsibility lay with the king and to criticise Wolsey's domestic policies is also to criticise Henry for his lack of involvement.

Ian Dawson, *The Tudor Century*, 1993

3 Now have a go at answering this question: Why did Wolsey fall from power in 1529?

The traditional view of Wolsey is that of an unpopular royal favourite who was constantly fighting to retain his hold over the King. This interpretation implies that Henry was relatively weak and easily manipulated by those around him. It suggests that in the end the nobility took their revenge on Wolsey when he lost favour with the King over the divorce crisis. It also suggests that there was a long-term noble conspiracy against Wolsey that manifested itself in the events of 1528–29.

Definition

Revisionist historian

A revisionist historian is one that challenges accepted historical lines of argument and puts forward new ideas.

The revisionist line on Wolsey plays down his unpopularity at court and asserts that Wolsey did not intentionally antagonise the nobility or directly harm the careers of ambitious young men in order to preserve his power over the King. Historians such as Peter Gwyn argue that Wolsey was too skilful a politician to needlessly offend anybody and create enemies. He suggests that rather than any long-term conspiratorial group at work in Wolsey's fall, there was a short-term opportunist faction led by the Dukes of Norfolk and Suffolk who acted on Henry's dissatisfaction with Wolsey over the Great Matter.

Was there a noble conspiracy against Wolsey?

Source X

Now not long afterwards, Christopher, Cardinal of York, died at Rome, and Wolsey, Bishop of Lincoln was next made archbishop of York, and shortly afterwards chancellor of the realm, from which office William Warham, archbishop of Canterbury resigned of his own accord. To have this abundant good fortune must be regarded as most estimable if it is showered upon sober, moderate and self controlled men, who are not puffed up by power, do not become arrogant with wealth, and do not give themselves airs because of their good fortune. None of these qualities appeared in Wolsey. Acquiring so many offices at almost the same time, he became so proud that he began to regard himself as the equal of kings.

Polydore Vergil, *Anglica Historia*, 1555

Question

What aspect of Wolsey's character, outlined in Source X above, may have created enemies for him?

It was entirely predictable that anyone in such a position of power as Wolsey in the Tudor court would create enemies, whether he intended to or not. As Gwyn suggests, claims that Wolsey deliberately kept ambitious courtiers such as Richard Pace away from Henry have been exaggerated and the evidence suggests that the Cardinal did consult leading nobles on important policy decisions.

Yet as John Guy points out, by the time that Wolsey debated policy with the nobility, the decision had already been made in private with the King. Wolsey may have paid lip service to conciliar government, but his close partnership with the King created envy and no little resentment.

Wolsey was unpopular with the Dukes of Norfolk and Suffolk, but they did not try to undermine his authority in the 1520s. **Anne Boleyn** (see page 85) too has often been seen as a key figure in Wolsey's fall. Certainly she had her reasons to despise the Cardinal as he had broken up her affair with Henry Percy in order that the King could claim his woman. Yet it was not in her interests to support any anti-Wolsey faction because until very late in the divorce proceedings he must have seemed like the one man who was capable of realizing her dream of becoming Queen of England.

Therefore it would be fair to say that although there was resentment and envy of Wolsey's position and wealth, there was no long-term noble conspiracy against him because such actions were pointless while he held the trust of Henry.

Source Y

I cannot comprehend, and the King still less, how your reverent lordship, after having allured us by so many fine promises about divorce, can have repented of your purpose, and how you could have done what you have, in order to hinder the consummation of it . . . The wrong you have done me has caused me much sorrow; but I feel infinitely more in seeing myself betrayed by a man who pretended to enter into my interests only to discover the secrets of my heart.

Letter from Anne Boleyn to Cardinal Wolsey, 1529

Questions

1 How would you describe the tone of this letter? Select some short quotations to reinforce your point.
2 Why is the date important in understanding the context of this letter?

Why did Henry lose faith in Wolsey?

There are two main reasons why Henry lost faith in his chief minister after almost fifteen years of loyal service:

1 In general Henry's government was becoming increasingly unpopular from 1527 to 1529. One reason for this was England's alliance with France, which had been in place since 1527. Wolsey had switched England's foreign allegiance from Charles V to Francis I after 1525 in a bid to break Habsburg control over Italy and cajole the Emperor into negotiations over Henry's marriage to Catherine. The Anglo-French alliance was unpopular with the leading nobility; it disrupted trade with the Low Countries, and ultimately it put Henry in a weak position regarding the Great Matter, after the sack of Rome in 1527 confirmed Imperial domination of Italy and the Pope.

2 In the end Wolsey fell from power as a consequence of his failure in the divorce crisis. Henry had always endorsed and supported Wolsey's rise through the ecclesiastical ranks because it extended royal influence over the Church. In 1527 Henry believed that Wolsey would be able to exercise his extensive legatine powers to attain an annulment of Henry's first marriage. In short, Wolsey's position as *Legate a latere* increased Henry's expectations of a quick resolution of the Great Matter.

Why was Wolsey unable to solve the King's divorce crisis between 1526 and 1529?

The crisis

By 1526 Henry wanted out of his marriage to Catherine of Aragon. With regards to his own future, Wolsey himself fully recognised the importance of attaining the divorce. Wolsey had the power to make the necessary judgement on Henry's case but needed papal confirmation of any decision that he made. Catherine would inevitably make an appeal to Rome and Wolsey had to be sure that the Pope would support his case.

The solution?

Wolsey proposed the idea of challenging the original dispensation issued by Pope Julius II that had allowed Henry to marry Catherine in the first place. Wolsey argued that this dispensation was issued on the grounds of consummation, yet Catherine was adamant that she came to Henry pure and virginal. This line had two distinct advantages in that first it was not directly challenging papal authority but merely picking up on a legal technicality, and second it was in line with Catherine's argument.

The problem

Henry wanted to seek a divorce based on the verses in Leviticus in the Old Testament that prohibited marriage to one's dead brother's wife. Wolsey should be given some credit for thinking up alternative solutions to Henry's problem, but he was in the end constrained by Henry's insistence on the Levitical route as a matter of principle.

Bad luck

In May 1527, Wolsey planned to use his powers as *Legate a latere* to annul the marriage in England before receiving confirmation from Rome. But Catherine heard of this meeting and immediately opposed any decisions taken in England about her marriage.

Wolsey had failed in his first attempts to quietly and secretly pronounce on the divorce in England. Now events in Italy turned against him. After Imperial troops sacked Rome in 1527, Charles V effectively held **Pope Clement VII** (see page 87) prisoner, and papal policy became imperial policy. Initially, Wolsey hoped to use this to his advantage by establishing a papal court in Avignon with the assistance of the College of Cardinals. Acting without Rome but with the assistance of the Church, Wolsey planned to pronounce in favour of the divorce. Yet the Cardinals were reluctant to help, and Clement's release in December 1527 rendered the plan obsolete.

Wolsey's last chance

Take it further

1 Pick out two phrases from Source Z which show that Wolsey was rather resigned to his fate in 1529.
2 In your own words explain Wolsey's advice to Master Kingston outlined in the last sentence.

Source Z

Well, well, Master Kingston quoth he, I see the matter against me how it framed. But if I had served God as diligently as I have done the King, He would not have given me over in my grey hairs. Howbeit, this is the just reward that I must receive for my worldly diligence and the pains that I have taken to do the King service and to satisfy his vain pleasures, not regarding my godly duty . . . I warn you be well advised and assured what matter ye put in his (Henry VIII's) head, for ye shall never pull it out again.

George Cavendish, *Thomas Wolsey, his Life and Death*

Wolsey's plan now was to get Clement to grant him the power to decide the case in England without the right of appeal. But the Pope was unwilling to openly support Henry's case and instead tried to find a compromise solution that would offend neither King nor Emperor.

In the summer of 1528, the Pope sent **Cardinal Campeggio** (see page 88) to oversee an ecclesiastical court in England with the necessary powers to annul the marriage. But Clement had privately told Campeggio not to use these powers and to delay proceedings for as long as possible. Before the court opened, Henry and Wolsey tried to convince Campeggio of the validity of their case, but by this time events in Italy once more favoured the Emperor and the Pope was convinced that he needed to align with Charles V. Campeggio, knowing that he could not decree on the Great Matter, looked for alternative solutions, even suggesting to Catherine that she retire to a nunnery and leave Henry free to remarry. Predictably, Catherine refused and many at court appeared to sympathise with her plight.

In October 1528 proceedings were held up further when it emerged that the Spanish had discovered a brief by Julius II from 1503 that cleared up any doubts over Catherine's second marriage to Henry. This brief would have severely damaged Henry's case and the English immediately proclaimed it to be a fake. Certainly, it does seem rather coincidental that it should appear at such an opportune moment, but its authenticity will never be known as the Spanish refused to give it up to the English for fear that it would disappear. With any hopes of attaining a divorce fading fast, and with them Wolsey's career, the court opened at Blackfriars on 31 March 1529.

Catherine maintained that her marriage to Arthur had not been consummated. She also made it clear that no court in England could decree her marriage invalid and she appealed to Rome before walking out. The proceedings dragged on until 23 July 1529 when Campeggio adjourned the hearing of Henry's case for the summer. It was clear to most onlookers that the case would never be heard in England and that Wolsey had failed in his bid to secure a divorce for Henry. Wolsey's fate depended on the continuance of Henry's confidence and that was now lost. Henry did not need Norfolk or Suffolk to alert him to the fact that Wolsey's divorce plans had failed.

On 9 October Wolsey was charged with praemunire, that is exercising his legatine power in England to the detriment of the King, a rather hypocritical charge given Henry's endorsement of Wolsey's ecclesiastical powers. The charge served not only to start Wolsey's fall from grace, but also to remind Clement of the independent traditions of the English Church. The Royal Supremacy was a long way off and at this stage not on Henry's agenda, but there was no harm in using Wolsey's public humiliation as a means of trying to pressurise Rome. The anti-clerical Acts passed in the first meeting of the Reformation Parliament in November 1529 could be seen as part of this policy. Wolsey was not ruined

Source AA

The King, who knew of his doings and secret communications, all this year pretended to ignore them to see what he would eventually do, until he saw his proud heart so highly exalted that he intended to be so triumphantly installed (as Archbishop of York) without informing the king, even as if in disdain of the king. Then the King thought it was not fitting or convenient to let him any longer continue in his malicious and proud purposes and attempts. Therefore he sent letters to the Earl of Northumberland, willing him with all diligence to arrest the cardinal.

Edward Hall, *The Union of the Two Noble and Illustre Families of Lancaster and York*, 1548

immediately as Henry believed that he might still be useful should circumstances change in Italy.

The end

Wolsey retired to his archbishopric of York where he continued to live in some splendour. Yet with Henry's ego dented by the failure to attain a divorce through Rome in 1529, Wolsey was always the likely scapegoat. The Cardinal had done all that he could to gain an annulment through Rome but in the end he was the victim of forces beyond his control. Blame for the failure at Blackfriars was placed on him and it was at this point that his enemies went into action. In November 1530 the council had Wolsey arrested, and on his way to face charges of treason in London, the Cardinal died at Leicester Abbey on 24 November 1530.

Take it further

1 What reason does Hall give for Henry finally losing patience with Wolsey?
2 Select phrases from the source which suggest that Hall was no friend of Wolsey.

SKILLS BUILDER

Draw up a detailed essay plan for the following question: how far can Wolsey's domestic policies be considered a success?

- Use the table you completed earlier in this chapter (page 50) to help you to structure your essay. Each paragraph should deal with one of the five key areas of Wolsey's domestic policy from your table: justice, finance, enclosure, nobility/councillors, Church.
- Think of each paragraph as a mini essay in which you make your point clearly at the beginning and then go on to reinforce your idea with well-selected evidence.
- This is where it becomes crucial that you have planned your essay clearly as it needs to hold together as an argument.
- At the end of the paragraph make sure you go back to the point that you wanted to make.

Exam tips

Remember that it is crucial you consider both sides of the argument here. One cannot completely dismiss Wolsey's domestic policies as hopeless, but neither would it be right to see them as a total success. Use your introduction to lay out the argument that Wolsey often had good intentions in domestic policy but rarely did his plans for reform actually come to anything.

Always include a conclusion that offers a judgement on the question. Your conclusion will not be radically different from your introduction but make sure that you address the demands of the question clearly and convince the marker that your essay is well focused. Perhaps the conclusion is the place to highlight the point that it is difficult to view Wolsey's domestic policy in isolation from foreign affairs as much of his financial policy was geared towards raising money for foreign expeditions.

KNOWLEDGE FOCUS

- Wolsey's rise to power was due to a combination of good fortune, opportunism and ability.

- That Wolsey remained in power for so long was largely down to the fact that he served Henry loyally and effectively.

- Wolsey's domestic policies took second place to his foreign affairs.

- Wolsey revolutionised the system of taxation in England.

- Wolsey planned a great deal of domestic reform but achieved very little in practice.

- Wolsey's relations with the nobility and parliament were strained as a consequence of his desire to raise money for Henry.

- Wolsey was in a strong position to reform the Church but did nothing of any substance.

- It is unlikely that Wolsey deliberately tried to monopolise power at the expense of other courtiers.

- Wolsey's fall was mainly down to the circumstances surrounding the Great Matter.

SKILLS FOCUS

- Source based answers need to use the documents to reflect a balanced argument. It is unlikely that all the sources will simply agree on the issue in question.

- Be prepared to structure your argument around the sources.

- Use a conclusion to make a clear judgement on the question.

4 Henry VIII and the quest for international influence: 1509–40

Key questions

- Can Henry's early foreign policy be considered a success?
- How far did Wolsey achieve his aims in foreign policy in the years 1514–29?
- To what extent was Henry isolated and vulnerable in European affairs 1530–40?
- Do the years 1521–40 in foreign policy merit their reputation as ones of expensive failure?

Timeline

1512	England joins Spain in an alliance against France.
1513	Emperor Maximilian joins Ferdinand, Henry and the Papacy against France
	August, Battle of the Spurs and capture of Therouanne
	September, Earl of Surrey leads a crushing victory over the Scots at Flodden
	September, Tournai captured
1514	Henry makes peace with France
1515	Accession of Francis I as King of France
1516	Princess Mary born
1518	The Treaty of London signed marking the centrepiece of Wolsey's peacemaking
1519	Charles V elected Holy Roman Emperor
1520	May, Henry meets Charles V in England
	June, Henry and Francis meet at the Field of Cloth of Gold
	July, Henry meets Charles at Calais
1521	Wolsey visits Charles V at Bruges, agreement reached for joint invasion of France
1523	English army under Suffolk lands at Calais. Siege of Boulogne abandoned to make an attack on Paris. The attack fails as winter sets in.
1525	February, Battle of Pavia: Imperial forces defeat the French. Francis I captured
	August, Henry makes peace with France
1527	April, offensive alliance against Charles V signed with France
1528	England and France declare war on Charles V
1529	July, Legatine Court presiding over the Great Matter adjourned
	August, Treaty of Cambrai seals peace between Charles V and Francis I
	October, Wolsey dismissed

1533	Diplomatic links made with Lutheran princes
1536	January, Catherine of Aragon dies
	May, Anne Boleyn executed
1537	Prince Edward born
1538	Papal bull of deprivation deposing Henry VIII
	Peace of Nice secures ten-year truce between Charles V and Francis I
1538/39	Purge of White Rose Party carried out
1540	January, Henry marries Anne of Cleves. Marriage remains unconsummated.
	July, Cromwell executed. Henry marries Catherine Howard.
1542	Henry declares war on Scotland
	November, English army defeats the Scots at Solway Moss
	December, James V of Scotland dies, leaving the infant Mary as heir
1543	July, Treaty of Greenwich signed with Scotland
	July, Henry marries Catherine Parr
	Henry declares war on France
1544	English invasion of southern Scotland
	September, Boulogne taken by English army
1545	French attempt to invade England fails
1546	Peace agreement between England and France at Ardres
1547	January, Henry VIII dies.

Source A

The twenty odd miles of sea between Dover and Calais were filled with a great concourse of ships carrying the King and queen and their suites (court) to France – leaving England emptied of most of its nobility . . . On 5 June Henry set out for Guines and two days later cannon sounded at the appointed hour on both sides to announce to each King the other's departure. When he reached the edge of the field Henry stopped. Francis was halted on the other side. The two kings stood still and silent, with their suites around them as if in battle array. The trumpets sounded. Both kings spurred their horses, galloped forward to the agreed point and embraced two or three times. In the following days there was much good cheer . . . they jousted and tilted without a break for nearly a fortnight apart from one day when they wrestled and danced instead. In all this Henry took superlative pleasure, except at the anxious moment when Francis threw him at wrestling.

A description of the meeting of Henry VIII and Francis I, King of France at the Field of Cloth of Gold in 1520, taken from J.J. Scarisbrick's 1968 biography, Henry VIII

Questions

1 What was the purpose of this meeting between the King of England and the King of France?
2 What does the source tell us about the character of Henry VIII?

Sixteenth-century Europe: The key players

France

In 1515 Francis I, from the house of Valois, became King of France. His kingdom was the largest in Europe at 460,000 square kilometres, with a population of 16 million people. The modern hexagon shape of France was just beginning to emerge with the acquisition through conquest or diplomacy of provinces such as Burgundy and Brittany. Francis inherited a conflict in Italy against the Habsburgs from his predecessor, Louis XII, and he was determined to uphold French honour and glory abroad.

Spain

In 1516 Charles of Habsburg became Charles I of Spain. The two kingdoms of Aragon and Castile had only recently been united by the marriage of Ferdinand, King of Aragon, and princess Isabella of Castile. Ferdinand and Isabella's only son, Philip the Fair, died suddenly in 1506 leaving their grandson Charles as heir. The Spanish kingdom was extremely diverse in terms of climate, language and culture. It housed 6.8 million people with a relatively large number living in towns such as Madrid, Toledo and Salamanca. Spain was a devoutly Catholic kingdom and in 1492 Ferdinand had succeeded in defeating the Moors of Granada and thus recovering the Iberian peninsula for Christendom.

The Holy Roman Empire (HRE)

The HRE was a collection of 400 semi-autonomous states in the heart of Europe, where Germany lies today. Technically, this area was ruled over by an Emperor, but in reality power was decentralised. Each state was ruled over by a prince who held a great deal of political power. Even the borders of the HRE were ambiguous with the Netherlands still in theory part of the Empire until 1548. The Empire housed 16 million inhabitants, some of whom lived in the 65 Imperial Free Cities, all of which enjoyed independence from the rule of the Emperor.

The office of Holy Roman Emperor brought with it great prestige, if not much actual power. Although an elected post, the Habsburgs had made it effectively hereditary. In 1519, Charles of Habsburg succeeded his grandfather Maximilian I to become Charles V. Charles now ruled over the HRE and Spain, as well as his lands in the Netherlands. Such a vast empire would provide Charles with major problems as he sought to wage war in Italy, defeat the Infidel Turk in the Mediterranean and repel the Protestant Reformation in the Empire.

The Papacy

The Pope was of course the spiritual head of the Catholic Church, and as such it was his duty to defend Catholic interests in Europe. It is therefore no surprise that we see successive popes in the sixteenth century calling for Catholic crusades against the increasingly powerful Ottoman Empire, which was a Muslim state. Yet the Pope, based in Rome, held great temporal power also as he was a major landowner in central Italy, ruling over the papal states. The papal court could rival that of any prince in Europe and at the beginning of the sixteenth century Pope Julius II (1503–13) was known as the 'warrior pope' as a result of his desire to expand papal territory through conquest.

The ongoing Habsburg–Valois conflict in northern Italy threatened papal interests in the first half of the sixteenth century and the papacy had to choose its allies carefully in order to prevent domination from either ruling dynasty. Indeed in 1527 an unpaid Imperial army sacked Rome and kept Pope Clement VII (1523–34) prisoner! This event was one of the key obstacles to Henry attaining a divorce from Catherine of Aragon through Rome and thus set England on course for the Henrician Reformation.

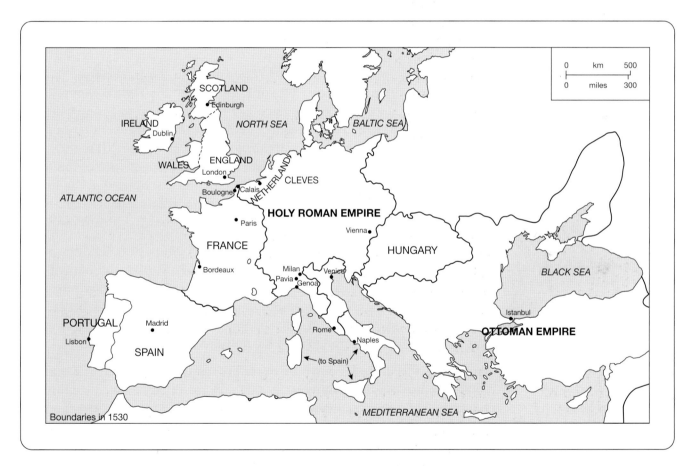

4.1 Europe in the sixteenth century.

Can Henry's early foreign policy be considered a success?

What was achieved by the French campaigns of 1511–14?

Henry was determined to lay claim to his title of King of France, which had been passed down through English kings since the fifteenth century. Having cemented the Anglo-Spanish alliance through his marriage to

Ferdinand II of Aragon (1452–1516)

The son of John II of Navarre and Aragon, Ferdinand married Isabella of Castile in 1469. After the death of Isabella's brother, namely Henry IV of Castile, in 1474 Ferdinand led Isabella's successful campaign for the throne of Castile. When Ferdinand's own father died in 1479, the Crowns of Aragon and Castile were united to form the basis of modern Spain.

Definition

Holy League

Formed by Pope Julius II in 1511, the Holy League consisted of Spain, Venice and England. In a bid to maintain the balance of power, Julius hoped that French influence in northern Italy might be weakened.

Catherine of Aragon, he now saw his father-in-law, **Ferdinand**, as a crucial ally in any future invasion of France. Henry was realistic in recognising that England's military capability was nowhere near that of France, Spain or the Empire, and that it would be impossible to replicate the glorious conquests of warrior kings such as Henry V without the aid of other countries.

War against France 1512–13

At first Henry found it difficult to detach himself from his father's old ministers. Important and wise old political figures such as Archbishop Warham and Bishop Fox were keen to stress the advantages of avoiding war, thus preserving English security and using neutrality to entice would-be foreign suitors who were eager to tip the balance of power in their favour. Such pragmatism resulted in a peace treaty with France in 1510, much to the frustration of the new young King. Yet Henry would not have to wait much longer for his bellicose ambitions to be fulfilled.

In 1508 the major European powers (France, Spain, Empire and the papacy) were brought together by Pope Julius II in the **Holy League** to attack Venice. Henry VII's diplomacy had for once failed to get England on board, but by 1511 the Holy League had largely run its course. France had emerged as the strongest power in northern Italy and Louis XII's dominance in that area was now threatening the independence of the papal states. The Pope now changed direction and put himself at the head of the Holy League to drive France out of northern Italy. Spain, Venice and the Empire along with England now directed their forces against France.

In order to win over the Great Council, Henry could portray the war as a papal one in defence of the liberties of the Church. Parliament granted the necessary money to wage war in April 1512 and an expeditionary force of 12,000 troops under the command of the Marquis of Dorset was dispatched to Bayonne. The plan was for England to gain control of Aquitaine in southwestern France through a joint Anglo-Spanish invasion.

But Henry was badly let down by his father-in-law, Ferdinand, who only wanted to use the English troops as a diversion so that he could capture Navarre. While the English waited for Spanish troops to arrive, dysentery and drunkenness engulfed their camp and Dorset's troops were soon recalled. Naval defeat at Brest (April 1513) capped an ignominious first entry into European affairs for Henry VIII. England's first serious continental campaign in sixty years had ended miserably after only a few months.

The Battle of the Spurs, 1513

Yet this failure only made Henry more determined to attain glory in France. With the papacy still keen to pursue victory over France, Henry had learned from the first campaign that he needed to be able to act independently from his so-called allies if English aims were to be met.

With that in mind the King personally led an army of 30,000 men that crossed over the Channel to Calais in June 1513.

The campaign that followed resulted in the capture of the towns of Therouanne and Tournai, with little French resistance. Therouanne was given over to the **Emperor Maximilian**, while Tournai was garrisoned at great expense by the English until 1518. There had been little real fighting to report apart from one minor skirmish with a small French expeditionary force, which was built up by English propagandists into a glorious victory and named the *Battle of the Spurs* in recognition of the speed at which the French had retreated. Some important French nobles were captured and returned to England in a bid to further enhance the prestige of what had been a relatively one-sided encounter.

The Battle of Flodden, 1513

Source B

Sir,

My Lord Howard hath sent me a letter open to your Grace within one of mine, by the which you shall see at length the great Victory that our Lord hath sent your subjects in your absence; and for this cause there is no need herein to trouble your Grace with long writing, but, to my thinking, this battle hath been to your Grace and all your realm the greatest honour that could be, and more than you should win all the Crown of France; thanked be God of it, and I am sure your Grace forgetteth not to do this, which shall be cause to send you many more such great victories, as I trust he shall do. In this your Grace shall see how I kept my promise, sending you for your banners a king's coat. I thought to send himself unto you, but out Englishmen's hearts would not suffer it. It should have been better for him to have been in peace than have this reward. All that God sends is for the best. My Lord of Surrey, my Henry, would fain know your pleasure in the burying of the King of Scots' body.

Your humble wife and true servant, Catherine

A letter from Catherine of Aragon to her husband, King Henry VIII, 16 September 1513

SKILLS BUILDER

1 Why is Catherine writing to Henry in September 1513?
2 To whom does Catherine credit the victory at Flodden?
3 What does Catherine send Henry as a trophy from the battle?
4 What advice does Catherine have for James IV of Scotland, now that he is dead?

Biography

Maximilian I (1459–1519)

German Emperor who, through marriage acquired Burgundy and Flanders. These territorial claims sparked war with Louis XI and in 1482 he was forced to give Artois and Burgundy to Louis. In 1486 he was elected King of the Romans, and in 1493 he became Emperor. His main territorial ambitions lay in Italy but after years of war he was forced to give up Milan to the French in 1515 and Verona to the Venetians.

Exam tip

Reading through a primary document source such as Source B above can be difficult. The language can be awkward and the meaning is not always clear. Try to pick out the key points from such documents and then put them into their historical context. The questions on this page should help you focus your reading.

Biography

James IV (1473–1513)

King of Scotland from 1488 and he stabilised the Scottish Crown and fostering good relations with the nobility. Married to Margaret Tudor (eldest daughter of Henry VII) in 1503. He embraced Renaissance values, and his court was a place of high culture and learning. His reign ended in disaster at the Battle of Flodden.

Back at home, a victory of far greater proportions had been achieved by an English army under the command of the Earl of Surrey. **James IV**, King of Scotland, had taken advantage of Henry's absence in France to launch an invasion of England. As the Scottish army crossed the border, Surrey moved to stop its progress. In September 1513, as the two armies confronted each other at Flodden Edge, Surrey was outnumbered and held the weaker position on the battlefield. Despite this the earl won a momentous victory that removed the Scottish threat for the foreseeable future. The core of the Scottish nobility lay dead on Flodden Field including James IV himself. James's son, James V, was only a boy and with Henry's own sister (Margaret) as regent, Henry could expect little trouble on the northern border for the rest of his reign.

The contrast between the key victory at Flodden and the seemingly pointless and expensive campaign in France is an easy one to make. What had Henry actually achieved by the end of 1513?

- Above all else Henry had stamped his mark on European affairs and announced his presence to the other powers. He had fulfilled one of the key tasks of a Renaissance prince in waging war. Henry himself had been at the head of an impressively large invasion force of France in 1513.
- He had laid claim to his inherited title of the King of France, and English victories on French soil had brought prestige and standing to his short reign. Henry had not given up hope of a renewed offensive in 1514.
- At the same time his attention had been drawn to the rising star of Thomas Wolsey who had organised the complicated logistics of raising this army, supplying it and sending it across the Channel.

Yet at the same time:

- Henry had been deceived and deserted by Ferdinand in 1512.
- Therouanne and Tournai were relatively soft targets, while the Battle of the Spurs (which Henry had missed) was nothing more than a skirmish.
- The costs of Henry's campaigns were extremely high. Henry spent £960,000 in 1511–13. Given that his ordinary income was only £110,000 per annum it was clear that Henry was severely stretching his fiscal resources. The reality of this situation hit home to Henry in 1514 when he realised that a further campaign in that year was unrealistic.

The Anglo-French Treaty 1514

In 1514 Henry was forced to make peace with France. Both Ferdinand and Maximilian had lost interest in attacking France and both had been negotiating with Louis XII behind Henry's back to conclude separate treaties. The new Pope, Leo X, favoured peace over war, and the state of Henry's coffers would seem to suggest that this was the sensible course of action.

The Anglo-French Treaty of 1514 gave England possession of Tournai, and at the same time Louis XII agreed to pay the arrears of the English pension handed out to Henry VII in the 1490s. Henry also proposed a joint Anglo-French attack on Spain to drive Ferdinand out of Navarre and claim Castile for Catherine of Aragon. Although an unrealistic proposal, which remained unfulfilled, it shows Henry's annoyance with Ferdinand's double-crossing over the previous three years. The peace treaty was sealed with the marriage of Henry's younger sister Mary to the elderly Louis XII.

How far did Wolsey achieve his aims in foreign policy in the years 1514–29?

There has been much historical debate over the guiding principles behind Wolsey's foreign policies.

- Traditionally historians argued that Wolsey pursued a policy designed to maintain the balance of power in Europe. This meant ensuring that no one side became too dominant in European affairs, and usually entailed promising support to those states seeking to curtail the power of a dominant force.

- Yet, as G.R. Elton pointed out, such a strategy was not always carried out by Wolsey who often allied England with the stronger power.

- A.F. Pollard challenged the balance of power theory by arguing that Wolsey's main principle in foreign affairs was to follow papal policy. Being a loyal papal servant, it was argued that Wolsey sought to defend the interests of the curia at every opportunity. It has also been suggested that Wolsey hoped to further his own ambitions of becoming Pope by aligning English ambitions with Roman ones.

- This idea was discredited by J.J. Scarisbrick who argued that Wolsey did not always follow papal policy and that his candidature for the papacy was unrealistic anyway. If at times England and the papacy shared common enemies or goals this was mere coincidence. Instead, Scarisbrick turned the initial balance of power argument around, and put forward the idea that Wolsey aimed to encourage peace by aligning England with the stronger side thus disrupting the balance of power still further and forcing the weaker combatants to seek terms.

- More recently, historians such as Steven Gunn have pointed out the flexibility of Wolsey's foreign policies, and argued that it is difficult to identify just one guiding principle throughout his period of pre-eminence. The diplomatic situation was a constantly shifting one, as deaths, marriages and wars all served to change the state of affairs on the continent, all of which meant that Wolsey could not stick to one policy.

Source C

Who that intendeth
France to win, with
Scotland let him begin.

Thomas Cromwell's address
to parliament 1523

Question

What does Cromwell mean by this statement?

Wolsey the peacemaker 1514–18?

In January 1515 Louis XII died to be succeeded by his twenty-year-old cousin, Francis I. Francis, like the young Henry, was eager to make his mark on European affairs, but with more monetary and material resources behind him he was more able to make an impression.

The Anglo-French peace soon began to evaporate as Francis stirred up unrest in Scotland by sending the Scottish claimant, the duke of Albany, to overthrow the **regency government** of Henry's sister Margaret, which he did successfully. Shortly afterwards Francis won a crushing victory over the Swiss at the Battle of Marignano in September 1515, which gave the French control of Milan, and most of northern Italy into the bargain. In 1516 Francis was in a strong enough position to negotiate the Concordat of Bologna with Leo X, which confirmed the right of French kings to appoint bishops to French sees.

Definition

Regency government

A government that rules a country on behalf of someone else. In this instance, Henry's sister Margaret, widow of James IV, ran Scotland on behalf of her infant son, James V.

Questions

1 What rumour does Skelton tell us about in this source concerning the young James V of Scotland?
2 What does Skelton think will come of these plans?

Source D

What say ye of the Scottish king?
That is another thing.
He is but an youngling,
A stalworthy stripling.
There is a whispering and a whipling
He should be hither brought;
But and it were well sought
I trow all will be nought

A poem by John Skelton

Although deeply envious of Francis's achievements and furious over his intervention in Scotland, Henry could do little to halt his progress. Wolsey was keen to avoid the expense of a full-scale invasion, but at the same time he wanted to support any pro-papal, anti-French alliance. The rather weak result of all of this was a secret subsidy to the Emperor Maximilian, in the hope that he could repel the French advance into northern Italy, but as was the case in the past, Henry was let down by his potential allies. Maximilian accepted the money and then defected to the French.

Wolsey's next proposal was to construct an anti-French league made up of Rome, Venice, Spain and the Empire. However, in January 1516 Ferdinand died, to be succeeded by his grandson, the Archduke Charles. Charles did not want to engage France immediately and saw little reason to renew terms with England. Instead Charles made peace with France at Noyon in 1516. Charles's other grandfather, Maximilian, joined the alliance in 1517 through the Peace of Cambrai. Despite the best efforts of Wolsey and Henry, England was left isolated and humiliated by the end of 1517.

The Treaty of London 1518

Wolsey was soon given the opportunity to redeem himself and that he did with the Treaty of London in 1518. Since the beginning of 1518, Leo X had been calling for a western crusade against the infidel Turk. Wolsey took these papal plans and modified them to suit the needs of the powers of Europe. In doing so he put together a settlement of universal peace, which seemed to put England at the centre of diplomatic affairs.

This Christian peace settlement bound France, the Papacy, Spain, the Empire and England to action against the Turk. More significantly the treaty:

- guaranteed non aggression between the major powers;
- built in the principle of collective security so that any aggressor would be rounded upon by the other states.

Twenty representatives of European powers were sent to London in October 1518 to sign the treaty and Wolsey had achieved a notable diplomatic success:

- the treaty heaped prestige onto Henry's reign;
- it ended the threat of English isolation in Europe;
- an Anglo-French treaty was signed that gave Tournai back to France in return for further French pensions;
- Henry's infant daughter **Mary** (see page 104) was betrothed to the Dauphin and the Duke of Albany was to be kept out of Scotland.

Not only had Wolsey hijacked Leo X's initial plans but he also received the commission of *Legate a latere*, a position that he had been pressing for since 1514. Indeed the papal representative to England, Lorenzo Campeggio, was not allowed to enter the country until Wolsey's new title had been officially confirmed by the curia.

Spain or France?

Given Europe's almost constant state of warfare in this period, it was unlikely that the Treaty of London would last long. In January 1519 the Holy Roman Emperor Maximilian died, which set up a power struggle between his grandson Charles of Burgundy, King of Spain, and Francis I. It was inevitable that the seven electors of the Empire would choose Charles, given his Habsburg lineage, and in doing so they upset the balance of power once again.

With France seemingly encircled by Charles's vast territorial inheritance, a Habsburg–Valois conflict appeared inevitable. Wolsey and Henry continued to present England as the arbiter of peace in Europe, while at the same time both France and the Empire looked to attract England as an important ally.

> **Take it further**
>
> - Find out more about the Ottoman Turk and the threat that they posed to Christian Europe in the sixteenth century.
> - How was Suleiman the Magnificent perceived in Western Europe?
> - What does the siege of Vienna in 1529 tell us about the military capabilities of the Ottoman Empire?
> - What do we know of Suleiman's domestic reforms?

The Field of Cloth of Gold, 1520

In June 1520 Henry and Francis met at the Field of Cloth of Gold, near Calais. Over 3,000 notables from each of the two kingdoms were present at this sumptuous feast of chivalric pageantry. No expense was spared in the creation of the royal pavilions, as both sides tried to show off their Renaissance credentials. Despite the rain and high winds, the jousting tournament went ahead and the two kings even wrestled against each other in an unplanned bout.

Aside from the splendour of the occasion, little of diplomatic value was achieved at the Field of Cloth of Gold. It was proving difficult to maintain English neutrality as Habsburg–Valois tensions mounted. Already Charles V had visited England in May 1520, and then again in July 1520 Henry and Wolsey met the Emperor at Gravelines. Charles was desperate for assurance that England would not be drawn into a French alliance. In reality England was likely to side with Charles for three key reasons:

1 England had a traditional hostility towards France, and Henry resented the success of Francis I since 1515;

2 England had important trade links with the Low Countries, which would be safeguarded by an alliance with Charles who ruled over the Habsburg Netherlands;

3 papal policy was anti-French at this time as the Holy See felt vulnerable in the face of French expansion in northern Italy.

In July 1521, Wolsey arranged a three-power conference at Calais, as England continued to act as the peace broker between the two main superpowers. Later, in August, Wolsey travelled to Bruges where a settlement was concluded with Charles. The agreement was that an English force would invade France unless the French King agreed to make peace. By the end of 1521 this agreement had been firmed up, although Wolsey had managed to negotiate a delay in England's entering the war against France until 1523. Wolsey hoped that by delaying any action, the situation might change and prevent the need for English assistance.

The situation was very different from 1513 when the last invasion plans had been drawn up. The conquest of France did not meet with such enthusiasm in England and one of the main reasons for this was that it would be funded through an increase in taxation. In 1522 England once more appeared to be committed to a war that did not directly serve her interests and might fuel domestic unrest.

The Earl of Surrey led a raiding party from Calais into Normandy and Picardy in 1522, but made no territorial gains and worryingly received little support from Charles's troops. However, in August 1523 another opportunity presented itself to undermine Francis's power when the French King was faced with a serious rebellion from Charles, Duke of Bourbon.

Bourbon was a leading French noble who felt that he had been denied his rightful territorial inheritance by Francis, and waged open rebellion in defiance of his King. A three-pronged assault was planned involving imperial and English troops as well as those of Bourbon. An English force costing £400,000 was sent under Suffolk, but the rebellion came to nothing and the English army fell apart due to a lack of supplies in the bad weather of winter. With money in short supply Wolsey was eager to release England from her obligations outlined in the Treaty of Bruges, and make a general peace with France. Charles was aware that England's loyalty was fading as between 1523–25 Wolsey did all he could to resist imperial demands for action.

The Diplomatic Revolution

In February 1525 the whole situation changed once more:

- Charles achieved a decisive victory over the French in northern Italy at Pavia
- The French army was annihilated
- Francis I himself was taken prisoner.

At first, both Wolsey and Henry hoped that they might profit from Charles's victory, and perhaps even lay claim to the French crown. Yet Charles was in no mood to allow England a share of the spoils, and there was little to be gained from his perspective of handing the French crown to Henry. Charles called off his proposed marriage to Mary and it seemed as if the Anglo-Imperial alliance was on the rocks. What happened next has been described as a diplomatic revolution by G.R. Elton, as Wolsey opened up negotiations with France. As a consequence of the Treaty of the More in 1525 Henry agreed to give up his claims to France in return for an annual pension.

Within a year Francis was released by Charles on condition that he did not threaten imperial interests in Italy and his sons were kept as hostage to support the oaths taken by the French King. Yet Francis had no intention of allowing Charles to dominate the northern peninsula, and in May 1526 the Treaty of Cognac was arranged that aligned England, France and several Italian states against Habsburg hegemony in Italy. Wolsey helped to construct the League and England financed it but never joined.

How far was 1525 a watershed mark in Henrician foreign policy?

Source E

Also it is spoken abroad, as I have been told, that it shall be the uttermost impoverishing of this realm, and the greatest enriching of the realm of France, if the King's Grace should have all this money that is required and should spend it not in this realm but in France, where his Grace must continually make his abode a long season and keep it, if he is fortunate to win it, or else it shall be soon lost again. I have heard say moreover that where the people be commanded to make fires and tokens of joy for the taking of the French king, several of them have spoken that they have more cause to weep than to rejoice. Also it hath been told me secretly that several have recounted and repeated what infinite sums of money the Kings Grace hath spent already invading France ... and little or nothing hath prevailed.

A letter from William Warham, Archbishop of Canterbury to Thomas Wolsey, 15 April 1525

Questions

1 What was Warham's purpose in writing this letter to Wolsey?
2 What reasons are given by Warham for his opposition to Wolsey's policy?
3 How useful is this source to historians studying Henrician foreign policy between 1518–25?

The year 1525 has often been seen as a key turning point in English foreign policy under Wolsey, as England moved away from her traditional Spanish/Imperial alliance towards France. In 1527 England and France cemented their alliance with the Treaty of Westminster in which Princess Mary was once more presented as a diplomatic marriage pawn for either Francis or his second son. Henry also threatened Charles with armed intervention if he refused to make an adequate peace with his enemies.

Yet England lacked the military power to threaten Charles, and the League of Cognac achieved nothing. In 1527 Imperial troops sacked Rome, and Pope Clement VII was taken prisoner. This was a disaster for Wolsey as now English foreign policy was closely tied to the King's Great Matter. Henry's need for a divorce from Catherine of Aragon was the most important issue and the King expected Wolsey to be able to deliver the annulment. Normally Wolsey would have been well placed to achieve the King's wishes but his diplomatic revolution in 1525 had moved England away from Charles, and now Wolsey was beginning to regret that decision.

Catherine of Aragon was Charles V's aunt, and he was unwilling to see a close family member wronged and humiliated. Henry needed the Pope to decree on the matter as only then could his marriage be legitimately annulled. With Clement a virtual prisoner of Charles there seemed little chance of success in 1527. Wolsey tried to act without the papacy, arguing that Clement's captivity provided extenuating circumstances under which the College of Cardinals could decree on the matter without Rome.

Yet by the end of 1527 Charles had released Clement, but maintained a tight grip over Italy. Wolsey declared war on Charles in 1528, but no English army was ever mobilised. Realising that English military capabilities were unlikely to worry Charles, Wolsey also considered a trade embargo on the **Low Countries**. Yet even here, this was more damaging to England's trade interests and a separate agreement was made with the Dutch markets to maintain trade despite the prospect of hostilities between Charles and Henry.

Although hopes of a French revival in Italy surfaced in 1528, these were put to rest by Charles's emphatic victory at Landriano in June 1529. In August 1529 France, Spain and the papacy signed the Peace of Cambrai. Wolsey was never informed and the settlement left Charles in effective control of Italy. Cambrai not only left England isolated but it also ended Wolsey's chances of attaining an annulment through Rome. With Clement now officially in the Imperial camp, and France also forced to sign up to Cambrai after Landriano, Wolsey was faced with ruin. Henry had called on him to deliver a divorce and he had failed and would now face the consequences of that failure. In the end, Wolsey's fate had depended upon the changing nature of foreign affairs, which had conspired against him from 1525–29.

Definition

Low Countries

The states of Flanders, Brabant and Holland, which would in time form the backbone of the sixteenth-century Netherlands. These provinces were very wealthy due to the manufacture and finishing of cloth.

How successful was Wolsey's foreign policy?

Successes

- The capture of Therouanne and Tournai in 1513 was a reflection of Henry's strong Renaissance kingship. The territories were not viewed as permanent acquisitions but rather as useful bargaining tools in any future relations with France.

- Wolsey was a successful peace broker, and the Peace of London in 1518 should be viewed as his single greatest achievement. The treaty bound the twenty foremost states in Europe together in a pact of perpetual peace. Wolsey was seen as the architect of the peace and treated as an almost equal of the heads of state. London was the centre of international relations and importantly England was no longer under threat of diplomatic isolation. Further events such as the Field of the Cloth of Gold additionally enhanced English prestige abroad.

- Given England's meagre resources and Henry's relatively low income, Wolsey and the King conducted a flexible and reactive foreign policy. No one more than Wolsey recognised the need to ally effectively with powerful countries in order to preserve English security and interests. To this end Wolsey courted both Francis I and Charles V in the period 1520–22, meeting with Imperial agents in secret at Bruges shortly after the Field of the Cloth of Gold. Wolsey's intentions were always to make a treaty with Charles in this period, but in order to get the best possible deal out of the Emperor and avoid a commitment to war, he kept communications with France open.

Failures

- Henry's aims and ambitions in foreign policy were often unrealistic. England's resources were small compared to her European counterparts. Henry was naïve to think that he could regain the Crown of France. In short, English foreign policy was costly, short sighted and out of date.

- Henry's campaigns yielded few gains. The French campaigns of 1512–13 were expensive and ultimately of little long-term value. Henry spent £1.4 million fighting wars in the period 1511–25. Henry squandered the secure financial legacy left to him by his father. The increasingly high cost of warfare in this period meant that Wolsey had to call upon parliamentary taxation and forced loans. Ultimately the Crown faced serious domestic disturbances in Suffolk and East Anglia as a consequence of Wolsey's Amicable Grant of 1525. The Amicable Grant was scrapped, proposed invasion plans of France were shelved and Wolsey suffered his first major setback in his relationship with the King.

- Henry was outmanoeuvred by more experienced monarchs in the early part of his reign. This can be seen by Ferdinand of Aragon using English troops in Aquitaine (1512) as a diversion so that he could capture Navarre from the French. Both Ferdinand and Maximilian signed separate treaties with the French, and often operated behind Henry's back in their own interests. Charles V was no more reliable as an ally, offering little military back-up to the English campaigns of 1523–25. Despite their alliance, Henry gained nothing from the Imperial victory at Pavia in 1525, nor did Charles stick to his agreement to marry Henry's daughter Mary.

- It has been argued that Wolsey was a self-interested diplomat in foreign affairs. Campeggio was not allowed into England in 1518 until Wolsey's position as *Legate a latere* had been confirmed by the Pope. This after Wolsey had essentially hijacked papal plans for a European crusade against the Turk. In 1518 at the talks held before the Treaty of London, Wolsey constantly wanted to attract attention to his achievements and be seen as the peacemaker of Europe. Similarly, in 1520 at the Field of the Cloth of Gold, Wolsey was as eager to promote himself as he was to promote the King.

- Further to this point, A.F. Pollard would contend that Wolsey used international relations as a means of furthering his own candidature for the papacy. After the deaths of Leo X in 1521 and then Adrian VI in 1523, Pollard argues that Wolsey followed a policy that was most likely to further his cause in Rome. This argument is now seen as flawed and outdated on three major counts. First, Wolsey did not always follow papal policy, even during times of papal elections. Second, Wolsey had no real plan or ambition to become pope. He regularly criticised and insulted leading cardinals in Rome who would have been crucial to his chances of election. Third, Wolsey only put forward his candidature for the papacy to satisfy Henry and because he heard that Charles V would also endorse his claim.

- In the final analysis, Wolsey's diplomatic revolution in 1525 was a failure because it gave him little chance of attaining an annulment of Henry's marriage to Catherine. After 1526 Wolsey hoped that the French would regain the upper hand in northern Italy, freeing the papacy from Imperial obligations and allowing Clement VII to decree the marriage null and void. Wolsey backed the wrong side, a point confirmed by the sack of Rome in 1527. Yet in some ways he was unlucky as it would have been very difficult in 1525 to foresee what way the Great Matter was going, and the centrality of the divorce issue subsequently gave Wolsey little room for manoeuvre in diplomatic affairs. The period 1525–29 was an undoubted failure for Wolsey in foreign affairs.

- The French alliance was unpopular and England simply did not have the military resources to frighten Charles. A trade embargo with Burgundy in 1527 only served to heighten the government's unpopularity as it coincided with a failed harvest. Hunger and unemployment combined to exacerbate Wolsey's unpopularity at home, forcing him to drop the embargo.

Conclusion

In some ways, given the circumstances and England's resources, Wolsey was able to direct an effective foreign policy. Few monarchs at the time worried about the financial implications of war, although the unrest of 1525 was a major blow to Henry's standing at home. The accession of Charles to the Crown of Spain and the Imperial throne made it more difficult for the balance of power to be maintained, and Wolsey was probably right to back the Emperor in 1521. As Habsburg–Valois rivalry intensified, the chances of following a policy of defensive neutrality were minimal. Wolsey attained an alliance with the strongest power in Europe, sealed it with a promise of marriage from Charles to Mary, and delayed England's entrance into war with France. The deal was a good one, but England's economic constraints prevented any direct action and Charles increasingly pursued his own aims and ambitions with little care for Henry. Wolsey's diplomatic U-turn in 1525–26 left him on the wrong side at the wrong time, and ultimately cost him his job.

Source F

Although there were some obvious large scale failures, especially between 1525 and 1529, there were many occasions on which both Henry and Wolsey had good reason to think that they had been very successful. After the campaign of 1513 Henry knew that he was internationally regarded as a figure of splendid chivalric kingship and his certainty was increased by events such as those at the Field of the Cloth of Gold in 1520.

Keith Randell, *Henry VIII and the Government of England* (2nd edn), 2001

Source G

Since Henry lacked the resources to wage war alongside these giants (France and Spain), Wolsey established England as the peacemaker between them. At the same time, he was careful not to ignore Henry's desire for military glory, especially at the expense of Francis I who was far too similar in character and ambition to Henry himself not to be regarded with jealousy.

Angela Anderson and Tony Imperato, *Tudor England 1485–1603*, 2001

Source H

Also it is spoken abroad, as I understand by relation, that it shall be the uttermost impoverishing of this realm, and the greatest enriching of the realm of France, if the Kings Grace should have all this money that is required and should spend it out of this realm in France, where his Grace must continually make his abode a long season and keep it, if it fortune him to win it, or else it shall soon be lost again. Which the Kings Grace long continuance there would be to the great decaying and desolation of this realm . . .

Thomas Wolsey writes a personal letter to William Warham, Archbishop of Canterbury in 1525 on the futility of invading France

Question

How far was Wolsey's foreign policy defensive?

Use Sources F–H and your own knowledge.

Exam tips

1 The best answers will be those that are balanced in their outlook. Make sure your response confronts both sides of the argument. There were aggressive aspects to Wolsey's foreign policy, especially in the early years. Sources F and G allude to this – highlight the key phrases and include them in your answer. Reinforce these ideas with your own knowledge. Source H, however, would seem to agree with the idea that Wolsey's foreign policy was defensive. Go through the same procedure as you did with the other two sources and incorporate some relevant own knowledge. Add a short and succinct judgement at the end of your answer.

2 Notice Source H is primary source. Use your own knowledge to contextualise this source. Think carefully about the date on which this letter was written and the financial pressures being felt by Wolsey at the time. Take into account also the fact that this was a personal letter – this clearly affects the reliability of the source.

How important was religion in shaping foreign affairs from 1530–40?

The successful conclusion of the Great Matter and the subsequent Royal Supremacy created problems in foreign affairs. The alliance with France, left over from Wolsey's time, began to fall apart in the years 1530–35. Francis I did not want to be associated with a heretical power (England was no longer viewed as part of the universal Catholic Church after the break with Rome), and more importantly France was eager to maintain peaceful relations with Charles at the beginning of the 1530s. After the break with Rome and the annulment of Henry's marriage to Catherine in England, enmity between Charles and the English King was inevitable. Catherine was the aunt of Charles V, and the Emperor was appalled at her treatment in England at the hands of Henry VIII. With France and Spain at peace, Henry began to fear the onslaught of a Catholic coalition. In this context Cromwell and Henry had two options:

1 Make an alliance with German Protestant princes. To this end, Lutheran princes were approached in 1533 and in 1534 Henry supported the Protestant town of Lubeck in the Baltic who were trying to stop an Imperial candidate from becoming King of Denmark. Again in 1535 negotiations with key Lutheran princes were opened up and significant reformers such as Philip Melanchton were involved in negotiations, but nothing concrete was decided upon.

2 Do nothing and allow Habsburg–Valois rivalry to take its natural course. The inevitable result would be war and both powers would be too busy fighting each other to worry about England.

In 1536 the second option seemed to be the one to choose for Henry and Cromwell. With the deaths of both Catherine of Aragon (see page 83) and Anne Boleyn (see page 85) in that year, there was a chance that Anglo-

Imperial relations might recover. Further reassurance was gained by the fact that war flared up once more between France and Spain over Milan. For Henry, the years 1536–38 were spent putting down the northern rising and continuing the dissolution of the monasteries. A new crisis emerged in 1538 when France and Spain signed the Peace of Nice, committing both sides to a ten-year truce. Again Cromwell (see page 92) and Henry felt vulnerable. English military defences were strengthened in anticipation of a Catholic invasion and links with German princes were reopened. Papal calls for an anti-English crusade were renewed, and **Cardinal Reginald Pole** once more urged Charles and Francis to overthrow England.

In a furious act of retaliation Henry carried out a brutal purge of Pole's family in England. Reginald's brothers Geoffrey and Lord Montague were arrested (the former pardoned after he gave incriminating evidence against the others), along with his mother the Countess of Salisbury. Other key figures such as Henry Courtenay and Sir Edward Neville were also arrested and all of them were executed for treason apart from the countess, who remained in prison until 1541 when she too went to the scaffold. In one bloody swoop Henry had removed the remainder of the Yorkist faction in England and silenced any thoughts of a pro-papal resurgence.

Biography

Cardinal Pole (1500–58)

Of Yorkist blood, Cardinal Pole was a stubborn opponent of Henry's divorce from Catherine of Aragon. In exile abroad, Pole used his influence to call for Catholic invasions of England to overthrow Henry and re-establish the true faith.

Source I

The state of this our kingdom is as follows: the ceremonies are still tolerated, but explanations of them are added. These things are retained for the sake of preventing any disturbances, and are ordered to be kept until the King himself shall either remove or alter them ... There is a report that we are to have war with the French, Italians, Spaniards and Scots, when this was reported to the King, he said that he should not sleep at all the worse for it; and on the day after he declared to his Privy Councillors that he now found himself moved in his conscience to promote the word of God more than he had ever done before.

Taken from a letter from a group of English Protestants writing to their friends in Protestant Zurich in 1539

Source J

We are all of us amazed at the sight of those decrees [the Six Articles] and at the rejection of the terms of the alliance between his Majesty and ourselves. We have altogether perceived a great change in England's views ... we suspect therefore, that something has blown over from France as you no longer appear to have any necessity for our alliance or even our friendship.

A letter from Martin Bucer (a prominent German Protestant) to Thomas Cranmer, October 1539

SKILLS BUILDER

How far do Sources I and J agree over the importance of religion in foreign affairs?

Exam tips

Look carefully at the authors of the two sources and be sure to place the content of the documents in its historical context.

Make sure you know what was in the Act of Six Articles (see pages 147–8) before you address this question. Think how someone such as Bucer would have reacted to news of the Six Articles. Now you can also begin to speculate as to whether Source I was written before or after the Six Articles.

Definition

The Act of Six Articles

Passed in 1539 the Act of Six Articles outlined the doctrinal position of Henry's Church in England. Unsurprisingly, the Six Articles came down on the side of orthodox Catholicism, reaffirming key aspects of Catholic doctrine such as transubstantiation. England had broken with Rome but Henry was no Protestant – the Six Articles reaffirms this point.

As Franco-Spanish amity continued into 1539, an interesting and seemingly contradictory policy emerged in England. Henry continued to display his belief in orthodox Catholic doctrine, as the passing of **the Act of Six Articles** showed. Perhaps the Six Articles were designed to reassure the rest of Catholic Europe that the English Church would not move towards Lutheranism. Yet at the same time as the Six Articles passed through the statute book, another Lutheran embassy was visiting England. No agreement had been made with the Lutheran princes in the past because Henry was reluctant to align England with heretics, and the Lutherans were rightfully sceptical of Henry's commitment to religious reform. The same sticking point remained in 1539, but Cromwell did succeed in proposing a marriage alliance between England and the duchy of Cleves.

Source K

Articles were decreed, commonly called the Six Articles (or the whip with six strings), in pretence of Unity. What unity followed, the groaning hearts of a great number and the cruel death of many, both in the reign of King Henry and Queen Mary.

From John Foxe's *Book of Martyrs*, 1563

SKILLS BUILDER

1 Select the adjectives or phrases that show us Foxe's Protestant bias in this source.

The Duke of Cleves was not actually Lutheran but was part of the Lutheran alliance, and could prove to be a useful ally on the Lower Rhine to counter any plans for an invasion of England. Henry was unsure, especially as Franco-Spanish relations were once more deteriorating. Yet, convinced by **Holbein's** (see page 145) flattering portrait of **Anne of Cleves** (see page 145), and persuaded by Cromwell of the diplomatic worth of the match, Henry went through with it. The subsequent marriage spelled the end for Cromwell. Henry detested the sight of Anne and the marriage remained unconsummated, while the need to court the German princes evaporated as the war in Italy resumed. Yet in contrast to the 1530s, Henry was not going to sit back and watch France and Spain fight it out. In the last years of Henry's reign he was to involve himself once more in continental affairs, and the old policies of invading France and conquering Scotland were again to the fore.

Do the years 1541–47 in foreign policy merit their reputation as ones of expensive failure?

Anglo-Scottish relations

Henry had come through the crisis years of 1538–41 unscathed. The renewal of war between Francis and Charles appeared to leave England safe once again. It is therefore surprising that Henry should choose to restake his claims to France in 1542. Ageing and with the Supremacy secure Henry perhaps viewed a re-entry onto the European scene as a final means of highlighting his chivalric kingship. Before any invasion of France, Scotland would have to be subdued. Relations between James V and Henry VIII were strained for a number of reasons.

- James thought little of Henry's attempts to advise him on the future direction of the Scottish church while Henry believed his young nephew to be uncouth and disrespectful.

- Scotland had an ongoing alliance with France, which was stronger than ever under the supervision of Cardinal Beaton.

- Diplomatic overtures from England to break the *auld alliance* were unsuccessful and in 1542 Norfolk was sent north of the border with an army to force James to submit to the English cause. Although some damage was done to towns and villages in the south of Scotland, little was gained by the expedition and Norfolk returned prematurely having run out of supplies.

In November 1542, convinced that Henry's armed forces were vulnerable to attack, James V decided upon a show of force himself, and his army marched over the English border. At the Battle of Solway Moss in November 1542, the Scottish forces were soundly beaten by an inferior English army.

Ridden with internal dissension and poorly led, the Scottish defeat at Solway Moss was a national humiliation. Many nobles surrendered, while James himself died only two weeks after receiving the news of the defeat in Edinburgh. He left behind an infant daughter, Mary, in the hands of a pro-French faction. Henry's victory at Solway Moss convinced him that Scotland was there for the taking, and he was now determined to impose English overlordship on her northern neighbour.

Henry bribed the prisoners captured at Solway Moss in a bid to create a pro-English party of Scottish nobles. A new Regent, the Earl of Arran appeared also to favour Henry's cause, and the pro-French Beaton was imprisoned. In July 1543 the Treaty of Greenwich was signed heralding peace between Scotland and England as well as the future marriage of Mary Stuart to Prince Edward. Henry appeared to be staking his claim to Scotland successfully through a combination of politics and diplomacy.

In reality, Henry's policies towards Scotland were naïve and short sighted. The captured nobles returned north with their bribes but did little to advance Henry's claims. The Treaty of Greenwich was weighted heavily in Scotland's favour because Mary did not have to go south to marry Edward until she was ten years old and in the meantime Scotland could maintain her treaty obligations with France. Arran was heir presumptive to Mary and therefore unwilling to put Henry into a strong position with regards to the Scottish throne. In reality, the negotiations for Greenwich did nothing more than buy the Scots time to rebuild their defences and strengthen their links with France.

By the end of 1543 the treaty had been repudiated, and it now became clear to Henry that only a concerted military campaign could subdue the Scots. The Earl of Hertford was sent north in 1544 to lay waste to the country and burn Edinburgh to the ground, but the *rough wooing*, as it was called, only served to unite the Scots against their southern aggressor and strengthen the auld alliance with France. Although English naval strength ensured that Edinburgh Castle remained in English hands until after Henry's death, the reality was that the Scottish campaign had been a failure. Henry had squandered a seemingly unbeatable position after Solway Moss, and by 1547 Scottish hatred of the English had never been greater.

Anglo-French relations

Yet Henry's initial campaign against Scotland had been designed to pave the way for an invasion of France. Since 1541 Charles had been encouraging Henry to join the continental war on his side against France. In February 1543 Henry agreed to join Charles in an attack on France, rekindling memories of the 1513 invasion. One year later a much larger English force of 40,000 invaded France from Calais, and joined the Spanish in a two-pronged attack on Paris.

An ageing and increasingly immobile Henry accompanied the army, which moved slowly and deliberately through Picardy. Although the coordinated march on Paris began at the same time, it became clear that neither Charles nor Henry would fulfil their obligations to each other. They had entered the war against France for different reasons and the break up of the alliance was inevitable.

Henry largely ignored the stated target of Paris and instead focused his attentions upon Boulogne. The English forces under Suffolk were able to capture Boulogne with relative ease. Charles, annoyed at being let down by his English ally, made peace with France. This allowed Francis to direct all of his military resources towards the English. Boulogne was garrisoned and the English army sailed home. For the next year the French sought to regain Boulogne and plans were set up for a French invasion of England. Indeed a French navy was assembled for that cause but poor weather and even worse leadership denied Francis the opportunity to turn the tables on Henry. There were one or two minor skirmishes in and around the channel, and one of Henry's most important warships, the *Mary Rose*, sunk itself in Portsmouth harbour when it attempted a sharp manoeuvre with its gunports open. Finally, in June 1546 a peace settlement was drawn up at Ardres. Again Henry was promised a sizeable pension from the French King and the English were to hold Boulogne until 1554 when France would buy the town back.

What was the cost of Henry's foreign policy?

Henry's honour was intact but the financial costs of the campaign had been vast.

- The cost of garrisoning Boulogne in the first year after its capture had been £130,000. The campaign in total had cost over £2 million.

- Henry had tried to finance his adventurous foreign policy through increased taxation and forced loans. But this was not enough and consequently crown lands, which had been vastly increased through the dissolution of the monasteries, were sold off. A steady income from future rents was lost forever.

- In addition, the coinage was debased, a process that involved collecting existing coins, melting them down and reissuing new coins with less silver in them but of the same value. Debasement gained over £1 million for Henry's government in the 1540s but it was no more than a quick cash-fix. Debasing the coinage also intensified inflation and reduced confidence in English financial markets. The future solvency and stability of the English monarchy had been compromised, and Henry's foreign adventures in his final years ensured that Edward would begin his reign in serious debt. Henry had impoverished the Crown and had little of lasting worth to show for the French campaign.

SKILLS BUILDER

Source L

4.2 Part of a painting made c.1520 showing the Field of Cloth of Gold during the meeting between Henry VIII and Francis I of France.

Source M

We have to tell your Grace that more and more knowledge is coming to us, that the joining together of many evil disposed persons of this town has extended to many other places, not only in Norfolk and in Essex, but in Cambridgeshire, the town and university of Cambridge, and many other counties. We think we never saw the time so needful for the King's Highness to call his council, to debate and determine what is best to be done.

From a letter written to Wolsey by the Dukes of Norfolk and Suffolk in May 1525, concerning the troubles associated with the Amicable Grant

Source N

English diplomacy between 1515–25 failed to bring great gains to the country, but it did thrust the county into a major role that its wealth and population scarcely justified and made hard to sustain. Wolsey's aim was to serve his master and maintain Henry's honor and influence. In hindsight this may well seem vainglorious, but the conflict between Francis and Charles may have been inevitable, and Henry and Wolsey did well to preserve an independent and active role and win glory, honour and prestige which meant so much to Henry.

From David Grossell, Henry VIII 1509–29, published 1998

Do you agree with the suggestion in Source N that Henry and Wolsey conducted an effective foreign policy in the years 1515–25? Explain your answer using Sources L, M and N and your own knowledge (40 marks).

Use the following adviceto help you answer this question.

- Remember to focus on the question – in this case an assessment of foreign policy 1515–25.
- Build your answer using the source material and your own knowledge. In your first paragraph you might want to set out the successes of Henry and Wolsey in foreign affairs using the sources and your own knowledge, e.g. Source L shows the magnificence of Henry's foreign policy at the Field of Cloth of Gold on French territory in 1520. But it cannot give us the historical context to the meeting between Francis and Henry. Add this in using your own knowledge. Now move onto the other source that shows that Henrician foreign policy was successful. Ignore Source M for now because that will be the main focus of the second half of our argument. Once you have done this, move onto the second half of your argument. It does not matter if you have already introduced some counter points arguing that Henry's foreign policy was not entirely effective.
- You do not have to deal with the sources in the order that they appear on the paper but think about fitting the sources to your agreement. Some sources might fit both sides of your argument – this is not a problem.
- Keep referring back to the source and use short, snappy quotations to reinforce your argument.
- Where relevant, evaluate the author in termsof situation, purpose and reliability. Look also at the tone of the source where necessary.
- Use your own knowledge to challenge or develop any points made in the source.
- Remember to make a judgement on the question at the end.

Evaluating a painting

When you deal with a painting make sure that you refer specifically to the imagery contained within it. Show the examiner that you are reinforcing your points from the source.

Just like any source, a painting can only reveal so much to us. We are not given the name of the painter for Source L but it is often useful to think about why such a painting may have been produced. Was it deliberatley painted in order to show the magnificence of the meeting?

KNOWLEDGE FOCUS

- Unlike his father, Henry VIII viewed it as his duty to wage war and win glory for England on the battlefield.

- England's resources did not match up to Henry's aims and objectives.

- Wolsey played a shrewd diplomatic game that involved offering England as the key ally in the Habsburg–Valois struggle.

- The Treaty of London might be seen as the high point of Henrician foreign policy.

- Foreign policy was expensive and by 1525 it began to impact upon domestic affairs.

- The years 1525–26 were crucial ones as England turned away from the Empire and towards France.

- This Anglo-French alliance was unpopular and did not serve Henry well in his Great Matter.

- The break with Rome (1534) left Henry in charge of the English Church but feeling vulnerable to a Catholic invasion.

- Victory over the Scots at Solway Moss in 1542 was not followed up effectively and English policy merely served to strengthen the Franco-Scottish alliance.

- The 1543 campaign against France was costly and ultimately achieved little of note.

SKILLS FOCUS

- Fit the sources around your argument rather than deal with them as they appear on the paper.

- Use your own knowledge to bring in new material as well as evaluate the source material.

- Use short, sharp quotations from written sources to reinforce your points.

- In a pictorial source, refer to the imagery and the purpose of the painter.

- Always finish your answer with a clear judgement on the question.

5 Henry's changing relations with the Catholic Church: the break with Rome Part 1

The King's Great Matter 1527–32

Key questions

- Why did Henry seek an annulment of his marriage to Catherine of Aragon?
- What were the consequences of Henry's failure to attain a divorce through Rome?
- What was the role of the Reformation Parliament 1529–32?
- How did royal policy change in the years 1529–32?

Timeline

1503	Julius II grants dispensation for Henry and Catherine's marriage
1509	Henry's accession and marriage
1516	Henry and Catherine's daughter, Mary, is born
1521	Henry writes the *Assertio Septem Sacramentorum* (In Defence of the Seven Sacraments)
1527	Henry commits himself to Anne Boleyn and decides to seek an annulment of his marriage to Catherine of Aragon Charles V sacks Rome and imprisons the Pope
1528	Cardinal Campeggio arrives in England
1529	June, Legatine court begins to try Henry's case July, Court adjourns. Case recalled to Rome August, Treaty of Cambrai, making peace between Charles V and Francis I October, Wolsey dismissed November, Reformation Parliament meets. Acts passed reducing probate and mortuary fees and attacking pluralities and non-residence
1530	Thomas Cromwell joins Henry VIII's Council October, Thomas Cranmer and Edward Foxe present Henry with the *Collectanea satis copiosa* November, Death of Wolsey at Leicester Abbey
1531	Convocation agree to Henry VIII becoming the Head of the Church in England as far as Christ's Law allows
1532	March, Supplication against the Ordinaries May, Submission of the Clergy followed by the resignation of Thomas More.

These words between Henry and Anne Boleyn were scrawled in the margins of a prayer book as they both took morning Mass in the royal chapel in 1527–28:

> If you remember my love in your prayers as strongly as I adore you, I shall hardly be forgotten, for I am yours. Henry R forever

> By daily proof you shall me find
> To be to you both loving and kind. AB

Question

What do these words tell us about the relationship between Henry and Anne by this time?

Why did Henry seek an annulment of his marriage to Catherine of Aragon?

Source A

And as touching the queen, if it be adjudged by the law of God that she is my lawful wife, there was never thing more pleasant nor more acceptable to me in my life both for the discharge and clearing of my conscience and also for the good qualities and conditions the which I know to be in her. For I assure you all that she is a woman of most gentleness . . . she is without comparison . . . so that if I were to marry again if the marriage might be good I would surely choose her above all other women. But if it be determined by judgement that our marriage was against God's law and clearly void, then I shall not more lament and bewail my unfortunate chance that I have so long lived in adultery to God's great displeasure, and have no true heir of my body to inherit this realm.

Henry's speech to the Lord Mayor and Aldermen of London,
8 November 1528

By 1527 Henry was convinced that his marriage to **Catherine of Aragon** was invalid before God and therefore unlawful. After a relatively happy eighteen years of marriage, Henry had decided that he wanted a divorce, the implications of which would be monumental for the Church in England.

Take it further

Anne Boleyn was not a catalyst in the English Reformation; she was a key element in the equation.

Eric Ives, *The Life and Death of Anne Boleyn*, 2004

Who was Anne Boleyn? Find out more about including her importance in the Henrician Reformation beyond her love affair with Henry. A good starting point would be Eric Ives's biography of Anne mentioned above.

Biography

Catherine of Aragon (1485–1536)

Catherine had married Henry VIII's brother Arthur in 1501 when she was only sixteen years old and he just fourteen. Arthur died shortly after the wedding, harbouring doubts that their marriage had ever been consummated. In 1509 Catherine married Henry VIII, thus maintaining the Anglo-Spanish alliance. Catherine fell pregnant on several occasions but bore only one child, a girl named Mary (b.1516). Henry's affections for Catherine were tested by her failure to produce a male heir and his increasing lust for Anne Boleyn. The whole issue of the King's Great Matter and the ensuing break with Rome revolves around Henry's desire to free himself from his marriage to Catherine of Aragon.

Questions

1 What does Henry mean when he says *for the discharge and clearing of my conscience*?
2 What was Henry's purpose in describing Catherine as a woman *without comparison*?

Definitions

Leviticus

A book of the Old Testament from which Henry VIII found scriptural justification for his divorce from Catherine of Aragon.

Canon law

Church law.

Consummate

The act of making a marriage legally valid through sexual intercourse.

Consanguinity

The relationship between one person and another person's relatives by the sexual union of those two persons. Henry argued that his marriage to Catherine was null and void because she had consummated her marriage with Arthur. This degree of affinity was a key part in Henry's argument as it was seen to contravene divine and natural law.

At the time Henry had no reason to believe that papal approval for his proposed marriage annulment would not be forthcoming. Partly this was based on Henry's justifications for the divorce. Henry believed that his marriage to Catherine contravened divine law. He based his case on scripture, citing verses from **Leviticus** that prohibited marriage to one's dead brother's wife.

Source B

Thou shalt not uncover the nakedness of thy brother's wife: it is thy brother's nakedness. xx, 21

If a man shall take his brother's wife it is an impurity: he hath uncovered his brother's nakedness; they shall be childless. xxv, 5

Texts from Leviticus supporting Henry's case for the divorce

To Henry and his supporters this was a clear-cut case. The papal dispensation that had allowed Henry to marry Catherine in the first place was invalid as their union contravened divine law and this was therefore beyond the authority of Rome. Furthermore, this text from Leviticus was altered to suit Henry's case even more snugly. Henry had heard that the Hebrew text translated the last line of Leviticus xxv, 5 as *he shall be without sons*, rather than *they shall be childless*. The King had no sons and clearly felt that the primary reason for this was God's displeasure at his unlawful marriage. Yet the invalidity of Henry's marriage to Catherine was not an open and shut case. A conflicting biblical text existed that appeared to contradict Henry's Levitical argument.

Source C

When brethren dwell together, and one of them dieth without children, the wife of the deceased shall not marry to another; but his brother shall take her, and raise up seed for his brother. xxv, 5

Text from Deuteronomy undermining Henry's case for the divorce

Henry had to find a way of neutralising the effect of Deuteronomy in order to uphold Leviticus. Henry's team of propagandists and theologians argued that Deuteronomy was Judaic custom and did not apply to Christians. Yet this was highly debatable and no matter how convinced Henry himself was by 1527 that his marriage was forbidden by divine law, his case in **canon law** was a weak one.

Henry would also face the difficulty of upholding Leviticus in the light of Catherine's previous marriage to **Arthur** (see page 85). Catherine argued that she came to Henry a virgin, and that her union with Arthur had not been **consummated**. Henry had to try to prove that her previous marriage to his deceased brother had been consummated because only through proving **consanguinity** would Leviticus hold water.

Was Henry motivated by lust or pragmatism?

Source D

Sire,

It belongs only to the august mind of a great king, to whom Nature has given a heart full of generosity towards the sex, to repay by favours so extraordinary an artless and short conversation with a girl. Inexhaustible as is the treasury of your majesty's bounties, I pray you to consider that it cannot be sufficient to your generosity; for if you recompense so slight a conversation by gifts so great, what will you be able to do for those who are ready to consecrate their entire obedience to your desires? How great soever may be the bounties I have received, the joy that I feel in being loved by a King whom I adore, and to whom I would with pleasure make a sacrifice of my heart , if fortune had rendered it worthy of being offered to him, will ever be infinitely greater.

Letter from Anne Boleyn to King Henry VIII, late summer 1526

Question

Seventeen of Henry VIII's famous love letters to Anne Boleyn exist but only one of Anne's letters to the King has survived. In this letter (above) Anne thanks the King for personally appointing her a maid of honour to his queen, Catherine of Aragon.

Why do you think this letter is so important to historians studying the relationship between Henry and Anne Boleyn?

Biography

Anne Boleyn (c. 1501–36)

Anne was the second daughter of Thomas Boleyn and granddaughter of the second duke of Norfolk. She spent some of her adolescent years in the French court, returning to England in 1522, with the intention of marrying Lord Henry Percy. Henry had Wolsey terminate the proposal and Henry became increasingly obsessed with Anne. Anne would not become Henry's mistress and it is widely believed that she played her cards wisely as the Great Matter unfolded. In January 1533 Henry married Anne in secret and she was crowned queen later that year.

Biography

Arthur, Prince of Wales (1486–1502)

Eldest son of Henry VII and his wife, Elizabeth of York and groomed by Henry VII for kingship. Arthur was betrothed to Catherine of Aragon in 1489, when he was only three years old. The marriage was designed to seal an Anglo–Spanish alliance and took place on 14 November 1501. On 2 April 1502, Arthur died suddenly. Catherine maintained that the marriage was unconsummated, but Julius II's dispensation for Catherine to marry Henry issued in 1503 suggested otherwise.

The question remains as to just what motivated Henry to divorce his wife of eighteen years. There is little doubt that he fell madly in love with **Anne Boleyn** some time between 1525 and 1527. Anne was the daughter of Sir Thomas Boleyn, a courtier and minister, as well as being the niece of the Duke of Norfolk. Henry even had to employ Wolsey to break up Anne's love affair with Henry Percy. More interestingly, Anne was also the sister of one of Henry's former mistresses, namely Mary. Anne was determined not to follow in her sister's footsteps and give in to Henry's lustful overtures. If Henry was to bed her he must first wed her and in doing so make her his lawful queen. Anne set out to allure Henry and she succeeded, but at the same time she played a clever game of cat and mouse in refusing to become merely another notch on Henry's bedstead. There is little doubt that Henry became infatuated with

Exam tip

There were two lines of argument that Henry could pursue with regard to the Great Matter.

1 The Levitical line was more radical as it actually challenged the right of the papacy to dispense on cases involving a man marrying his brother's widow. This argument was favoured by Henry, but many believed that it was too much of an affront to papal authority to be successful.

2 The less radical line was to argue that the original dispensation issued by Julius II was technically insufficient. Wolsey believed that this did not offend the papacy as it was merely drawing attention to a technical error in the original dispensation, and therefore had more chance of success.

Questions

1 What were the weaknesses of Henry's Levitical argument?

2 How far do you think Henry was motivated primarily by lust for Anne or genuine conviction that his marriage to Catherine was unlawful?

Anne. Perhaps he had grown tired of Catherine who was six years Henry's senior and over the age of forty by the time that the sprightly young Anne appeared on the scene. Certainly the numerous love letters written by Henry to Anne testify to his desires to win her over, and she remained the prize throughout the struggle for an annulment of his first marriage. Yet, Henry's love for Anne and her unwillingness to yield to his desires until they were man and wife were not the only reasons for the divorce.

Henry's conscience probably was troubled by his marriage to Catherine of Aragon. Henry had an enormous ego, and once he was convinced that his marriage to Catherine was against God's law and illegal, he was not going to move from that position. He had fallen in love with Anne and he was concerned over the succession, but at the heart of his justification remained the Levitical line.

Despite eighteen years of marriage and multiple pregnancies Catherine had provided Henry with only a daughter, named Mary. By 1525 it was clear that Catherine was ageing and unlikely to conceive of another child. The future stability of the realm appeared to rest on the succession of a legitimate son and heir. The instability and chaos of the Wars of the Roses were a recent part of English history, and Henry had no wish to reignite civil war. In this context a female sovereign was unthinkable as it would weaken the Tudor dynasty and perhaps encourage Yorkist contenders to stake their claims once more. The last attempt by a woman to succeed to the throne had been made in the twelfth century by Henry I's daughter, Matilda, and this had resulted in years of conflict. The omens were not good and the fact that two of Henry's sons had died in infancy only served to confirm to the King that God was angry with his marriage.

Henry knew that he could sire a son as he had an illegitimate boy called Henry Fitzroy through an illicit relationship with Elizabeth Blount. This served to convince Henry that he was not at fault, and that God must be deeply unpleased with his marriage to Catherine.

Precedents for papal annulments existed:

• one was granted to Louis XII of France to release him from marriage to Anne of Brittany;

• a decree of nullity was given to Henry's sister, Margaret of Scotland.

Yet the circumstances of Henry's case made the prospect less straightforward.

Why did Henry have problems attaining a divorce through Rome 1527–29?

Source E

Our trusty and wellbeloved subjects, both you of the nobility and you of the meaner sort, it is not unknown to you how that we, both by God's provision and true and lawful inheritance have reigned over this realm of England almost the term of 20 years, during which time we have so ordered us, thanked be God, that no outward enemy hath oppressed you nor taken anything from us . . . so that we think that you nor none of your predecessors never lived more quietly, more wealthy, nor in more estimation under any of our noble progenitors. But when we remember our mortality and that we must die, then we think that all our doings in our lifetime are clearly defaced and worthy of no memory if we leave you in trouble. For if our true heir be not known at the time of our death, see what mischief and trouble shall succeed to you and your children.

Henry's speech to the Lord Mayor and Aldermen of London, 8 November 1528

Questions

1 What was Henry's purpose in addressing the important citizens of London in November 1528?

2 In your own words explain what Henry's main point is in this extract of his speech?

Henry required a divorce through Rome as only a papal annulment of his marriage to Catherine would be seen as legitimate across Europe. Henry had to demonstrate that his marriage to Catherine had been unlawful from the very beginning.

- Catherine's nephew was **Charles V**, Holy Roman Emperor and the most powerful political figure in Western Christendom. Charles held real influence over **Pope Clement VII** as a consequence of military superiority in the Habsburg–Valois conflict and it would have been unwise for Clement to disgrace the Habsburg emperor by granting an annulment. In May 1527 Imperial troops sacked Rome and the Pope was held a virtual prisoner. Papal policy was now shaped largely by the wishes of Charles, and the chances of an annulment for Henry seemed slim as long as Imperial power held sway in Italy.

Biography

Charles V (1500–58)

Holy Roman Emperor 1519–56. Son of Philip of Burgundy and Joanna of Castile, he inherited vast territorial possessions including the Netherlands, Spain, Naples, Sicily, Sardinia, the Americas and the Habsburg dominions in 1519 when he was elected Holy Roman Emperor. Charles was unquestionably the most powerful ruler in Western Christendom, but his enormous inheritance upset the balance of power in Europe and provoked antagonism with Francis I of France.

Biography

Clement VII (1478–1534)

Pope from 1523. The illegitimate and posthumous son of Giuliano de Medici, he was brought up by Lorenzo de Medici. His cousin, Pope Leo X, elevated him to the cardinalate and to the position of papal legate in Florence. In 1523, after the brief pontificate of Adrian VI, he became the second Medici Pope at an awkward time. Charles V was in the ascendancy in Italy and his advance threatened papal lands. In 1527 Imperial troops sacked Rome. Partly as a consequence of this, Clement was unable to resolve the issue of Henry VIII's divorce, leading to England's break with Rome in 1534.

Key information

Wolsey's diplomacy

It is important to recognise that the fate of the Great Matter was also bound up in foreign affairs. England had ditched her long-standing alliance with Spain in 1525–26 after Charles refused to cut Henry in on the spoils of his great victory at Pavia. Wolsey had negotiated a new alliance with France, just as the Great Matter was beginning to emerge as the key domestic issue of the Tudor court. In the end Wolsey backed the wrong side at the wrong time.

- Wolsey hoped that he would be able to use his credentials as a papal legate and cardinal to attain what his master so desperately desired. With the Pope a prisoner, Wolsey wanted to call a council of leading archbishops to pronounce on the divorce without the Pope (*capto papo*). However, the French cardinals were reluctant to play along and in December 1527 Clement was technically freed from imprisonment even if he was still under Habsburg control. Wolsey's hopes of pronouncing on Henry's case without the Pope were dashed and he now depended upon a revival of French fortunes in northern Italy.

- Wolsey's next strategy was to have the case heard in England, with papal approval of course. The Pope wanted nothing to do with the Great Matter, as he did not want to antagonise Charles V for fear of losing papal independence in Italy. At the same time Clement wanted to pacify Henry, and to that end he suggested that Henry get divorced in England, marry Anne and then attain an official annulment from the Pope sometime in the future, possibly after Catherine had died. Essentially this amounted to bigamy and Henry was not interested in such solutions. Clement also told his legate Cardinal Campeggio, who was on his way to England to hear Henry's case, in 1528 that Catherine might enter into a nunnery and take her monastic vows, leaving Henry free to remarry. Yet again, this would not suffice as Henry wanted the annulment to be given through Rome, thus legitimising all future heirs through his subsequent marriage. There was even the suggestion that the succession might be secured through the marriage of Henry's illegitimate son Fitzroy to his daughter Mary, but once again this idea was never really taken seriously by Henry as the succession had to be watertight.

Biography

Cardinal Campeggio (1472–1539)

Lorenzo Campeggio was made a Cardinal in 1517 and papal legate to England in 1518. Subsequently he also became Bishop of Salisbury and Archbishop of Bologna, both in 1524. Best known for his role in the legatine court at Blackfriars that aimed to resolve Henry's Great Matter. European politics dictated that Campeggio was in no position to decree on the divorce, and Clement VII had told him as much. He adjourned the court in July 1529 for the long, hot Italian summer, despite the location being England! The failure of the court marked the end of the road for Wolsey and the beginnings of the break with Rome.

Biography

John Fisher (1469–1535)

A devoted servant to Lady Margaret Beaufort and her son Henry VII, Fisher was less of a comfort to Henry VIII. Fisher was a staunch supporter of the Papacy and Catherine of Aragon, arguing that the Pope had every right to dispense on the issue of a man marrying his dead brother's wife. He also denied outright the idea of Royal Supremacy over the Church, a view revealed in the wording of the Pardon of the Clergy (1531) where Fisher insisted on *as far as Christ's law allows* being added to Henry's title of sole protector and Supreme Head of the Church. On 17 June 1535 Fisher was condemned to death under the new Treason Act, and five days later he was beheaded.

- Catherine had powerful supporters at the English court and her plight won her much sympathy. Catherine was determined to defend the validity of her marriage and the legitimacy of her daughter Mary. Catherine consistently argued that she was a virgin when she married Henry and that the King's Levitical line did not apply to an unconsummated marriage. Influential and important men such as **Bishop John Fisher** (see page 88) and Thomas More supported her cause while she was in regular correspondence with Rome and Charles V. Catherine was quite simply unprepared to accept that after eighteen years her marriage was somehow unlawful. To do so would have been an acceptance that she had been no more than a royal mistress and her daughter a royal bastard. Her loyalty to Henry remained unwavering and was a source of embarrassment to the King when she appeared before Wolsey and Campeggio's legatine court in 1529. The King's infatuation with Anne Boleyn further gave claim to the idea that Catherine was being cast aside by Henry in favour of a younger woman. Catherine's determined opposition along with her bloodline was a central reason why Henry was unable to attain an annulment.

- In April 1528 after much procrastination, Clement VII finally granted a commission to hear the case in England. Cardinal Campeggio was dispatched to join Wolsey, but by the time he arrived in October 1528 Imperialist power in Italy was assured and the likelihood of a papal annulment decreased still further. The actual trial was delayed again by the discovery of a Spanish brief. This was a letter from Julius II in 1503 to Catherine's mother, Isabella of Spain, which reportedly cleared up any discrepancies surrounding the marriage of Catherine to Henry. The English court believed the brief to be fake, and its discovery at such a crucial time does appear to be more than good fortune for the Spanish party. Henry demanded it be sent to England for examination but the Spanish would not let it out of their sight. Wolsey was desperate to get proceedings under way before Charles V had the case revoked to Rome. On 31 March 1529 the court opened at Blackfriars, although Campeggio was already under strict orders from Rome not to dispense on the Great Matter.

The Blackfriars court proceedings lasted until July 1529, with no resolution of the problem. Despite the case being heard in England, Campeggio used papal jurisdiction to adjourn proceedings for the long, hot Italian summer! The Treaty of Cambrai confirmed the ascendancy of Charles in Italy, and at the same time ensured that Catherine's case would indeed be revoked to Rome. The year 1529 therefore marks a turning point in the Great Matter. Although Henry would continue to pursue an annulment through Rome for the next two or three years he would also be open to the idea of a unilateral decision on the divorce being made in England.

What was the royal policy in the years 1529–32?

Some historians such as **G.R. Elton** see the years 1529–32 as ones without a clear policy. In some ways Elton is right as there does not seem to be

Biography

G.R. Elton (1921–94)

G.R. Elton was Regius Professor of Modern History at Cambridge University from 1983–88. He is regarded as one of the leading historians on the Tudor period. His works include *The Tudor Revolution in Government* (1953), *England under the Tudors* (1955) and *Reform and Renewal* (1973). Elton's thesis on the Tudor revolution in government is an important and contentious analysis of the administrative reforms of Thomas Cromwell, although some of his ideas are now regarded as slightly outdated.

any clear direction to Henry's plans for an annulment in these years. Moreover, Henry's new Lord Chancellor was Thomas More, a brilliant man in many ways but one who could not bring himself to support the King's case.

- The drift in policy is therefore understandable given the nature of the problem that Henry faced. On the one hand he would ideally have liked to attain a watertight annulment through Rome freeing him to marry Anne Boleyn. Yet this looked out of the question.

- On the other hand he is increasingly attracted by the proposition of an internal solution to the problem that would increase his own powers over the Church at the same time. Just exactly when Henry decided to take this radical step to break with Rome and establish a Royal Supremacy over the Church in England is highly debatable, although it is clear that by 1532 his mind was all but made up.

Throughout the period 1529–32 Henry still applied pressure on Rome to make a decision on the Great Matter in his favour.

- Wolsey's fate is sealed with the failure of Blackfriars in 1529. Henry has his once-favoured servant minister charged with **praemunire**. The charge against Wolsey was based on him supposedly exercising his power as cardinal legate in England to the detriment of the Crown. Henry had been more than happy for Wolsey to use his influence at Rome when it appeared to be in the interests of the Crown to do so, but now Wolsey was going to pay for his failure to attain an annulment with his life. At the same time the charge of praemunire made a point to Rome that Henry's authority was total in England.

What was the role of the Reformation Parliament?

- **The Reformation Parliament** opened in November 1529 and the legislation that it passed was anti-clerical in nature. The Probate, Pluralities and Mortuaries Act tapped into anti-clerical sentiment in England and again put pressure on Rome. Henry hoped through this legislation that the Pope might feel threatened by the consequences of not granting Henry his divorce.

Definitions

Praemunire

Praemunire was the treasonable crime of acknowledging a foreign power, such as that of the papacy, over the Crown.

The Reformation Parliament

The name given to the seven sessions of parliament that met on and off 1529–36. Known as the Reformation Parliament because by the time it closed Henry had broken with Rome and established the Royal Supremacy. The legislation began as an attack on the clergy and a warning to Rome, but it increasingly served to sever links with the Papacy and assert Henry's control over the Church in England.

Question

What are the major grievances outlined by Fish in Source F above?

Source F

And what do all these greedy sort of sturdy, idle, holy thieves with these yearly exactions that they take of the people? Truly, nothing but exempt themselves from the obedience of your grace. Nothing but translate all rule, power, lordship, authority, obedience and dignity from your grace unto them. Nothing but that all your subjects should fall into disobedience and rebellion against your grace and be under them.

Simon Fish, *A Supplication for the Beggars*, written in 1529

Fish, a common lawyer, gives us an insight into the kind of anti-clerical material that was being disseminated throughout the south of England at this time. One should view the legislation of 1529 in the context of Wolsey's fall and such literature as that cited above. Fish called on Henry to reform a clergy that was idle and corrupt. Henry for his part began to become increasingly convinced that the Church needed to be brought to heel on the issue of the Great Matter and he began to assert his authority over the English clergy.

Were Henry's views on the Great Matter changing by 1530?

- In 1530 Henry collected the opinions of the finest universities in Europe, including Oxford and Cambridge, on the Great Matter. The findings were published in 1531. Seven universities returned favourable verdicts on Henry's case, reiterating his Levitical line that his marriage contravened divine law, and that the Pope had no authority to dispense such marriages. Most of these universities had been bribed to support Henry's case. Thomas More was given the job of reporting the findings to parliament. Increasingly, his duty as Lord Chancellor was being compromised by his own personal opposition to the King's case.

However, Henry was also beginning to consider a more radical option to solving his Great Matter.

- In 1530 some of Henry's leading clerical supporters, led by Edward Foxe, Bishop of Hereford, and **Thomas Cranmer** (see page 92), future Archbishop of Canterbury, put together the *Collectanea satis copiosa*. The *Collectanea* referred to ancient English manuscripts and Anglo Saxon chronicles in supporting the concept of the King as head of state and Church. In short, historical precedents were found or perhaps invented to support the idea of the Royal Supremacy. Henry was unquestionably intrigued and excited by the possibility of extending his power over the Church and using the English clergy under his authority to pronounce on the divorce.

At the same time pressure on the Church was exerted.

- In February 1531 the Church in England was forced to pay a subsidy as a monetary fine for their endorsement of Wolsey's papal posts. The whole clergy were charged with praemunire and as a result stumped up £118,000. The clergy were thereby pardoned for their offence of unlawfully exercising their spiritual jurisdiction in Church courts. Once more pressure was being brought to bear on Rome, and Henry was stamping his authority on the clergy.

- In the 1531 Pardon of the Clergy, mentioned above, Henry insisted that he be referred to as *sole protector and Supreme Head of the English*

Take it further

Find out about other anti-clerical lawyers such as Christopher St German (John Guy assesses the importance of St German in his book, *Tudor England*). What was the impact of such thought at this time on the progress of Henry's policy?

Definition

Radicals v conservatives

This was the key factional battle at court during the journey towards divorce. The radicals were men such as Foxe, Cranmer and, by 1531, Thomas Cromwell. They supported Anne Boleyn and advocated the Supremacy. This entailed a break with Rome, which suited the religious stance of these men as most leaned towards Protestantism. The conservatives were mainly traditionally minded bishops such as Fisher, Tunstall and Standish. Thomas More was also part of this group that supported Catherine of Aragon. The two groups fought for control of the King's policy. Both sides supported their case in print.

Church and clergy. The diehard conservatives such as John Fisher were outraged and insisted that this title be tempered with the line *as far as Christ's law allows.*

- Nevertheless, these two factors highlight the point that Henry was becoming increasingly won over by the idea of Royal Supremacy. As Henry became more convinced of his authority over the Church, so the radical faction at court began to hold sway over the conservatives.

Biography

Thomas Cromwell (1485–1540)

Thomas Cromwell served in Wolsey's household until 1529, and his administrative efficiency was sufficient to gain him the attentions of the King. By 1532 he had worked his way into the inner council and had become Henry's willing servant on the issue of the divorce. From 1533–40 Cromwell was Henry's leading minister and the man behind the break with Rome and the Royal Supremacy. As Henry's Vicegerent in Spirituals he also masterminded the dissolution of the monasteries between 1535–39, and introduced reforms such as the English Bible in 1538.

Biography

Thomas Cranmer (1489–1556)

Cranmer was a key figure in the Henrician Reformation. In the early stages he discussed with Foxe and Gardiner the King's Great Matter and proposed an appeal to the universities of Europe in 1530. Henry was pleased with Cranmer's contribution to his problem and he was appointed a royal chaplain and attached to the household of Anne Boleyn's father. On an embassy to Germany to meet with Charles V, he met and married a niece of the reformer Osiander. As he had entered the priesthood, this had to be done secretly. In 1533 he was recalled by Henry VIII to succeed Warham as Archbishop of Canterbury. In May 1533 Cranmer pronounced Catherine's marriage null and void and the private marriage to Anne Boleyn, four months earlier, valid. Religiously, Cranmer was very much an evangelical and was eager to promote the accessibility of scripture to the masses. In 1538 injunctions were issued by Cromwell for a Bible in English and in 1544 Henry authorised the use in English of Cranmer's Litany.

How important was Thomas Cromwell in introducing the Royal Supremacy?

In 1532 the whole fabric and structure of the Church in England began to change as the break with Rome hit the statute book and the Royal Supremacy gathered pace. The architect was **Thomas Cromwell**.

In 1532 Cromwell introduced a petition against Church courts and clerical jurisdiction into the Commons. The petition was known as the Commons

Question

Why would Chapuys report on Cromwell's origins and upbringing?

Source G

Sir, Master Cromwell, of whose origin and antecedents your Secretary Antoine tells me you desire to be informed, is the son of a poor blacksmith, who lived in a small village four miles from this place, and is buried in a common grave in the parish churchyard. Cromwell in his youth was an ill conditioned scapegrace. For some offence he was thrown into prison, and was obliged afterwards to leave the country.

A letter from Eustace Chapuys to Charles V, 1535

Supplication against the Ordinaries, and Cromwell's political skill lay in the fact that he convinced the Commons that this was their Bill and nothing at all to do with the King or the government. In reality they were endorsing Henry's proposed attack on the legislative independence of the Church in England.

Source H

Firstly the prelates and other of the clergy of this your realm, being your subjects, in their Convocation by them holden . . . have made and daily make divers fashions of laws and ordinances concerning temporal things; and some of them be repugnant to the laws and statutes of your realm; not having nor requiring your most royal assent of the same laws by them so made, nor any assent or knowledge of your lay subjects is had to the same, nor to them published and known in the English tongue.

Supplication against the Ordinaries, 1532

Question

What is the major grievance drawn up in the Supplication against the Ordinaries?

Convocation naturally defended its right to make laws, but Henry appeared determined to assert his supremacy over the Church. On 15 May 1532 the Submission of the Clergy was drawn up in which the legislative independence of the Church was surrendered to the Crown.

- convocation could only meet with the permission of the King
- new canon laws had to be approved first by the King
- existing canon laws were to be inspected and any that undermined royal authority were to be removed.

Why was the year 1532 a turning point in royal policy?

Thomas More resigned the chancellorship as a consequence of the Submission of the Clergy and slipped out of the political limelight for the time being. Ultimately, he could not reconcile his loyalty to the Crown with his loyalty to the Church. The Church in England was now effectively under Henry's control and the way to the Supremacy was becoming clearer. First Henry and Cromwell had to sever links with Rome in order that Catherine's appeal to the papacy could be nullified. Already this process was under way as in March 1532 parliament passed the Act in Conditional Restraint of **Annates**.

The very fact that the legislation was made conditional shows us how much opposition and controversy was caused by such a decree. It was not merely the economic aspect of papal power that was being challenged but also papal rights of consecration. The statute stated that should the Pope refuse to consecrate bishops as a result of annates being abolished, those bishops would be consecrated by English authority. Traditional bishops voted against the legislation. Although they stood to benefit

Definition

Annates

Annates were the payments made to Rome by bishops when they took up their post for the first time. In return for papal consecration a payment was made that roughly equated to one-third of a year's income. Annates were paid across western Europe and deeply resented. They were at the same time a lucrative source of income for the papacy.

financially, they were reluctant to see Papal power dissolved and the power of the monarchy over the Church increased still further. Henry and Cromwell had to tread carefully in 1532, as such radical legislation as the Act in Conditional Restraint of Annates challenged centuries of tradition and worship. Even as late as 1532 Henry had some doubts about asserting Royal Supremacy over that of the Pope. The repercussions within England and across Europe could have been serious. Therefore the Act remained on the statute book as conditional until 1533.

Nevertheless, 1532 can be seen as a watershed mark in Henry's policy towards Rome. He had now all but given up on his annulment being granted by the papacy. Moreover, Anne Boleyn was pregnant by December 1532 and it became a matter of urgency to secure a divorce and marry Anne so that any offspring would be legitimate. However, even without the pregnancy it seems likely that the legislation and actions of 1533 would have occurred anyway. Henry was growing impatient; the idea of the Supremacy appealed to his enormous ego and Cromwell was determined to find a solution to the Great Matter. The year 1532 saw the break with Rome and the Royal Supremacy become Henry and Cromwell's first choice solution to the Great Matter. The following five sessions of the Reformation Parliament would see the policy become a reality.

SKILLS BUILDER

Do you agree with the view expressed in Source K that the diplomatic situation was the main reason for Henry's failure to attain an annulment of his marriage to Catherine by 1529?

Explain your answer using Sources I, J and K and your own knowledge.

Source I

After I had exhorted her [Catherine] at great length to remove all these difficulties, and to content herself with making a profession of chastity, setting before her all the reasons which could be urged on that head, she assured me that she would never do so; that she intended to live and die in the estate of matrimony, into which God had called her, and that she would always be of that opinion, and would not change it. She repeated this many times so determinately and deliberately that I am convinced she will act accordingly. She says that neither the whole kingdom on the one hand, nor any great punishment on the other, although she might be torn from limb to limb, should compel her to alter this opinion. I have always judged her to be a prudent lady, but her obstinacy in not accepting this sound counsel does not much please me.

From a letter written by Cardinal Campeggio to Pope Clement VII,
26 October 1528

Source J

Anne Boleyn is at last come hither, and the King has lodged her in a very fine lodging, which he prepared for her himself. Greater attention is now paid to her every day than has been to the Queen for a long time. I see they mean to accustom the people by degrees to endure her, so that when the blow comes it may not be thought strange. However the people remain quite hardened, and I think that they would do more if they had power. Wolsey uses all his means to bring the Emperor into hatred, and Francis into favour; but it is hard work to fight against nature.

From a letter written by the French Ambassador, December 1528

Source K

The diplomatic situation was running hard against Henry by March 1529. Pope and Emperor were fast coming together and in a few weeks Clement would confess to a close friend that 'I have quite made up my mind to become an imperialist and live and die as such.' In the face of all this Henry was not likely to make much headway with a programme which in even the most favourable circumstances, would have been a thorny one to handle.

From J.J. Scarisbrick's biography, *Henry VIII*, 1968

We are going to plan this answer together:

- Read the question carefully and then read all the sources.
- Use a grid like the one below to record information about the sources.

	Diplomacy	Other factors
Sources		Catherine's stubbornness: 'live and die in the estate of matrimony'
		Popular approval of Catherine: 'people remain quite hardened' against Anne
Own knowledge		

- First of all, use the grid to note down any information from the sources that fits in each column. A couple of examples have been included to get you started.
- Note that one source may provide material for both columns – that is no problem. In this case you should have material from Source J in both columns.

- Once you have collected all the material, identify short quotations from each source that reinforce these points. In the exam, highlight them on the page or underline them.

- Once you have analysed the sources, add your own knowledge into the grid. Bullet-point three or four key points of relevant own knowledge that are not in the sources, e.g.:

  1 Catherine of Aragon was Charles V's aunt;

  2 Henry's Levitical argument was flawed and contradicted in Deuteronomy;

  3 the Pope had been a virtual prisoner of Charles V after the sack of Rome in 1527;

  4 the Pope had told Campeggio not to dispense an annulment on his visit to England.

- Your answer is now taking shape. The final thing you need to think about is the provenance of the source material. Look at the author and date of each source and make some notes on the context of the source and the purpose/situation of the author. Think about who wrote the source, when and why. E.g.:

  1 Cardinal Campeggio was a key figure in the divorce crisis as he was sent by Clement VII to pronounce on the matter – he is therefore well informed;

  2 he is clearly trying to find alternatives to having to annul the marriage which shows us that the Pope was not keen to make a positive decision;

  3 it is hardly objective as Campeggio was a servant of Rome;

  4 the date is significant as it comes eight months before the legatine court opened at Blackfriars, showing us that the papacy was desperately trying to find more convenient solutions to the problem and delay official proceedings for as long as possible.

- Your plan is now complete. This will be much fuller than that you would expect to put together in an examination and it will have taken you much longer. However, you should now be able to go away and write up your answer.

Here is a reminder of the structure:

Paragraph one
- use your material on the diplomatic situation being against Henry;
- remember to add own knowledge;
- remember to evaluate the author and the date.

Paragraph two
- use your material on other important factors obstructing Henry's divorce proceedings;
- add own knowledge;
- evaluate the author and date.

Finally, write a short conclusion in which you pass judgement on the question. Start that conclusion with the phrase,

To a certain extent diplomacy was important in assessing Henry's failure to attain an annulment by 1529 but ...

KNOWLEDGE FOCUS

- Henry's desire for an annulment was down to his love for Anne Boleyn, a practical wish to maintain the Tudor dynasty and a belief that his first marriage to Catherine contravened the laws of God.

- Henry always wanted to pursue the Levitical argument, challenging papal authority.

- Wolsey's suggestion of finding a legal hitch in the original dispensation was therefore ignored.

- Foreign affairs severely hampered Henry's chances of attaining an annulment through Rome.

- The failure at Blackfriars signalled the end for Wolsey.

- When the Reformation Parliament first opened there was no indication that Henry intended to break with Rome.

- The years 1529–32 can be seen as ones without a policy as Henry still wanted to pressure Rome into granting an annulment but at the same time he was open to more radical suggestions.

- Radicals such as Cromwell and Cranmer become more important at court from 1530–32 because they could offer a solution to Henry's problem.

- The Submission of the Clergy in May 1532 marks the first step on the road to the Royal Supremacy.

SKILLS FOCUS

- Independent reading is an important skill to develop. Be prepared to go beyond the textbook and research key individuals such as Anne Boleyn or Thomas Cromwell.

- Build up character profiles of these important individuals and this will help you identify with their policies and significance.

- Source-based answers consist of three major components:

  1 Think about the content. What is the source telling us? What is its message?

  2 Analyse the context. What was happening around the time the source was written? Use your own knowledge to place the source in its historical context. The date is clearly very important.

  3 Evaluate the provenance of the source. Think carefully about the situation and purpose of the author.

- A successful answer is one that builds on all of these components.

6 Henry's changing relations with the Catholic Church: the break with Rome Part 2

The Royal Supremacy 1532–35

Key questions

- How was the attack on the English Church carried out?
- How did Acts of parliament secure the break with Rome and the Royal Supremacy?
- How serious was opposition to the break with Rome and the Royal Supremacy?
- Why was there so little opposition to the Royal Supremacy and the break with Rome?

Timeline

1532	March, Supplication against the Ordinaries
	May, Submission of the Clergy followed by the resignation of Thomas More from his post as Lord Chancellor
	May, Act in Conditional Restraint of Annates
1533	January, Henry and Anne secretly marry
	March, Thomas Cranmer appointed Archbishop of Canterbury
	March, Act in Restraint of Appeals
	May, Cranmer annuls Henry's marriage to Catherine of Aragon
	July, Henry excommunicated
	September, Anne gives birth to a daughter, Elizabeth
	November, The Holy Maid of Kent, Elizabeth Barton executed
1534	January to March, First parliamentary session. Acts for the Submission of the Clergy, in Absolute Restraint of Annates, forbidding Papal Dispensations and payment of Peter's Pence. Succession Act.
	November, Second parliamentary session. Act of Supremacy. Act annexing First Fruits and Tenths to the Crown. Treasons Act.
1535	May, Leading Carthusians executed
	June, Fisher executed
	July, More executed.

The Trial Scene from Robert Bolt's play *A Man for All Seasons* (1960)

> **The Duke of Norfolk:** Repeat the prisoner's words!
>
> **Richard Rich:** He said *Parliament has not the competence.* Or words to that effect.
>
> **Cromwell:** He denied the title?

Rich: He did.

Thomas More: In good faith, Rich, I am sorrier for your perjury than my peril.

A Man for all Seasons covers the life and death of Thomas More. The play was made into a famous film in 1966 and it won six Academy Awards.

How was the attack on the English Church carried out?

The uncertainties of the years 1529–32 gave way to a more definite policy whereby the legislative independence of the English Church was destroyed and the Royal Supremacy established. Threats gave way to real blows, and the man at the heart of this destructive process was Cromwell.

How important was Thomas Cromwell in the formation and execution of the Royal Supremacy?

> **Questions**
>
> 1 Why was More on trial?
> 2 What was the title he supposedly denied?
> 3 What is perjury?

> **Take it further**
>
> Find a copy of the film, *A Man for all Seasons*, and watch it. How reliable do you think it is as a historical source?

Source A

Henry's ministers were broken reeds, without ideas to offer or sufficient skill even to take the burden of government from Henry's shoulders; as early as 1530 he had talked pointedly of recalling Wolsey. But Wolsey was dead, and these Norfolks and Wiltshires, Gardiners and Suffolks, had no answer to the royal perplexities. It was at this point that Henry discovered among his lesser councillors a man who knew exactly how the problem could be solved, and who was an even better administrator than Wolsey. In December 1531, Thomas Cromwell was promoted to the inner ring of the council, and the Tudor revolution was about to begin.

G.R. Elton, *England under the Tudors*, 1955

Source B

By early 1531 Henry VIII saw his Royal Supremacy as a fact rather than a novelty. He could see no objection to it, and interpreted the clergy's resistance as culpable disobedience. Perplexing at first sight, his attitude can be explained. For some months Henry had been studying a manuscript known as *Collectanea satis copiosa*. A collection of sources for pro royal propaganda, it was prepared by members of the Boleyn faction . . . he (Henry) applauded the document because, setting out to validate the divorce, Foxe and Cranmer had justified it from legal and historical principles, not simply personal or dynastic needs.

John Guy, *Tudor England*, 1988

Questions

1 What does Elton suggest about the influence of Thomas Cromwell?
2 How important was Cromwell in putting together the concept of the Royal Supremacy as opposed to putting it into action?

Questions

1 How does John Guy's interpretation of the origins of the Supremacy differ from that of Elton?
2 Why might that be the case?

Make sure that you:
- understand each source and the context in which it was produced
- make links between what the sources are saying
- show how and why the sources agree or disagree.

Source C

At least as far as the central event of the 1530s is concerned, namely the establishment of the Royal Supremacy, Cromwell was the executant of the King's designs. In executing them he doubtless left his own imprint on them . . . he may have determined timing and sequence, shown what was possible and what was not, what was necessary and what was not, and intervened with decisive suggestions. But he neither worked alone nor was the true initiator of these royal undertakings.

J.J. Scarisbrick, *Henry VIII*, 1968

Question

Where does Scarisbrick stand on the Cromwell debate?

The Royal Supremacy

In 1531 the Church had been forced to acknowledge a relatively meaningless title and agree to a heavy fine in the so-called submission of the clergy. Henry was, on paper, Supreme Head of the Church in England as far as the law of Christ allows, but in reality there was still much ambiguity and confusion surrounding the King's position in relation to the Church.

Source D

In the devising of his caesaro papal claims, Henry was a student, applying himself diligently to studying the manuscript which contained the dubious historical precedents for his Supremacy. Edward Foxe and John Stokesley (who would be rewarded with the bishoprics of Hereford and London) had been compiling evidence to support the King's position, including legal judgements, chronicles, scriptures, and arguments from the Church Fathers and the General Councils of the Church. This was the *Collectanea satis copiosa*. Ubi hic? (Where does this come from?); Hic est vera (Here is the truth), the King wrote in the margins. Henry was now convinced – he needed little convincing that England had long been, and still was, an empire, within which he had both temporal and spiritual jurisdiction. By October 1530 the King had convinced himself that his imperial authority empowered him to prevent appeals outside his realm.

Susan Brigden, *New Worlds, Lost Worlds*, 2000

Questions

1. What do you think Brigden means when she talks of the *dubious historical precedents for his Supremacy*?
2. What can Henry's jottings in the margin of the *Collectanea* tell us about his attitude towards the Supremacy?
3. What do you think Henry understood by *imperial authority*?

Definition

Convocation

An assembly of clergy in the provinces of Canterbury (south) and York (north) to regulate the affairs of the Church.

Supplication against the Ordinaries

In 1532 Cromwell re-drafted a document known as the Supplication against the Ordinaries (see page 93) that asked the King on behalf of the Commons to curb the legislative power of the Church. The power of Church courts and the abuse of that legislative authority were called into question. Essentially the government was attacking the power of **Convocation** to make laws without the consent of the laity.

Henry was supposed to be an impartial observer at this stage but there was little doubt that he approved of the Commons attack on convocation. Henry demanded that convocation should pass no new legislation unless he licensed them to do so. All future changes in canon law (Church law) would also require the monarch's consent. Existing canons were to be examined closely by a royal commission of thirty-two members, half of whom were laymen, and those that stood contrary to the royal prerogative were to be annulled.

The Church's legal system was now effectively under royal control. Convocation was stunned by the removal of their age-old legislative powers, but could do little to resist this attack. Archbishop Warham was ageing and could only offer token resistance, while Henry continued to increase the pressure on convocation by stating that the clergy were only half his subjects since they took an oath to the Pope. With the threat of a further assault on canon law from the Commons, the clergy capitulated on 15 May 1532 in what became known as the Submission of the Clergy (see page 93).

Thomas More resigned as Lord Chancellor the next day while many of the leading clergy disassociated themselves from the Submission by refusing to turn up to the session at which the deciding vote was taken on the issue. Henry did not care. He was now established as the supreme legislator in England. Cromwell and Henry had manipulated the emotions of the Commons brilliantly in gaining the surrender of convocation. The Church was now powerless to withstand further attacks on its position, and the road to the break with Rome and the Supremacy was now clear.

How did Acts of parliament secure the break with Rome and the Royal Supremacy?

Act in Conditional Restraint of Annates, 1532

Henry still did not have his divorce and he knew that even if he demanded his clergy to pronounce it, Catherine would appeal to Rome. As the Commons discussed the legislative powers of the Church in England, the lords considered the Bill of Annates. Annates were the payments made by bishops to the Pope on taking up their sees, at the rate of one third of their annual income. Annates were the papacy's main source of income from Henry's kingdom, and their proposed abolition was likely to cause consternation in Rome. Henry knew that in retaliation the Pope may well refuse to offer **bulls** of consecration for new bishops, and as a result the Bill stated that bishops could be consecrated by English authority.

The fact that the Act was made conditional demonstrates that Henry had not given up hope of persuading the Pope to grant him his divorce from Catherine of Aragon. Henry had some trouble getting both Houses to agree to the Bill. It is most likely that the clergy were conveying their bitterness towards the Supplication, while the Commons feared economic reprisals, such as the disruption of the wool trade with Charles V's Flanders. Either

Definition

Papal bulls

Papal bulls were legal pronouncements from the Pope in Rome concerning the Church.

way Henry felt the need to be present in the House as the Bill was being passed, such was the division in parliament. The message to Rome however was that parliament was desperately pressuring the King to end payments to the Pope. For now he was holding the Commons back but he could not stand in their way indefinitely.

A new Archbishop of Canterbury

Biography

Stephen Gardiner (1483–1555)

Gardiner served as Wolsey's secretary before embarking on several missions to Rome to try to further Henry's chances of attaining an annulment. Bishop of Winchester from 1531, Gardiner was a keen supporter of the Royal Supremacy, writing *De Vera Obedientia* in 1535. However, Gardiner remained a conservative in his religious views and opposed any radical change.

Source F

Cranmer has married the King to the Lady in the presence of the father, mother, brother and two of her favourites. If it be so, the King has taken the best means of preventing him from changing his opinions when raised to the dignity of the archbishopric.

From a letter by Chapuys to Charles V, 23 February 1533

Source E

Dr Cranmer, recently ambassador with your Majesty, had not been here a week before the King, to the great astonishment of everybody, promoted him to the Archbishopric of Canterbury. It is suspected that the object of this haste is that the archbishop, as legate of this kingdom, may authorize the new marriage in this parliament and can grant the necessary divorce. It is reported here that Cranmer, being a Lutheran, will renounce all the temporalities of his benefice to the King which is a good way of forcing the rest to do the same.

From a letter by Eustace Chapuys, the Imperial Ambassador, to Charles V, 27 January 1533

SKILLS BUILDER

How far do the contents of the letter in Source E suggest that Chapuys was well informed of the goings on at the Tudor court? Think about what this source tells you, what it suggests, but also what you cannot find out from it – its limitations.

On 23 August 1532 Archbishop Warham died, which meant that Henry could appoint someone who was more sympathetic to his divorce and the Supremacy. Thomas Cranmer was the new appointment, a man closely linked to the Boleyn family, and one who was known to hold reformed views. **Stephen Gardiner**, Bishop of Winchester, had been in line for the job but had opposed the Submission of the Clergy, and Cranmer's rise from relative obscurity can only be explained by the King's need to appoint a compliant cleric quickly.

The need for haste was due to the fact that by January 1533 it was clear that Anne was pregnant, and on the twenty-fifth of that month, Anne and Henry were married in secret.

Importantly, Henry had received from the Pope the necessary bulls for Cranmer's consecration, yet he still had no word from Rome on the validity of his first marriage. Anne's pregnancy and her marriage to Henry added impetus to Cromwell's statute-making in 1533. In reality the decision to break with Rome had already been taken, and it is likely that Anne's decision to sleep with the King was the result of this policy being affirmed.

The Act in Restraint of Appeals, 1533

This Act ended appeals to Rome, and ordered them to be heard by English Church courts instead. Appeals relating to the King were to go straight to convocation where they would be heard by the Archbishop of Canterbury. The Act clearly prevented Catherine from challenging any legal decision made on the Great Matter in England, and allowed Cranmer to open his court at Dunstable to preside over the legitimacy of the King's first marriage. On 23 May 1533 Henry's marriage to Catherine was declared void on the grounds that the papal dispensation was invalid. On 1 June Anne was crowned Queen, but the much-anticipated son would not follow. In September Anne gave birth to a baby girl, Elizabeth.

The Act of Appeals did more than just prohibit appeals to Rome. It also clarified the Royal Supremacy in full for the first time. It stated that:

> Where by divers sundry old authentic histories and chronicles it is manifestly declared and expressed that this realm of England is an empire, and so hath been accepted in this world, governed by one Supreme Head and King having the dignity and royal estate of the imperial crown of the same . . . unto whom a body politic, compact of all sorts and degrees of people, divided in terms, and by names of spirituality and temporality, be bounden and owe to bear, next to God, a natural and humble obedience.

The preamble justified the Supremacy on the basis of old English histories and chronicles in a bid to convey the idea that nothing new was being created, but rather old rights were being reasserted. Henry could celebrate a sovereign state free from foreign authority. Unsurprisingly the Pope did not see things Henry's way and in July 1533 Clement declared that Anne was not the King's wife and Henry was excommunicated. The sentence was suspended until September to give Henry time to see the error of his ways.

Further Acts in 1532

- The clergy's submission of 1532 was put into statutory form
- Appeals to Rome were forbidden in any form rather than in certain cases
- The Act in Conditional Restraint of Annates was made permanent
- English bishops were no longer to be appointed by Rome but by the King.

The Act of Dispensations, 1534

This stopped all payments to Rome including Peter's Pence. All future dispensations allowing for exemptions or departures from canon law would be issued by the Archbishop of Canterbury not Rome. Failure to abide by this decree would result in a charge of praemunire.

Take it further

Research Mary Tudor's religious policy between 1553–58. Most people associate her with the bloody persecution of Protestantism. How accurate is her nickname *Bloody Mary*? You could use Foxe's *Book of Martyrs* to find out about those Protestants who were burned in Mary's reign. Foxe's book, first published in the reign of the Protestant Queen Elizabeth (1558–1603), did much to shape our view of Mary.

The Act of Succession, 1534

This registered the invalidity of Henry's marriage to Catherine and the validity of his marriage to Anne. The heirs of the second marriage were legitimised and Mary was bastardised. The Act proposed to bind the nation by an oath, swearing allegiance to the new Queen and her offspring. At the same time it was made a treasonable offence to speak maliciously against Henry's second marriage. The papal response on 23 March 1534 was to re-affirm the validity of Henry's marriage to Catherine, an act that prompted Henry to order that the Pope's name be struck out of all prayer books.

Biography

Mary I (1516–58)

Queen of England from 1553, first daughter of Henry VIII by his wife Catherine of Aragon. As a result of the annulment of Henry's first marriage, Mary was ousted from the line of succession by Act of parliament in 1533, deprived of her title of Princess of Wales and declared a bastard. After enduring two torrid years between 1534–36, when Mary was finally forced to agree to the Supremacy and her own bastardisation, life began to improve for her. In 1544 she was restored to the succession, after Edward but before Elizabeth.

The Act of Supremacy and the Treason Law, 1534

Source G

Be it enacted by the authority of this present Parliament, that the King our Sovereign Lord, his heirs and successors, kings of this realm, shall be taken, accepted, and reputed the only Supreme Head in earth of the Church of England.

Act of Supremacy 1534

Henry now had complete administrative and legislative control over the Church. The Act of Supremacy was to be enforced by a new Treason Act that made it a capital offence to slander the Supremacy or to deny the King's new title. Treason could now be committed in word as well as deed. This gave Cromwell an instrument of terror to wield against opponents of the regime if and when they arose.

The economic consequences of the Royal Supremacy

With the Supremacy laid down in statute, Henry sought to exploit the wealth of the Church.

- Payments to Rome such as annates had been outlawed on the grounds that they were too burdensome for the Church to bear, yet this did not stop Henry passing the Act annexing **First Fruits and Tenths** to the Crown. This meant that any new benefice holder was to pay one year's income to the Crown and an annual levy of one-tenth the annual value of that benefice thereafter.

- Cromwell was commissioned to carry out a survey of ecclesiastical wealth (the *Valor* Ecclesiasticus), which detailed all clerical incomes, in order that Henry had an up-to-date and accurate picture of just how much property and areas of revenue the Church possessed.

- Between 1485 and 1534 the clergy paid £4,800 a year to Rome, but in 1535 they paid £46,052 and in 1536 £51,770 to Henry.

- In 1536 the Royal Supremacy was finalised with the Act Extinguishing the Authority of the Bishop of Rome, which removed papal rights to preach and teach in England.

Definition

First Fruits and Tenths

Any new benefice holder (e.g. a bishop) originally paid one year's income to the papacy, then after the 1534 Act of Supremacy, to the Crown. They also paid an annual levy of one-tenth the annual value of that benefice thereafter.

How serious was opposition to the break with Rome and the Royal Supremacy?

It was one thing to pass the Royal Supremacy through the statute book, but quite another to enforce it on the ground. Yet in the final analysis, clerical and lay opposition to the Royal Supremacy was limited, which may come as some surprise given the momentous nature of the changes enacted by Henry and Cromwell. Although there were some high-profile opponents of the Supremacy, there was no coherent, organised party that attempted to resist change. Therefore we might argue that opposition was not serious. There are two main reasons why opposition was scarce:

1 fear of what would happen to opponents of royal policy;

2 loyalty to the Tudor dynasty ahead of Rome.

It is also difficult to comprehend whether lay folk merely gave in to the religious and political change, or the extent to which they were enthusiastic about what was passing through the statute book.

How did the Crown make sure that people were loyal to the Supremacy?

Henry, the key architect of the Supremacy, was also the man who ensured obedience. To this end:

- all adult males had to swear an oath to the terms of the Act of Succession;

- all clergy had to make a declaration that the Pope had no greater God-given authority in England than any other foreign bishop.

These oaths were reinforced using the printing press and the pulpit to convince the nation of the legality of Henry's Reformation. Sermons were preached in support of the Supremacy and the Boleyn marriage. Government control of the pulpits allowed hitherto marginal radicals such

Biography

Hugh Latimer (1485–1555)

Hugh Latimer was Bishop of Worcester from 1535. He was an evangelical, capable of fiery sermons denouncing Rome and the immorality of the Catholic Church. Latimer was an enthusiastic supporter of the Supremacy and probably hoped that it might be the first stage in a more radical Reformation. He resigned in 1539, along with Nicholas Shaxton, Bishop of Salisbury, after the Act of Six Articles outlined an entirely orthodox doctrinal position for the English Church.

as **Hugh Latimer** and Nicholas Shaxton to come to prominence as they were more than willing to extol the virtues of Henry's caesaropapism and denounce papal power.

The Treason Act 1534

Added to this was the fear factor created by Henry's instrument of terror: the Treason Act. Originally passed in 1534, but strengthened in 1535, the Act served to silence potential opponents. The Treason Act made it treasonable to speak out maliciously against Henry or his queen, thus extending the definition of treason to include threatening words as well as deeds.

High-profile opposition

There were some high-profile opponents of the new order, which often lead us to believe that opposition was widespread, when in fact it was not.

Elizabeth Barton, known as the Holy Maid of Kent, had visions of the Virgin Mary, and soon her notoriety grew in popular and learned circles. Archbishop Warham regarded her as a true messenger from God, and it was not long before opponents of the divorce tried to use her as a means of undermining Henry's proposed marriage to Anne Boleyn. For example, she gained support from John Fisher (see page 88) and Henry decided he could not allow her to carry on with her harmful prophecies.

In November 1533 Barton was sent to the Tower, to be executed along with four of her adherents the following April. Symbolically, and not by chance, Barton was executed on the same day (21 April 1534) that Londoners were required to swear to the Oath of Succession.

Source H

This unknown 16 year old girl was rocketed to national fame in 1525 by a vision of the Virgin Mary that she had while suffering from a mental illness. Her visions continued and she rapidly came under the spiritual guidance of Dr Edward Bocking. Her later prophecies were chiefly exhortations against the King's marriage to Anne Boleyn . . . She remained important until 1533 when her claim that the King would cease to be on the throne in a month forced Cromwell into action.

David Rogerson, Samantha Ellsmore and David Hudson, *The Early Tudors*, 2001

Source I

Edward Bocking frequently railed against the King's marriage before the false nun of St Sepulchre's. She to please him, pretended to have a revelation from God that the King would not live a month after his marriage. When this did not come true, she claimed to have another revelation to the effect that the King was no longer accepted as King by God to the King's marriage. The Nun also met with the Pope's ambassadors and the obstinacy of the Bishop of Rochester's opposition to the marriage was confirmed and strengthened by her revelations.

The charges drawn up by Cromwell against the Nun of Kent, January 1534

Source J

I thank you for telling my son in law Roper that you wished to hear from me concerning my communications with the lewd nun of Canterbury. It is 8 or 9 years since I first heard of her, at which time the Archbishop of Canterbury sent to the King a letter containing certain words spoken during her trances. The King gave me the letter and asked my opinion. I told him there was nothing in it, since there was nothing there that a simple woman might not speak of her own wit.

From a letter written by Sir Thomas More to Cromwell in March 1534

SKILLS BUILDER

Use Sources H, I and J and your own knowledge.

Do you accept the view expressed in Source H that the Holy Maid of Kent remained important until 1533?

Explain your answer using Sources H, I and J and your own knowledge. (40 marks)

Planning your answer:

- Read the sources carefully and highlight key phrases that show both sides of the argument.
- Draw up two columns, one headed *important* and the other *not important*. Compile evidence from the three sources in each of the columns.
- Remember, material from one source may be used on both sides of the argument. For example, Thomas More's letter in Source J largely makes out the Nun of Kent to be an insignificant threat, yet the very fact that he is having to write to explain himself to Thomas Cromwell suggests that the authorities were taking her extremely seriously.
- Do not forget to evaluate the context of the sources. The years 1533–34 were crucial ones in the establishment and consolidation of the Supremacy. How does that affect the tone and language in these sources?
- Finally, think about the relevant own knowledge that you might use to develop your answer. Add in two or three significant pieces of own knowledge to your plan.

Writing your answer:

Now write your answer. Construct one paragraph on Barton being a serious threat, incorporating the source material and your own knowledge. Write a second paragraph on Barton being an insignificant threat, using the same style and technique. Offer a judgement on the question in a two-sentence conclusion.

Swap answers with someone else in your class. What have they done well? What could they improve?

Definition

Charterhouse

A Carthusian monastery.

Biography

Cuthbert Tunstall (1474–1559)

Tunstall was Bishop of Durham from 1530–52. He was a leading conservative clergyman who opposed any calls for more radical religious reform. Initially against the Supremacy, his loyalties to the Crown and instinct for self preservation brought him round to Henry's point of view.

Biography

Pope Paul III (1468–1549)

Originally Alessandro Farnese, he was Pope from 1534–49. He is traditionally seen as the first of the popes of the Counter Reformation, issuing a bull instituting the Order of the Jesuits in 1540. In 1538 he issued the bull of excommunication and deposition against Henry VIII.

Religious orders

Henry also faced some opposition namely from two religious orders located in London, the Carthusians and the Observant Friars. The Observants were potentially dangerous to Henry because their friary was alongside the King's most frequented palace at Greenwich, and as itinerant preachers they could spread the word of dissent quickly. All seven Observant houses were closed down, and a number of the friars imprisoned. The Carthusians appeared less dangerous and were not united in their opposition to Henry's policies. Yet Cromwell was unable to silence dissenting opinion and reasoned persuasion soon gave way to imprisonment and torture. Over a period of three years eighteen members of the **Charterhouse** were either executed or starved to death. Six leading Carthusians were executed between May and July 1535 in a brief period of terror that saw more high-profile victims mount the scaffold.

John Fisher, Bishop of Rochester

Fisher was the only bishop to oppose the Supremacy to such a degree that he was to be executed for his beliefs. There had been some disagreement among the bishops as the break with Rome became apparent. Archbishop Warham and **Bishop Tunstall** of Durham had both spoken out against Henry's motives and desire for a divorce as well as the move away from papal supremacy. Yet both ultimately realised as time wore on that they were not going to succeed in changing Henry's mind, and to resist would put them in a very dangerous position indeed. As Warham himself declared, 'the wrath of the King is death', and most dissenters decided to fall into line.

However, Fisher was steadfast in his support for Catherine, writing and preaching in her defence. Henry loathed Fisher, and saw his chance to strike when the bishop was heavily implicated in the Holy Maid of Kent affair (see page 106). Yet Henry let Fisher off the hook with a fine of £300, perhaps as a consequence of Fisher's status and standing. It was one thing to send a Kentish prophetess to the scaffold but another to execute a bishop.

But with little chance of compromise between Fisher and Henry, it was only a matter of time until they crossed swords again. Predictably, Fisher refused to swear the Oath of Succession in April 1534 (see page 104), which demanded condemnation of Henry's first marriage and an implied denial of papal supremacy. Fisher was imprisoned in the Tower, an act which in itself caused alarm in Catholic circles abroad. Fisher was known to be in close correspondence with Charles V's imperial ambassador, Eustace Chapuys.

Chapuys appealed to his master on several occasions for armed intervention, and although an invasion of England was highly unlikely, the rumours served to irritate Henry still further. In May 1535 **Pope Paul III** announced that Fisher was to be made a Cardinal. Before his Cardinal's hat arrived, Fisher had been tried and found guilty of high treason. He was executed in June 1535, the first high-profile martyr of the Henrician Reformation.

Fisher's execution caused outrage across Europe and convinced many of Henry's tyrannical ways. Henry had shown that no one was beyond the law of the land, but at the same time the execution of a relatively old and respected clergyman did little for his reputation.

Thomas More

Source K

In More's eyes, to defend the Catholic Church was a religious obligation. Before the break with Rome it was also a secular one . . . The main target of More's campaign against heresy was the traffic in prohibited books. Over a hundred titles were formally proscribed on an index of heretical books. When the distributors of Tyndale's New Testament and other colporteurs were caught and brought before More in Star Chamber, he applied the full severity of the law in the punishments which he handed down. The booksellers were fined . . . and forced to perform public penance: being paraded on market days through the streets of London on horseback, sitting back to front, their coats *pinned thick* with the proscribed books, while they were pelted with rotten fruit.

John Guy, *Thomas More*, 2000

Source L

Many things more were said on both sides. In the end, when they saw they could not persuade him to change his view by these arguments, they began more terribly to press him. They told him that the King had commanded them to charge More with great ingratitude; that there never was a man so villainous and traitorous as he. He had caused the King to magnify the power of the Pope in the King's book called the Assertion of the Seven Sacraments.

When they had laid forth all the terrors they could imagine against him. Sir Thomas said, My lords, these terrors be arguments for children and not for me.

Sir Thomas More is interviewed in March 1534, taken from the *Life of Sir Thomas More* by William Roper, written in Queen Mary's time (1553–58)

Two weeks later, Thomas More would follow Fisher to the scaffold, but his case was much less clear-cut. More was reluctantly willing to accept the change in succession as it had already happened and to do otherwise would have been pointless. However, he would not compromise his conscience by swearing to the idea that the King of England had always

SKILLS BUILDER

Make a note of what this Source tells us about the character of Thomas More.

SKILLS BUILDER

1 Why should we question the reliability of the author of this source?

2 Why was the King being rather hypocritical in using the Assertion of the Seven Sacraments as a means of attacking More?

3 How does this excerpt agree with the account given by John Guy in Source K?

been supreme head of the Church of England, and that parliament was simply re-asserting Henry's right to something which had always been the case. He was held in the Tower alongside Fisher, until the Treason Act, passed later in 1534, made it possible for the government to strike.

More was a dangerous opponent for Henry in that he was one of the most respected humanists in Europe. Legally trained, More was a scholar of some renown, and the publication of *Utopia* in 1516 had advanced his reputation still further. It was not long before he came to the notice of the royal court and he helped Henry write a tract against the emerging Lutheran threat in Europe (see pages 22–3) entitled the *Assertio Septem Sacramentorum*, and subsequently showed himself to be a merciless persecutor of heretics. In 1529 he was in many ways the obvious candidate to succeed Wolsey as Lord Chancellor. Still his appointment surprised many as More was known to oppose the King's Great Matter on principle. More accepted the role on condition that he did not have to become directly involved in the Great Matter, but as the break with Rome unfolded, More became increasingly uncomfortable. More's resignation after the Submission of the Clergy in 1532 marked a turning point in his relationship with Henry. Thereafter More tried to retire from public affairs and he deliberately remained silent on the key political issue of the day, namely the Supremacy.

Cromwell and Cranmer tried to save More, and both were willing to accept assurances from More that he would remain the King's loyal servant and do nothing to assist Henry's enemies. Yet this was not enough for Henry who insisted that More take the oath in April 1534.

More simply would not approve the Boleyn marriage against his conscience, nor would he condemn papal jurisdiction. At the same time he maintained his silence, and would not actively speak out against the Supremacy. In the end More was tried and found guilty of treason on the unsupported and perjured evidence of Sir Richard Rich, the solicitor general.

More defended himself brilliantly at his trial, maintaining his line that parliament had no right to bind men's consciences by making them swear an Oath to the Supremacy. More attacked the tyrannical nature of Henry's England that did not allow for freedom of conscience, and there is little doubt that on this point More held the moral high ground. He had shown no signs of inciting opposition, unlike Fisher who had urged Charles V to invade England, nor had he actively spoken out against the King's policies until this point. As a result of Rich's perjured testimony and a rigged jury, More's conviction was inevitable. His trail had been somewhat of an embarrassment for the Crown and his execution on 6 July 1535 again did little for Henry's reputation abroad.

Historical reputations

Thomas More: saint or sinner?

Source M

More was a complex, haunted, and not altogether admirable man. We may assume that he endured a lifelong inner torment because of the contradictions in his character and his experience. His fury at the Protestant heretics has a touch of hysteria about it . . . for he cried for them to be burned alive, and he rejoiced when some of them went to the fire. This fury was not a bizarre lapse in an otherwise noble character; it was almost the essence of the man. Yet he seduces biographers. We all end by liking him. That in itself is one of his mysteries.

Richard Marius, *Thomas More*, 1984

Take it further

Why do you think that biographers often tend to end up liking their subjects as Marius suggests?

Thomas More's reputation in history owes much to his courageous refusal to swear to the Oath of Succession and his subsequent martyrdom at the hands of Henry VIII. He is seen as a man of principle who was willing to die for his beliefs. The popular view of More has largely been shaped by Robert Bolt's play, *A Man for All Seasons* (1960), which hit the big screen in a film version starring Paul Scofield as More, and Robert Shaw as Henry VIII. The film won six academy awards but cannot be regarded as historically accurate.

Rather it relies heavily for its historical grounding on early biographers of More such as William Roper and Nicholas Harpsfield. Both of these accounts of More's life are flawed, in that they present a very sympathetic and personal overview of More's career designed to elevate him to Catholic martyrdom and sainthood. That is not to say that many historians have not also called on Roper's account to substantiate their ideas on More.

Much of what Roper writes can be validated, but importantly his description of More's trial lacks accuracy and is embellished with accounts of More endorsing papal supremacy and of the perjury of Sir Richard Rich. Clearly More's early biographers were eager to secure More's place in history.

More's subsequent reputation in Protestant England was largely defined by John Foxe's *Acts and Monuments* (1563), which recounts Protestant martyrs throughout English history. In this popular and influential work, More is portrayed as a harsh and cruel hunter of good, honest Protestant men. Foxe describes More as a 'wretched enemy against the truth of the Gospel and a bitter persecutor of good men'. This view of More was to an extent carried forward in recent works by Jasper Ridley and Peter Ackroyd.

Yet More's Protestant reputation is not as straightforward as all that. In 1684 Gilbert Burnet, Bishop of Salisbury, produced a new translation of More's *Utopia* which implied that the author was not a slavish follower of the papacy but rather a reformer who might be claimed by the Anglican Church as a forerunner of the Reformation.

Source N

From John Foxe's *Book of Martyrs* and other post Reformation sources we learn that he tied heretics to a tree in his Chelsea garden and whipped them; we read that he watched as *newe men* were put upon the rack in the Tower and tortured until they confessed; we learn that he was personally responsible for the burning of several of the *brethren* in Smithfield. Stories of a similar nature were current even in More's lifetime and he denied them forcefully. He admitted that he did imprison heretics in his house, but he utterly rejected claims of torture and whipping.

Peter Ackroyd, *The Life of Thomas More*, 1998

Source O

I cannot tell whether I should call him a foolish wise man or a wise foolish man, for undoubtedly he beside his learning had a great wit, but it was so mingled with taunting and mocking that it seemed to them that best knew him, that he thought nothing to be well spoken except he had ministered some mock in the communication.

Edward Hall, *The Union of the Noble and Illustre Families of Lancaster and York*, published in 1548.

Source P

During the dozen years when More was increasingly in power and favour, there were no death sentences for heresy pronounced in his diocese; during the few months when he was still in office, but certainly neither in power nor favour, there were three; during the three years of his retirement, disgrace and imprisonment there were fifteen or sixteen. The figures do not suggest that the London persecution had anything to do with More; they suggest that it depended upon Stokesley replacing Tunstall as bishop.

R.W. Chambers, *Thomas More*, 1935

SKILLS BUILDER

Do you accept the view that More was a cruel man with little compassion for others? Explain your answer using Sources N, O, P and your own knowledge. (40 marks)

Exam tips

This is a b) type question. Make sure you refer to the three sources, but also remember to include your own knowledge.

1 Use the material in the sources to build up a balanced argument. Sources N and O would appear to agree with the statement – find relevant quotations to reinforce this point.

2 Source O is written by Edward Hall after More's death and after the Royal Supremacy has become a reality. How does this affect the reliability of Source O?

3 In what way does Source P contradict the statement in the question? Does Source P explicitly praise More's character? What own knowledge can you think of which might be used in this answer?

4 In the context of the sixteenth century is it fair to condemn More as cruel because he did not care for heretics?

Why was there so little opposition to the Royal Supremacy and the break with Rome?

Ultimately it seems that most people showed loyalty to Henry even if they disagreed with his policies.

No change

In reality one has to ask how much the reforms actually changed the nature of everyday worship, and the answer here is very little. The central difference in the new Church was the absence of the Pope, yet as Robert Whiting has shown, the Pope was a remote and distant figurehead to most of the English populace. In most regions people appear to have acquiesced in the removal of Roman authority, and records from churchwardens' accounts demonstrate that people rapidly stopped paying the Peter's Pence.

Local affairs

Ordinary lay folk cared about their local affairs and their own everyday world. If that world was intruded upon in a negative way they were likely to resist such change, but the Henrician Reformation did little to change the spiritual or material world of the common man. Only in 1536 when rumours abounded in the north that parish churches were to be plundered alongside smaller monasteries did serious insurrection occur. In the end it was clear that people identified more readily with the Tudor regime and their King than they did with the Pope and there were few popular objections to the Royal Supremacy.

Loyalty to the King

It is not surprising that people showed both loyalty and respect to the Crown. The King was divinely ordained, and he preserved internal order as well as protecting his kingdom from the threat of foreign invasion. To resist the King was treasonable and sinful. The execution of high profile opponents of the regime, combined with the amendment of the treason law in 1534–35, served to frighten people into submission.

Oaths of loyalty

Important clerical and political figures were required to take oaths to the succession and the Supremacy, which in some ways highlights the insecurities of the government. At the same time, such oaths commanded loyalty from the populace and bound men's consciences to the Crown. More may not have approved and indeed doubted the legality and morality of such a strategy, but it served its purpose as no one could sit on the fence and adopt a middle ground – Henry required the public and outright support of his subjects and he got it.

Cromwell

Cromwell was a key figure in the whole process because he controlled the pulpits and the printing presses of London. Royal letters were sent out to bishops, nobles and JPs instructing them to imprison any clergy who showed signs of dissent against royal policies. Later, Cromwell's Injunctions attempted to place a Bible in English in every parish church, another propaganda exercise to highlight the national identity of the new English Church. Assize judges and JPs kept watch in the localities, and there were few instances of popular opposition in the south.

No mercy

Any opposition that did emerge tended to come from the more conservative north. Our prime example of this comes in 1536 with the Pilgrimage of Grace, but aside from that major insurrection there were 197 cases of treason reported from the north in the period 1532–40 compared with 224 cases in the more densely populated south. Cases reached their peak in 1537, perhaps reflective of the perceived radicalism and destruction of royal policy at that time, and then tailed off towards 1540.

Again people quickly recognised that opposition was dangerous and relatively futile. Henry showed no mercy to opponents of the regime and made an example of them to others who might be contemplating resistance. In the wake of the Pilgrimage of Grace in 1537, Henry ordered the Duke of Norfolk 'to cause dreadful execution upon a good number of the inhabitants, hanging them on trees, quartering them, and setting their heads and quarters in every town'. Henry would not compromise on the issue of the Supremacy. Indeed, there were even advantages in supporting the Supremacy as the acquisition of confiscated monastic property showed.

Source Q

I find his grace my very good lord indeed, and I believe he doth as singularly favour me as any subject within this realm . . . however may I tell you that I have no reason to doubt that if my head could win him a castle in France, it should not fail to go.

Sir Thomas More in conversation with William Roper 1515, from The Lyfe of Sir Thomas More, first printed 1626

SKILLS BUILDER

How far do Sources Q and R suggest that Henry's ruthlessness was the reason why there was little opposition to the Supremacy?

Source R

Anti papal progaganda gained momentum as the need to combat resistance grew . . . yet resistance to the government's programme continued despite executions and other public spectacles. Uprisings such as the Pilgrimage of Grace, in which thousands of armed men were led against towns and royal strongholds by disaffected members of the northern aristocracy, posed an especially grave threat and clearly identified the religious reforms as central to the opposition.

Seymour Baker House, *Literature, Drama and Politics in The Reign of Henry VIII* (ed. Diarmid MacCulloch), 1995

KNOWLEDGE FOCUS

- The break with Rome and the Royal Supremacy were carried out from above by Act of parliament.

- Henry VIII was the main architect of the process, although the actual theories and justification behind the supremacy had been put together by a team of radicals.

- Thomas Cranmer was elevated to Archbishop of Canterbury because he was willing to marry the King to Anne Boleyn. He becomes an important figure in pushing the Henrician Reformation in a more radical direction.

- The power of the Crown was significantly increased by 1534.

- The Crown also stood to gain financially from the break with Rome and the Royal Supremacy.

- Opposition to the Crown over the Supremacy was limited due to fear, loyalty and acquiescence.

- Bishop Fisher was a more obvious threat to the Crown than Thomas More but not necessarily a more serious one.

- The years 1534–40 were concerned with consolidating the Supremacy and increasing the wealth of the Crown at the expense of the Church.

SKILLS FOCUS

- Use own knowledge to evaluate the context of the source. The date of the source can act as a clue as to why the source was written and go some way to explaining its tone.

- Think carefully about the purpose of foreign ambassadors reporting back to their masters from Henry's Court. Consider also just how much such men were privy to high level political information.

- It is crucial that you have a good grasp of the religious and political loyalties of the key figures in Henry's reign.

- Being able to distinguish between conservatives and radicals will allow you to evaluate the source with greater confidence.

- Repeated practice of source based questions under timed conditions is the only way to improve and hone your technique.

7 The dissolution of the monasteries

Key questions

- What was the condition of monasticism in England in 1530?
- How and why were the monasteries dissolved?
- What were the effects of the dissolution of the monasteries?
- How serious a threat to the Crown was posed by the Pilgrimage of Grace?

Timeline

1535	*Valor* Ecclesiasticus. Royal visitation of the monasteries
1536	Act for the Dissolution of the Lesser Monasteries
	Ten Articles published
	Cromwell issued first set of Royal Injunctions
	October, Pilgrimage of Grace
1537	*Bishops' Book* published
1538	First official English Bible published
	Cromwell issued Second Royal Injunctions
1539	Act for the Dissolution of the Greater Monasteries
	Act of Six Articles

Questions

All of these statements come from the wisdom of St Benedict and his teachings are closely adhered to by his monastic followers, the **Benedictines**.

1 What can these observations tell us about the life and work of a Benedictine monk?

Definition

Benedictines

A religious order following the rule of St Benedict of Nursia. The order has a long tradition of scholarship and the promotion of learning.

The Rules of St Benedict

- There are times when good words are to be left unsaid out of esteem for silence
- We must know that God regards our purity of heart and tears of compunction, not our many words. Prayer should therefore be short and pure
- Earnestly competing in obedience to one another, no one is to pursue what he judges better for himself but instead what he judges better for someone else
- We descend by exaltation and we ascend by humility
- As we progress in this way of life and in faith, we shall run on the path of God's commandments, our hearts overflowing with the inexpressible delight of love.

What was the condition of monasticism in England in 1530?

In 1530 there were at least 825 religious houses in England and Wales. Of these, 502 were houses of monks, 136 were nunneries and 187 were friaries. Some houses were closed, meaning that the occupants spent all their times in the confines of their abbey or nunnery.

The monks included Benedictines, **Carthusians** and **Cistercians**. Such monasteries were usually found in the countryside. The open houses were urban-based and in these friaries the inhabitants could carry out good work away from the cloister, particularly in hospitals caring for the sick and needy. Monks and nuns devoted their life to prayer for the souls of their founders and their heirs. All of them took vows of poverty, chastity and obedience, which were upheld with varying degrees of success across the land.

Contact and communication with local communities varied from region to region, although it is likely that most lay folk knew of their local monastic institution and may well have had some material or indeed spiritual connection with it. Certainly there seems to have been little popular antipathy towards monastic houses as there was in Germany during the Reformation, and the reaction to dissolution in the north in 1536 reveals a degree of loyalty towards the religious houses in that particular part of England.

The collective wealth of the monasteries was vast. In 1535 Cromwell commissioned a survey of all ecclesiastical property and wealth in England, which was known as the **Valor Ecclesiasticus**. It revealed that the total income of the religious houses was over £160,000 a year, and about one-third of landed property was in monastic hands. Much of their wealth came from rents but there was also a spiritual source of revenue in the form of **tithes** and the profits of pilgrimage. To put things into context, monastic income was more than three times the income from royal estates. Therefore, it is no surprise that a recently nationalised English Church should look to exploit this area of clerical revenue.

However, this task was not as easy as it seemed. One must not forget that the monasteries themselves were established features of the English countryside. Admittedly most peasants did not have regular contact with monks or nuns but most knew of their activities and existence. After all there were nearly 10,000 men and women who had taken their vows of poverty, chastity and obedience in a total population of only 3½ million. They were a visible and noticeable minority within the spiritual life of England.

How and why were the monasteries dissolved?

Henry VIII and Cromwell had a number of reasons why the monasteries should be dissolved. Apart from financial gain, the monasteries were also perceived as one of the last bastions of popery. Many of England's religious houses owed obedience to Rome first and the Crown second. Many were exempt from visitations by English bishops and looked for spiritual and temporal guidance to Rome.

Allegiance to Rome

It is unsurprising that subsequent Protestant historians have viewed the dissolution of the monasteries as the natural and next logical step in the

English Reformation. To them monasticism was both outdated and unnecessary in its existence and beliefs. Monks and nuns devoted much of their time to prayer for the souls of the dead, a practice deemed unnecessary by Protestants. The laity were encouraged to give money to monks and nuns so that they might pray on their behalf or on behalf of their dead relatives. In the eyes of the lay folk this would lessen time in purgatory and speed their accession into heaven. The new revitalised English Church needed to sweep away such deadwood in its relentless drive towards Protestantism.

Such ideas were problematic, however, because religious houses did not really owe a special obedience to Rome, but to continental mother houses (leading monasteries in Europe). The Crown itself was the founder and patron of many abbeys and priories, while most monks had shown their loyalty to the Crown over Rome by agreeing to take the Oath of Supremacy. Moreover, Henry himself hardly subscribed to the doctrines subsequently put forward by Protestant writers. Henry even re-founded two monasteries in order that frequent prayers were said for him and his family, thus revealing Henry's inherent faith in the monastic ideal.

The idea then that a monastic revival in favour of the Pope was an impending threat seems unlikely, and it is more the case that Protestant historians have placed an unhelpful emphasis upon the religious reasons for dissolution in order to neatly fit the episode into the process of the English Reformation.

Abuses and decay

In some ways linked to this idea of religious renewal comes the issue of moral and spiritual laxity within the monasteries. In other words, the reason for dissolution was that the monks and nuns were simply not fulfilling their vows of chastity, poverty and obedience but rather living in a corrupt and ostentatious manner.

The issue of reform is a complex one. There is no doubt that in some monasteries moral standards and actual numbers had begun to dip, but at the same time it was true that most monks and nuns continued to live up to Christian ideals as they had done for centuries. Records survive of diocesan visitations in the 1520s, before the break with Rome, that reflect the variations in standards of behaviour across the country. Reports of monks living the life of country gentlemen or others having strings of mistresses and illegitimate children did exist but so did accounts of well-disciplined religious houses where silence was observed in cloister and good works carried out within the community.

The point here is that little had changed over the past 200 years in monastic life, but once the Crown had made up its mind to carry out the process of dissolution, the issue of corruption was used as an excuse or justification for the despoiling of England's religious houses. The *Valor Ecclesiasticus* provided the ammunition that Cromwell required as it revealed that nearly one quarter of each monastery's income was paid directly to the head of the house.

At the same time as the *Valor* was being compiled, royal commissioners reported sordid tales of depravity and immorality within the monasteries. The findings of these visitations were read out in parliament and convinced many notables of the need for dissolution, especially in the smaller houses. There is little doubt that Cromwell's visitors knew what they were to find before they entered the monasteries and that many of these tales were sensationalised to justify dissolution on the grounds of reform.

Source A

I went to Godstow where I found all things well and in good order, both in the monastery and in the convent, except that one sister, 13 or 14 years ago, when in another house, had broken her chastity. For her correction and punishment, the Bishop of Lincoln sent her to Godstow, where she has now lived in virtue ever since.

From there I went on to Eynsham where I found a raw sort of religious persons. All kinds of sin had been committed by them, for which offences they have been punished by their Ordinary (church official) in his visitation. However, as far as I can tell, the abbot is chaste of his living and right well supervises the repairs of his house. He is negligent in the overseeing of the brethren but claims that this is because of his daily illness, which infirmity did appear, by his face to be true.

From a letter written by John Tregonwell to Thomas Cromwell, September 1535

Source B

Basedale – Superstition – there they had the Virgin's milk. Founder Sir Ralph Everes. Rents £18

Meaux – Founder the King. Rents £98. Superstition – here singulum of S Bernard is sometimes lent for pregnant women

Nunburnholme – Founder Lord Dakers. Rents £7. Here they have part of the Holy Cross

Haltemprice – Founder the Duke of Richmond. Rents £104. Here is a pilgrimage to Thomas Wake for fever and in veneration they have the arm of St George and part of the Holy Cross and the girdle of St Marie healthful for childbirth.

Reports on the value and foundation of monasteries in Yorkshire, delivered to Cromwell, 1535

SKILLS BUILDER

1 Assess the state of the monasteries based on these two accounts.

2 What was the purpose of these accounts?

Despite not all commissioners reporting unfavourably, the *Valor* did not present a balanced picture of events. Reports of sodomy were misleading in that the majority of cases were described as solitary vice, presumably masturbation, rather than the homosexual orgies that the House of Commons were lead to believe were taking place. The monastic cause was not helped by the fact that intellectual opinion was also largely negative as humanist thought at the time tended to follow the line put forward by Erasmus that the monastic way of life had little to recommend it.

Wealth

Source C

The main motive for the dissolution was financial. A memorandum of 1534 in the State Papers shows that the nationalisation of all Church property was being considered as a way to provide for the defence of the realm and an army to put down the Geraldine rebellion in Ireland. Dissolution of the smaller monastic houses was no new idea. Thomas Cromwell had already helped Cardinal Wolsey to dissolve twenty-nine selected monasteries between 1524 and 1528, and just before his fall Wolsey was granted a papal bull which permitted him to dissolve all houses with less than twelve monks or nuns. There was also the example of Sweden, where Gustavus Vasa secured the conversion of a substantial proportion of Swedish Church property.

M.D. Palmer, *Henry VII*, 1971

Although one cannot ignore cases of immorality or indeed spiritual arguments that view the dissolution in the context of the Reformation, it would be hard to argue against the idea that at the heart of the dissolution lay the issue of monetary gain. Henry might not have been entirely sure of the doctrinal direction that his Reformation was taking but he was eager to fill the Crown's coffers and bolster England's defences against the threat of foreign invasion. Henry and Cromwell had already benefited from the financial gains of the break with Rome, through measures such as the Act for First Fruits and Tenths (see page 105). The prospect of transferring the enormous wealth of the monasteries to the Crown was just too good for Henry to miss out on as it would double his income and at the same time free him from any dependence on parliamentary grants.

Was the dissolution of the monasteries pre-planned?

There are two key questions regarding the dissolution of the monasteries that have provoked much debate among historians. Both of these are interrelated and an understanding of one clearly enlightens our appreciation of the other.

1 What were the King's motives for dissolution and did they change?

2 To what extent did Cromwell and Henry plan the total dissolution of the monasteries in England from the outset?

- One school of thought argues that Cromwell had a masterplan for dissolution in place from the 1530s and that he always intended to dissolve all the religious houses in England. This school would see the vice gerent's motives as both financial and evangelical. Cromwell had promised to make Henry wealthy at the expense of the Church and the monasteries were a relatively easy target in Cromwell's eyes. Moreover the liquidation of monastic houses was in line with Cromwell's own evangelical views that saw monasticism as corrupt, anachronistic and failing.

- A second school argues that only once the full extent of monastic wealth had been revealed in the *Valor* Ecclesiasticus of 1535 did Cromwell and Henry decide upon dissolution. The motives here are again clearly financial but the nature of governmental decision making is more reactive than planned. The initial reason for the *Valor* was to assess how much each clerical institution would have to pay to meet the 10 per cent of ecclesiastical income granted to Henry by the Reformation Parliament, not to reveal the landed assets of the religious houses. Indeed, Cromwell was not able to pull together all the evidence that he had received from his visitors regarding the state of the lesser monasteries in time to present his damning verdict to parliament in 1536. If the whole process was pre-planned one might have expected everything to be in place. That it was not suggests a highly opportunistic and reactive process.

- A third line of argument develops this point further, and states that although Henry and Cromwell planned the dissolution of those houses with an income of under £200 per annum, they had no intention of dissolving the larger houses. Only when it became clear throughout 1538 and 1539 that the larger houses could be swept away with relative ease did total dissolution enter the minds of both King and vice gerent. Henry was mightily impressed with the amount accrued from the dissolution of lesser houses and once the Pilgrimage of Grace was swept up, he encouraged Cromwell to finish off the job and swell the royal coffers still further.

Source D

Cromwell's government acted likewise against the monasteries, not so much because they were so utterly corrupt as because they wished to prepare the ground for the dissolution. The visitation of 1535 was never intended to mend but always to end; it was an hypocritical weapon. Equally hypocritical was the pretence in the bill introduced into the parliament of February 1536 that only the lesser houses were corrupt; the bigger ones served religion, maintained discipline, and knew no vice. It appeared from the bill that the line between virtue and depravity followed with curious fidelity the line which divided £200 a year from incomes larger than this: realising well that he could not carry out the whole dissolution at one stroke, Cromwell first attacked only the smaller monasteries.

G.R. Elton, *England under the Tudors*, 1955

Source E

Cromwell's object was partly to encourage voluntary surrenders and partly to collect incriminating data that could be used to manipulate Parliament into authorizing mandatory dissolution. He was successful: an Act was secured in March 1536 which dissolved all religious houses worth under £200 per annum – some 372 institutions in England and twenty seven in Wales fell into this category. Initially there was no plan to reduce all the greater houses; some isolated surrenders were induced at the end of 1537. In the latter part of 1538, however, Cromwell and some thirty agents entered upon a systematic campaign of total dissolution.

John Guy, *Tudor England*, 1988

SKILLS BUILDER

1 Look at Sources D and E. How far do Elton and Guy agree over the process of dissolution?

The dissolution of the smaller monasteries (1536)

Source F

. . . so that without such small houses be utterly suppressed and the religious persons therein committed to great and honourable monasteries of religion in this realm, where they may be compelled to live religiously, for reformation of their lives, there can else be no reformation in this behalf:

. . . considering also that divers and great solemn monasteries of this realm wherein religion is right well kept and observed, be destitute of such full numbers of religious persons as they ought and may keep . . .

The first Act for the dissolution of the lesser monasteries, 1536

Question

What does the first Act for dissolution suggest about the condition of the greater houses?

Definitions

Secular clergy

Churchmen who worked outside of monasteries, e.g. priests.

Court of Augmentations

Bureaucratic office set up by Cromwell to deal with the transfer of Church lands to the Crown. Administered by Sir Richard Rich.

In the spring of 1536, parliament passed an Act for the dissolution of all religious houses with a net income of less than £200 a year. These smaller monasteries were seen as *dens of vice* and places of *manifest sin, vicious, carnal and abominable living.* The emphasis here was very much placed upon reform, and to that end the inmates of these smaller houses might be transferred to the greater houses of their orders for correction. Indeed the greater houses were praised in the Act as places where 'religion is well kept and observed', thus suggesting to many subsequent historians that the process of dissolution was not meant to be wholesale. Just over 300 houses fell within the category specified by the Act, but not all were immediately dissolved. The King granted exemptions to those 67 houses that were still perceived to be carrying out their spiritual duties effectively, although such houses had to pay a substantial sum for their royal reprieve. Other houses such as the Gilbertines escaped closure because their Master, Robert Holgate, was a friend of Cromwell's!

The displaced monks and nuns either moved to the larger houses as the Act had intended or they were released from their vows of poverty and obedience by the suppression commissioners, allowing them to take up employment as **secular clergy** men or seek a lay occupation. Note that they were not released from their vow of chastity and were expected to uphold it even after their release from the cloister. Heads of the houses were granted a pension whereas ordinary monks and nuns were given a grant of twenty to thirty shillings.

Soon after the Act hit the statute book royal commissioners were appointed to each county to oversee the closures. Moveable goods such as gold and silver plate were sent up to London before the locals could help themselves, while land was rented out or sold for the enrichment of the Crown. The overall supervision of monastic property was the task of the **Court of Augmentations** (see page 122), set up by Cromwell in April 1536.

Source G

I send you supposed religious relics – God's coat, Our Lady's smock, part of God's supper – and all this from the priory at Maiden Bradley. Here you will find a holy father who has six children. His sons are all tall men who wait on him, and he thanks God that he never meddled with married women, but only with maidens (the fairest that could be got). The Pope, considering this holy father's weakness, has given him licence to keep a whore.

From a report by Richard Layton, one of Thomas Cromwell's commissioners, on a visit he made to the priory of Maiden Bradley in 1535

Source H

Manifest sin, vicious, carnal and abominable living is being daily used and committed among the small abbeys, priories and other religious houses. The governors of such religious houses spoil, destroy, consume and utterly waste their properties to the high displeasure of almighty God. And although many continual visitations have been made for an honest and charitable reformation, yet their vicious living shamelessly increases, so that unless such small houses are utterly suppressed there can be no reform of these matters.

From the Act of 1536, dissolving monasteries with an income of less than £200 a year

Source I

The said Aske says that he opposed the suppression of the monasteries because the abbeys in the North have great alms to poor men and laudably served God. And by the suppression the service of God is greatly diminished. The church of God is damaged and pulled down, the ornaments and relics of the church are irreverently treated, and tombs of honourable and noble men pulled down and sold. There is no hospitality now kept in those parts, nor places for travellers to stay, and the profits of the abbeys now go out of the area to the King.

From the deposition of Robert Aske, leader of the Pilgrimage of Grace, in 1536. His statements were taken before his execution in 1537

SKILLS BUILDER

Study Sources G, H and I. How far do these sources suggest that the smaller monasteries were dissolved in 1536 because of their corruption?

Explain your answer using the evidence of Sources G, H and I. (20 marks)

Exam tips

1 Read the question before you read the sources – that way you know what to be looking for as you read through the documents.
2 Always take five minutes to plan your answer – this way you will have an idea of which of the sources agree and which of them disagree with the statement.
3 Unlike the (b) question that we looked at in the foreign policy chapter, the (a) question does not require own knowledge. You are only using the material in front of you. That said, you may occasionally need to use your knowledge to evaluate the author and date of a particular source.
4 Write a one-sentence introduction in which you match up the sources to the statement. This immediately gives your answer a focus.
5 First deal with the sources that agree with the statement. Use short quotations from both sources to demonstrate how they agree but always use your own words to explain the quotations.
6 Examine the context as well as the content of the sources that agree. Remember to look at the provenance of the sources; that is the situation and purpose of the author.
7 Then move on to the source(s) that disagree with the statement. Go through the same process as you did in the paragraph(s) above.
8 Bring your answer together with a short and snappy conclusion.

The surrender of the greater houses (1538–40)

Source J

Even at that time, one said in the parliament house that the lesser monasteries were as thorns, but the great abbots were putrified old oaks, and they must needs follow.

Edward Hall, *The Union of the Two Noble and Illustre Families of Lancaster and York*, 1548

SKILLS BUILDER

1 How does Hall's account compare to what was said about the greater houses in the first Act of dissolution (see page 122)?
2 How reliable is Hall as a historical source? Do not forget to think about when and why he was writing.

Towards the end of 1537, the government decided to make total dissolution its aim. Some houses were implicated in the Pilgrimage of Grace (see pages 128–9), and the heads of such houses were declared traitors by Acts of attainder. They were to be executed and their associated monasteries turned over to the Crown in the same way that the smaller houses of 1536 had been.

In the wake of the failure of the Pilgrimage of Grace, other abbots gave up hope of resistance and surrendered freely. Still, hundreds of houses survived as 1538 approached and it was Cromwell's aim to suppress them all. Some monasteries were aware of the threat and began to lease out land themselves and sell-off gold plate in an attempt to cater for their future financial security. Cromwell wrote to the heads of surviving houses to reassure them that a general suppression was not planned, and that all recent suppressions had been voluntary. Underlying these words was the threat of force should the sale of monastic property and possessions continue.

In 1538 Cromwell sent out more royal commissioners to visit the remaining religious houses and invite the heads of houses to hand over their property freely to the King. Again undertones of terror accompanied the visitiations, but Cromwell made it clear to his trusted servants that no time was to be wasted on those who showed any signs of resistance. This sweep of the remaining monasteries was to clean up those abbots and abbesses who were willing to resign their positions and give up their lands to the Crown. Most abbots saw the advantages of signing the prepared form of surrender, not least the generous pension on offer if they entered the secular world. Those who proved more obdurate were forced to resign by royal orders and quickly replaced with men whom Cromwell knew would be more amenable to his overtures. The end came quickly for most religious houses with many of the monks and nuns taken by complete surprise when Cromwell's commissioners appeared.

In 1539 an Act of parliament was passed ratifying the legality of voluntary surrenders. Effectively the Commons was presented with a *fait accompli* as most of the larger religious houses were now dissolved. In this light any opposition was unlikely in political circles. Still there was some resistance on the ground. The Priory of Lenton and the Abbey of Woburn were not surrendered but passed into royal hands by forfeiture after the condemnation of their heads of houses. In the autumn of 1539 the abbeys of Colchester, Reading and Glastonbury went the same way. The Abbot of Glastonbury was accused of robbing his abbey of its treasures and he was subsequently executed in the grounds of his abbey.

In November 1539 two of Cromwell's most trusted servants, namely **Thomas Legh** and **Richard Layton**, were given instructions to suppress or alter all remaining religious houses. These two men had been involved in the compilation of the *Valor* Ecclesiasticus in 1535 and knew their business well. Alteration might mean the conversion of an existing monastery into a secular one or the conversion of a monastery into a cathedral. The will to resist was fading in light of the punishments handed out to the likes of the Abbot of Glastonbury. The continued justification of reform based on the profits of dissolution convinced many that dissolution was a force for progress. Waltham Abbey in Essex was England's last surviving house and it surrendered in March 1540. In less than five years over 800 monasteries had been dissolved, in a process of startling administrative efficiency.

Biographies

Thomas Legh and Richard Layton

Two of the leading royal commissioners who carried out visitations of monastic property in 1535. Cromwell issued them with a list of questions to ask the abbots and monks and it is likely that they were given instructions by their master to detail any moral shortcomings which they came across in their visits. They returned with a detailed *comperta*, highlighting sinful excesses of monks and nuns. Legh and Layton were regarded as being particularly fierce and unscrupulous in their work.

Source K

I was minded at divers times to mention certain abuses and excesses committed by Dr Thomas Legh. At Bruton he behaved very insolently. At Bradstock and elsewhere he made no less ruffling with the heads than he did at Bruton. Wherever he comes he handles the fathers very roughly.

A monastic visitor complains about a colleague, 1536

What were the effects of the dissolution of the monasteries?

Source L

Cromwell administered the dissolution of the monasteries over which the Tudor monarchy had control with remarkable speed and efficiency between 1532 and 1540, thus destroying monastic life throughout England and Wales and in about half of Ireland. The Pilgrimage had been in large measure a cry of anguish at this process: the Pilgrimage's defeat only speeded it up, and may have decided King and minister on making it total. The King no doubt regarded the dissolutions chiefly as a welcome source of cash, but they had the incidental effect of eliminating much traditional religion.

Diarmaid MacCulloch, *Reformation*, 2003

Cultural impact

The dissolution of the monasteries is often viewed, particularly by Catholic historians, as an act of cultural vandalism. Architectural treasures were lost forever, and only the existing ruins of abbeys such as Fountains in Yorkshire give some idea of their splendour and grandeur. Monastic libraries, religious art, stained-glass windows and furnishings were all sold off to fill the Crown's coffers. Nearby mansion houses such as that at Woburn often sprung up, built as they were from the materials taken from the despoiled monastery.

Perhaps one should also note that some monastic buildings such as that at Tewkesbury were bought by local communities and continued to serve the lay population as parish churches. Other abbey churches survived to become cathedrals in new dioceses such as Bristol and Westminster.

Certainly it would be true to say that part of England's architectural heritage was lost forever with the dissolution, but one must be wary of such subjective viewpoints; it could be argued that many of the monastic buildings which were dissolved were in a state of disrepair and held little in the way of architectural beauty.

Impact on the local population

The dissolution also put an end to monastic charity, and this is often cited as a reason for increasing levels of poverty in sixteenth-century England. Monasteries gave alms to the poor, acted as places of refuge and shelter for travellers and pilgrims, and cared for the sick and needy.

Yet according to the *Valor* Ecclesiasticus the average proportion of a house's income dispensed to the poor was just over 2 per cent. A rising population, pressure on land and rapid inflation were more likely causes of poverty than the loss of monastic charity. Indeed there is evidence that laymen continued to endow charities and fund hospitals.

Still, on a humanitarian note, one must also consider the fate of the monks and nuns who were unceremoniously turned out of their abodes:

- It has been estimated that all but 1,500 of the 8,000 monks and friars who were dispossessed managed to find alternative paid employment, often among the ranks of the secular clergy.

- The Crown also awarded most monks pensions proportionate to their standing although it is undeniable that some ex-monks must have come across hard times.

- It is more difficult to estimate just how many monastic servants joined the ranks of the unemployed after 1540, but one would assume that those who worked monastic lands could easily transfer their skills and allegiance to the new proprietor.

Related to this very point is the idea that dissolution created a new, ruthless breed of landlord who unlike the monks cared little for the local population. It has been argued that these landlords enclosed land for sheep rearing and increased rents dramatically. Yet again there is little evidence to reinforce this claim as monks, too, had engaged in the process of enclosure, and its impact on the rural population has been exaggerated anyway. Furthermore, rents were always likely to rise in a period that witnessed rapid inflation, and the monks would have acted no differently had they continued to oversee the land.

One final related social change involves the rise in the number of landowners as a consequence of dissolution. Some historians argue that as a result of the redistribution of landed property at this time, many wealthy merchants or second sons of leading gentry were able to buy up land. Such an increase in the landowning class can be linked to England's relatively peaceful long-term development as a **constitutional monarchy**.

Other historians contend this point arguing that very few new estates were built up solely out of ex-religious land and that there was no revolutionary change in the size of the landowning class. Indeed those who bought monastic property were often already landed people who sought to extend their estates.

Impact on the Crown

With regards to the impact on the Crown the effects of dissolution were almost entirely financial. The dissolution did little to consolidate the break with Rome as this had already been achieved by the time that the process began. In terms of reform, the actual achievements predictably came up short of Henry's promises:

- six new dioceses were established upon the remains of monastic buildings and cathedral churches were re-established

- new cathedral schools were established

- grammar schools were re-endowed

- Trinity College at Cambridge was founded and five Regius Professorships were set up at both Oxford and Cambridge universities.

Definition

Constitutional monarchy

A constitutional monarchy, or a limited monarchy, is a form of constitutional government, wherein either an elected or an hereditary monarch is the head of state, unlike in an absolute monarchy, wherein the king or the queen is the sole source of political power. Most constitutional monarchies are parliamentary, the monarch is the head of state, but the elected prime minister is head of government.

However, this was some way off the original agenda of educational and spiritual reform that had been lined up in the years 1538–39, and which had so attracted many learned men to the idea of dissolution.

The Crown's primary aim in dissolving the monasteries was monetary gain. Although some of the land and wealth went to key administrators, such as Cromwell, most of it went to the Crown and contrary to popular belief little land was sold off immediately. Cromwell himself recognised the long-term benefits of leasing-out land in order to bring in a regular source of income.

It was only after Cromwell's death in 1540 that lands were sold off to finance Henry's fruitless wars with France and Scotland. The years 1543–47 saw the sale of two-thirds of all ex-monastic land and it has often been argued that Henry squandered the opportunity to secure the financial independence of the Crown for the foreseeable future. This argument can be extended to the point of saying that the Crown would not have come under threat from the Commons in the seventeenth century if the profits from dissolution had been safeguarded.

Yet, once more, such views owe much to hindsight and one must remember that Henry viewed parliament as a submissive and pliant institution rather than a threat to his power. It is all too easy to criticise Henry in selling-off valuable assets, but at the time the need to bolster coastal defences and engage the enemy was seen as being of paramount importance.

How serious a threat to the Crown was posed by the Pilgrimage of Grace?

Timeline

1536
- 2 Oct, Start of Lincolnshire rising
- 13 Oct, Rising in South Yorkshire; Aske becomes leader and adopts the title of the *Pilgrimage of Grace* for the rebellion
- 16 Oct, Rebels seize York and there are risings in Northumberland, Durham, North Yorkshire and Cumberland
- 21 Oct, Pontefract Castle is surrendered to Aske by Lord Darcy
- 27 Oct, Pilgrim Army (30,000) confronts the royal army (8,000) at Doncaster The royal commander, Norfolk, meets the Pilgrim leaders on Doncaster Bridge Two pilgrims take a petition to Henry VIII
- 21 Nov, Pilgrims return from meeting with Henry and report to the Pilgrims' Council
- 4 Dec, Pilgrims issue detailed articles
- 6 Dec, King grants a general pardon for the Pilgrims and agrees that parliament will meet to address their grievances

1537
- 10 Feb, Rising in Cumberland fails to take Carlisle
- June, Darcy executed
- July, Aske executed in York

Source M

The false flatterer [Cromwell] says he will make the King the richest prince in Christendom but I think he will make him the poorest prince for by his pillaging he has lost the hearts of his baronage and poor commons.

From an anonymous petition, October 1536

The Pilgrimage of Grace refers to those events that took place in the north of England from October to December 1536; it does not include the Lincolnshire rising of early October 1536, nor the Cumberland Rising of early 1537.

The Pilgrimage of Grace, so often seen as a direct reaction to the proposed dissolution of the smaller monastic houses, was not solely religious in origin. It is no surprise that the most serious rebellion in Henry's reign took place in the north, an area that was largely conservative in its political and religious outlook. The dissolution was one of many reasons why the pilgrims revolted in 1536, with other socio-economic concerns of equal importance. That said, the sight of monks and nuns being turned out of their monasteries and monastic treasures being taken away fuelled local rumours that parish churches were also going to be targeted and their gold plate plundered.

The Lincolnshire rising, October 1536

Trouble first broke out in Lincolnshire in October 1536 at Louth, and it was clear from the list of grievances drawn up by the rebels that religious concerns were closely intertwined with political and economic ones. Certainly there had been successively bad harvests in the years 1535 and 1536, which always served to exacerbate social tensions.

The Lincolnshire rising was **popular in character**, and in part prompted by a fiery sermon from a local priest highlighting the dangers faced by the local community from the Crown. Parish property and rights were perceived to be under threat and demands were made for Cromwell's dismissal. Common gossip and rumour fuelled ideas that the government planned to ban the consumption of white bread, pigs and capons without a licence!

Clearly there was resentment of central government interference in local affairs heightened by the impending dissolution of the monasteries. At the same time the list of grievances drawn up by the rebels also cites high taxes and hatred of the **Statute of Uses**, demonstrating that no one cause motivated the rebellion, although it would be fair to say that its timing and impetus owe much to the dissolution of the monasteries and religious change in general.

Definitions

Popular in character

Ordinary people were behind the Lincolnshire rising rather than the nobility or gentry.

Statute of Uses (1536)

Law that changed the way in which property could be left in wills. Highlighted the King's feudal right to claim property on the death of a tenant. Resented by the gentry.

SKILLS BUILDER

Make a list of socio-economic factors that might have contributed to the Pilgrimage of Grace. For each one, decide how important you think it was in causing the Pilgrimage of Grace in 1536.

Source N

Recent taxation was much disliked and the new subsidy, unusually, had come in peacetime . . . Coming after two years of dearth, following bad weather and poor harvests, resentment at the new subsidy may have been particularly important in prompting support for the rising in the Yorkshire dales and in Marshland: the evidence of the tax assessments in the early Tudor period has shown that these were the poorest areas of the West Riding. Yet taxation can hardly be accounted a major element in the rebellion.

A. Fletcher, *Tudor Rebellions*, 1983

Biography

Robert Aske (d.1537)

Leader of the Pilgrimage of Grace in 1536, Aske visited London to discuss the rebel grievances with Henry. In the end Aske was content to accept the King's assurances that rebel grievances would be addressed. By May 1537 after the failed Bigod Rising in Carlisle (which Aske had actually helped to disperse) Aske was in prison in London. He was tried and found guilty of treason and executed.

Source P

Alack! Alack!
For the church sake
Poor commons wake,
And no marvel!

For clear it is
The decay of this
How the poor shall miss
No tongue can tell.

A Pilgrim ballad from 1536

The Lincolnshire rebellion ended as quickly as it had started, with the rebels dispersing on hearing of the imminent arrival of a royal army under the command of the Duke of Suffolk. Henry was in no mood to negotiate with the rebels and the Lincolnshire rising was over by 18 October.

The Pilgrimage of Grace, October–December 1536

However, the rebellion had already spread north and from October to December 1536 a more serious revolt took place in Yorkshire. It is this rising that is normally referred to as the Pilgrimage of Grace and the religious imagery associated with the rebellion in the northern counties should not be lost on us.

Under the leadership of the lawyer **Robert Aske**, some 30,000 men marched on York. It was Aske who declared the rebellion to be a pilgrimage and it was he who chose the banner of the Five Wounds of Christ as its standard. The rebels swore a religious oath that contradicted the Supremacy and sang ballads in favour of the monasteries.

Source O

And that ye shall not enter into our said Pilgrimage for no particular profit to yourself, nor to do any displeasure to any private person, but by counsel of the commonwealth, nor slay nor murder for no envy, but in your hearts put away fear and dread, and take afore you the Cross of Christ, and in your hearts His faith, The Restitution of the Church, the suppression of heretics and their opinions, by all the holy contents of this book.

The Pilgrims' oath taken in October 1536

Source Q

They called this, their seditious and traitorous voyage, a holy and blessed pilgrimage; they also had certain banners in the field whereon was painted Christ hanging on the cross on one side, and a chalice with a painted cake in it on the other side, with various other banners of similar hypocrisy and feigned sanctity . . . only to delude and deceive the simple and ignorant folk.

Edward Hall, *The Union of the Two Noble and Illustre Families of Lancaster and Yorke*, 1548

SKILLS BUILDER

1 What do Sources O and P tell us about the motivating factors behind the Pilgrimage of Grace in 1536?

2 In what way does Source Q disagree?

3 Why might Hall be in disagreement with the first two sources? Think about when and why he was writing.

Manifestos were drawn up at York in October 1536 that called for:

- the removal of evil councillors from Henry's government
- the restoration of the Old Faith
- the protection of the monasteries.

In many ways the demands of the rebels at York were the same as those weeks earlier in Lincolnshire. Perhaps Aske's followers were more politically aware as they called for a free parliament in the north to discuss religious and political issues.

Certainly there was far more support for the Yorkshire rising with almost 30,000 men marching behind Aske. Moreover, there was more support for the actual Pilgrimage among the local nobility including **Lord Darcy**. With Norfolk's army numbering only 8,000 it was clear that the advantage lay with the rebels.

Why was the Pilgrimage of Grace a serious threat?

- Firstly it was the largest numerical uprising of the Tudor period.
- Furthermore the pilgrims were far from being an unorganised rabble. Many had previous experience of fighting the Scots. Had the rebels wished to engage the royal forces in battle it is likely that they would have won.

Why did the rebellion fail?

The rebellion failed because its leaders wanted to negotiate and subsequently put their faith in Henry's word. Aske had intended for a show of force to bring Henry to the negotiating table and make the King listen to his demands. In this aim Aske and the other rebel leaders were successful.

Yet Henry was no fool, and knowing that he was outnumbered he instructed Norfolk to play for time and agree to any of the demands made by the rebels. Acting from a position of strength in York, Aske was certain that he could take Norfolk's concessions in good faith.

Biography

Thomas, Lord Darcy (1467–1537)

A northern nobleman with large landholdings who fell foul of the Cromwell regime in 1532 for questioning the Supremacy. By 1534 he was in treasonable correspondence with Chapuys, the Imperial Ambassador. Darcy played an important role in the Pilgrimage of Grace in surrendering Pontefract Castle to the rebels.

Source R

Led by Robert Aske, their Grand Captain, who was both visionary and politic, the Pilgrimage united the grievances of a whole society against alien innovations from the South, devised by heretic evil counsellors around the King. The pilgrims' grievances were inevitably economic, social and political, as well as narrowly religious, but only the defence of Holy Church, *now lame and fast in bounds,* could have united so many different groups in this mass demonstration and overlaid it, through long waiting days, with an almost mystical aura.

Susan Brigden, *New Worlds, Lost Worlds*, 2000

Question

What reason does Brigden give for emphasising religious issues above all else in 1536?

Agreement was reached with the Duke of Norfolk on 6 December 1536 at Doncaster and the rebels agreed to disperse peacefully, convinced that their demands had been met. The government allowed a free and general pardon for the participants of the Pilgrimage, highlighting the weakness of Henry's position. The government stopped the collection of the 1534 subsidy and were quick to quell rumours that parish property was under threat. Importantly, the rebels also secured the promise of a parliament to be held by free election in York to consider their complaints. Until this parliament met, existing royal policies were to be suspended including the suppression of lesser monasteries.

Take it further

1 In your own words explain the point being made here by Morrison.
2 Find out about other rebellions in the Tudor period. How were they dealt with?
3 What were the concerns of the elites regarding rebellion in the sixteenth century?

Source S

When every man will rule, who shall obey? An order must be had and a way found where those who are the best rulers and Councillors should rule. It is most necessary for a commonwealth that those of the worser sort should be content that those who are wiser should govern them. They must realize that God has given to those who rule special virtues and good fortune and raised them to a high position in society.

A Remedy for Sedition, written by Richard Morrison and printed by the King's printer in 1536

In many ways this would appear to be a total victory for the rebels. Central aspects of royal policy had been successfully challenged and there were optimistic signs that religious reform might be turned back. Yet the sheer size and scale of the revolt meant that Henry could not back down indefinitely and he never meant the concessions to be anything other than temporary.

The outbreak of unrelated revolts in Westmorland and Cumberland in early 1537 gave Henry the excuse he had been looking for to carry out reprisals and renege upon earlier promises. Norfolk declared martial law in Carlisle and seventy-four rebels were hanged on the spot. Ringleaders from the Pilgrimage were arrested and taken to London for interrogation. Among those leaders executed in the early months of 1537 were Robert Aske, Sir Thomas Percy, Lord Darcy and Lord Hussey.

Historical debate on the Pilgrimage of Grace

The three main areas of historical debate on the Pilgrimage of Grace are as follows:

1 What were the causes of the Pilgrimage of Grace?
2 How important were the local nobility and gentry in leading and spreading the revolt?
3 How far can the Pilgrimage of Grace be considered a success for the rebels?

1 What were the causes of the Pilgrimage of Grace?

The first modern historical work on the Pilgrimage was compiled by two sisters, Madeleine and Ruth Dodds. Their two-volume history of the Pilgrimage of Grace and the Exeter Conspiracy was published in 1915, and offers a full narrative of events from a relatively sympathetic standpoint. The Dodds argue strongly that religious change caused the Pilgrimage of Grace, and that the dissolution of the lesser monasteries brought to the boil simmering discontent in the north.

C.S.L. Davies, Christopher Haigh and J.J. Scarisbrick, all writing in the second half of the twentieth century, largely reinforced the Dodds' line that the Pilgrimage was essentially a religious uprising.

Other historians such as R.R. Reid and to a lesser extent A.G. Dickens have put forward social and economic motivations as being of paramount importance in the Pilgrimage.

2 How important were the local nobility and gentry in leading and spreading the revolt?

Moving on to the leadership of the revolt, both M.E. James and R.B. Smith have emphasised the importance of the local nobility and gentry in the spread of revolts. They argue that the central areas of the West Riding revolted as a consequence of the fact that the Percies and Lord Darcy rebelled. On the other hand Hallamshire remained loyal to the Crown, perhaps as a consequence of the example set there by the Earl of Shrewsbury. The same was true in Lancashire where the loyalist Earl of Derby was in control of events. Therefore this model presents a gentry rebellion that was assisted by the lower orders.

G.R. Elton has suggested that Pilgrimage was in fact a courtly plot orchestrated by the conservative faction and transplanted to the north where support was assured. Out of favour with the King and suffering under the administration of Cromwell, figures such as Darcy, Hussey, Constable and Stapleton planned armed rebellion. Just how much influence this courtly faction had over events is debatable.

John Guy argues convincingly that noble and gentry supporters of Princess Mary joined forces with Catholic lawyers from the inns of court in revolt against Cromwell's regime. Yet, whereas for Guy an element of noble conspiracy existed in the lead up to the events of 1536, those concerned, such as Darcy and Hussey, were in fact taken by surprise when the revolt started in Lincolnshire. Therefore, although evidence of noble pre-planning and intended gentry leadership exists, it was the ordinary people who lit the fuse. Only mass popular participation and commitment to the cause can explain the speed at which the revolt spread.

3 How far can the Pilgrimage of Grace be considered a success for the rebels?

Michael Bush's important work, entitled *The Pilgrimage of Grace* (1996), challenged the traditional assumption that the Pilgrimage was a failure for

Read through the following three accounts of the Pilgrimage of Grace carefully. In answering the question below think carefully about the perspective and purpose of the author in each source.

Study Sources T, U and V. How far do these sources suggest that the Pilgrimage of Grace was a serious threat to Henry VIII? (20 marks)

the rebels. Although it cannot be denied that few, if any, of the rebels' demands were ultimately carried out by the government, Bush maintains that the very size of the pilgrim armies combined with the fact that Norfolk did agree to meet their grievances means that we ought to view the rebellion as an enormous achievement on the part of the rebels.

Bush's research reveals that the rebel army at Doncaster was over 30,000 strong, while in Cumberland there was a force of 15,000. Elsewhere two armies defended Sawley Abbey and a force of some 15,000 besieged Skipton Castle. Bush writes that 'the secret of success for the pilgrims had lain in their mobilisation of a large force'.

Bush takes this point further when he asserts that clearly the rebels were well organised and showed signs of advanced planning in order to mobilise such a large force so quickly, and that the gentry were clearly important in instructing the commons to raise arms. Hierarchy and order were key concepts in sixteenth-century society, and Bush argues that either the commons were responding to orders from their social superiors or they actively persuaded the lesser nobility to lead the protest.

It is crucial to understand that the aim of the Pilgrimage was to raise a large enough force to be able to dictate terms to the Crown. The rebellion was not intended to challenge the Crown on the battlefield, but rather to pressurise the government into changing its policy and personnel.

Source T

We have received your letters and perceive that the late insurrections have been reported in a very exaggerated manner. They were attempted in consequence of false reports spread among the people by certain seditious persons who are in danger of the laws . . . When the people learned from those who were sent to represent them that they had been deceived, they lamented their offences and desired our pardon.

We do not intend to use any rigour towards the Yorkshire men who lament their traitorous attempt but will force them to follow the example of the Lincolnshire men in the apprehension of the ringleaders. Both shires are at our mercy. Thank God my subjects were so ready to fight against the rebels that we were rather forced to keep them back than spur them on. People are now in great quiet without a blow being struck.

From a letter by Henry VIII to his ambassador in France, dated 5 November 1536

Source U

All the nobility of the duchy of York have risen. They number 40,000 combatants and among them 10,000 horse. They are in good order and have a crucifix for their principal banner. Norfolk and his colleagues do not wish for battle, showing tacitly that the petitions of the rebels are lawful . . . The men of the North are able to defend themselves and their number will probably grow every day. However they have little money and the Pope ought to help them.

From a letter by Eustace Chapuys, the Imperial Ambassador to Charles V, dated November 1536

Source V

We have received your sundry letters via Sir John Russell. We wonder you all write in such desperate tones as though the world would be turned upside down if we do not agree to the petitions of the rebels especially for a free pardon and a parliament. Even if the rebels be as bitterly disposed and in as good a readiness as you write, we marvel that neither you, our cousin of Shrewsbury, have been so careful in viewing and fortifying the fords of the River Don as we desired in our former letters, nor that you, our cousin of Norfolk and our Admiral, have devised upon the same since your arrival, knowing that we had the doing therof so much to heart . . . We marvel still more that if you have certain knowledge that the rebels have levied such forces that you have not raised other forces to withstand or at least to stay them. If by your negligence the rebels should march forward and cross the Don, we should think ourselves ill served.

From a letter by Henry VIII to the Dukes of Norfolk and Shrewsbury

KNOWLEDGE FOCUS

- The monasteries were generally in a good condition, especially in the north.

- Cromwell's visitors exaggerated reports of abuse and corruption in order to provide the ammunition for dissolution of the smaller houses in 1536.

- Financial gain rather than reform was the main reason for dissolution in 1536.

- It is unlikely that there was ever a blueprint in place for total dissolution.

- Cromwell and Henry were so impressed with the financial results of the 1536 dissolutions that they went on to suppress the greater houses.

- The Pilgrimage of Grace was a serious rising in the north of England in 1536 against Henry's regime.

- The main cause of the Pilgrimage was religion although there were other socio-economic grievances.

- Henry's standing army was not strong enough to cope with the uprising and the Crown had to make serious concessions to the rebels.

- In the end Henry did not stick to his word and used a follow-up rising in 1537 to deal with the ringleaders of the Pilgrimage.

SKILLS FOCUS

- Read the question before you read the sources.

- Recognise the difference between questions that want own knowledge and those that do not.

- Evaluate the provenance of source material and think about why the source takes the line that it does.

8 How Protestant was England by 1540?

Key questions

- Was there a move towards Protestantism in the years 1534–39?
- Why were Anne Boleyn and Thomas Cromwell executed?
- How far did 1539 mark a setback for the evangelical cause?
- What was the religious future of England likely to be after Henry's death?

Timeline

1534	Thomas Cromwell is appointed the King's vice gerent in spirituals, giving him day-to-day control of the Church Treasons Act passed through parliament making it unlawful to oppose the King in deeds or words
1535	Fisher and More executed
1536	January, Catherine of Aragon dies May, Anne Boleyn executed Ten Articles published Cromwell issued First Royal Injunctions Pilgrimage of Grace
1537	October, Edward born; death of Jane Seymour The *Bishops' Book* (*Institution of a Christian Man*) published
1538	First official English translation of the Bible published (known as the Matthew Bible) Cromwell issued Second Royal Injunctions
1539	Act for the Dissolution of the Greater Monasteries Act of Six Articles
1540	January, Henry marries Anne of Cleves July, Thomas Cromwell executed July, Henry marries Catherine Howard
1542	Catherine Howard executed
1543	The *King's Book* published Henry marries Catherine Parr Act for the Advancement of the True Religion Attempts to remove Cranmer fail
1544	The English Litany
1545	Act vesting chantry property in the Crown
1546	Gardiner excluded from the Council Norfolk arrested for treason
1547	January, Henry VIII dies

Exam tip

Remember, the specification goes up to 1540 and you will only be required to answer on the period 1509–40 in the exam. However, information about the period 1540–47 is included here to provide you with a full understanding of what happened during Henry's reign.

Look back at the title page of the Great Bible on p. iv. It shows Cranmer at the King's right hand ready to receive the Bible and lead his fellow bishops. On the King's left hand is Cromwell, also receiving the Bible with a group of noble councillors behind him, ready to follow his lead. Below them are the laity receiving the word of God from above.

How far had the break with Rome changed the nature of the Church in England?

The Henrician Reformation was essentially an act of state motivated by political, personal and financial motives rather than religion. Nevertheless, the road towards the break with Rome and the Royal Supremacy had allowed evangelicals such as Cranmer and Cromwell to rise to prominence, as they were the ones who were willing to endorse and promote Henry's new policies.

The fabric and structure of the English Church had been fundamentally altered in the years 1532–34, but the nature of worship at a popular level remained predominantly Catholic. Henry himself remains a Catholic at heart, and doctrinally conservative. Yet at the same time he was willing to flirt with evangelical ideas if they underpinned his **caesaropapism**.

This leads to quite a confused situation, as it becomes difficult to determine precisely where Henry stands on religious matters. Such ambiguity also paves the way for a fierce factional struggle at court between those who want to use the Supremacy as a vehicle to advance evangelical doctrine and those who want to maintain Catholic rituals and worship. The result of this factional struggle determines the direction of religious policy in the reign of Edward VI.

Was there a move towards Protestantism in the years 1534–39?

Clearly one must first acknowledge the obvious point that the English Church in 1534 was fundamentally different to that in other western European kingdoms. The break with Rome and the Royal Supremacy had severed English connections with the papacy and removed Roman influence from English shores.

A national English Church had essentially been created, but whereas much in the way of papal authority had been destroyed and financial payments redirected to the Crown, nothing new had been enacted in the way of reform. The break with Rome clearly encouraged more radical reformers abroad, and made some believe that Henry was going to take England towards Lutheranism.

Yet in reality Henry had no such intentions. The Henrician Reformation was orchestrated from above, and as such it was created by the King in parliament.

Unlike Germany or indeed Switzerland at this time, there was little popular support for reformist ideas. As historians such as A.G. Dickens have

Questions

1 What is the significance of Henry's position in this illustration?

2 The laity proclaim VIVAT REX at the bottom of the illustration. What does this mean?

3 Why did Henry allow for a Bible in English?

Definition

Caesaropapism

The authority of a monarch over the clergy and the Church in his dominions.

Definitions

Evangelical

A term used to describe a reformer who believed in the authority of Scripture or God's Word. Key figures such as Cranmer and Cromwell were evangelicals, and indeed they may have been Protestants. Yet Protestants were burned in Henry's reign, so any radical views had to be kept secret. Furthermore the term Protestant did not reach England until 1553. Evangelical therefore becomes a useful term to describe religious reformers in England during the 1520s and 1530s.

Grassroots level

How ordinary people on the ground reacted to religious change.

Temporal

Secular or non clerical.

pointed out there were pockets of active **evangelicals** in the southeast, but they were few in number.

Essentially, the changes enacted by the Reformation Parliament did little to alter popular worship on the ground, which remained Catholic, nor did they encourage a popular outpouring of anti-clericalism. Therefore, with a monarch who was essentially conservative in his beliefs, combined with a populace that was essentially satisfied with its spiritual lot, it was unlikely that further positive evangelical change would follow the legislation of 1532–34.

The factional struggle: evangelicals v. conservatives

Yet leaving aside the situation at **grassroots level**, one must not forget the significance of royal patronage at court. Ultimately, the key men in power throughout the 1530s were evangelicals.

- On the spiritual side, Thomas Cranmer had risen from relative obscurity to the highest ecclesiastical position in England.
- On the **temporal** side Thomas Cromwell had shown his worth in masterminding the Royal Supremacy.
- Alongside these men were others of a reformist nature who had similarly come to light as a result of the break with Rome. Men such as Nicholas Shaxton, Hugh Latimer, **Robert Barnes** and William Jerome had all been given special licences to preach by Cromwell.
- One must not forget the role of Anne Boleyn here in patronising key evangelical figures, and the historian Eric Ives has shown just how important she was in protecting and promoting reformers at court.

Biography

Robert Barnes (1495–1540)

An Augustinian friar in his early years, Barnes soon provoked controversy with his non-conformist religious views. A Christmas Eve sermon in Cambridge was reported to the authorities on the grounds that his ideas were heretical. He was forced to recant before a tribunal in 1526, before fleeing to Luther's home town of Wittenberg in 1528. After the Royal Supremacy passed through the statute book, Barnes was able to return to England. Henry and Cromwell saw Barnes as a potentially useful link with the Lutherans, and he was employed on diplomatic missions to Germany. Although Barnes was a Lutheran and advocated the authority of scripture, he was not sacramentarian in that he continued to recognise the real presence of Christ in the Eucharist. He even turned in the radical John Lambert who was subsequently burned at the stake. In 1540 Barnes himself was condemned to the flames. Caught up in the conservative resurgence at court. Barnes was called to account for a verbal attack on Gardiner, and under examination his views were deemed heretical. He was burned at the stake on 30 July 1540.

Yet opposite these men were conservatives such as Stephen Gardiner and Thomas Howard, who did not see the Supremacy and doctrinal reform as the same thing.

Evangelicals were always aware that they could push the boundaries of reform only so far, and in that sense they were playing a dangerous game. Henry never wanted to feel as if he was being deceived, nor did he want to feel subject to the forces of faction. He was master in his own kingdom and both reformers and conservatives alike would pay with their lives if they overstepped the mark.

The Ten Articles 1536

Henry's outlook towards Lutheranism had already been shown in 1521 when he penned the *Assertio Septem Sacramentorum* with the help of Thomas More. This tract constituted a stinging attack on Luther's doctrine and works. In 1536, Henry's attitude towards Luther's doctrine had not changed but the nature of the English Church had.

In 1536 it was important that this new national Church produced a statement of faith and defined its doctrinal position. It was now not

What the Articles stated	*Significance*
• The Articles included only three sacraments, namely baptism, penance and the Eucharist. • No mention was made of the remaining four, which were confirmation, ordination, marriage and extreme unction.	To deny the existence of four of the seven sacraments was overtly Protestant. Continental reformers including Luther upheld only three sacraments in the belief that they were the only ones to be found in the New Testament. For evangelicals and reformers, doctrine and belief had to be grounded in Scripture, as that was the only test of true validity. In losing four sacraments Cromwell had taken up a Lutheran stance, and on other matters, too, England seemed to be veering towards Lutheranism.
• The central Catholic position on the Eucharist, transubstantiation, was not mentioned by name although the **real presence** of Christ was reaffirmed. • The Lutheran concept of justification by faith alone was outlined, but in a sufficiently moderate fashion as to make it acceptable to conservative clergy also.	Therefore, the official religion of England in 1536 was left ambiguous and unclear. It did not condemn the Mass nor the Catholic call for good works in attaining salvation, but at the same time a deliberate emphasis was placed on the authority of scripture and on the merits of a simple Christian existence.

Definition

Real presence

Orthodox Catholic doctrine asserting the actual presence of Christ in the Eucharistic sacrament. More radical Protestant doctrine, especially that emanating from Switzerland, stated that Christ is only present symbolically.

inconceivable that Henry might look to the Lutheran princes as allies, given how badly the break with Rome had gone down with the rest of Catholic Europe.

In 1536 the Ten Articles were produced as a formulary of the new Church's faith, and there is little doubt that Cromwell was behind their completion. They were as significant for what they left out as they were for what they included.

A month later, Cromwell's injunctions took a moderate stance against images in churches and against pilgrimages, while the number of holy days and saints' days were limited in number.

At best the Ten Articles were a tentative move in an evangelical direction, but they are also an indication of the need for compromise and unity. In his position as vice gerent Cromwell was able to push the evangelical cause forward, but more often than not he had to couch doctrinal definitions in conciliatory and ambiguous terms in order to satisfy all parties.

The Bishops' Book 1537

In 1537 a second attempt was made at a formulary of faith (an outline of what the English Church believed in). This time it was entitled the *Institution of a Christian Man* or the *Bishops' Book* (it was issued under the bishops' authority not the Kings). It looked to deal with the contentious issues of justification, purgatory and the status of the four missing sacraments.

- The *Bishops' Book* found the four lost sacraments again and admitted their validity, but they were deemed to be lesser sacraments because they were not to be found in scripture.

- It also emphasised the idea that justification through the merits of Christ did not dispense with the need for good works. On the issue of transubstantiation the *Bishops' Book* was adamant that 'under the form and figure of bread and wine, which we there presently do see and perceive by outward senses, is verily, substantially and really contained the very selfsame body and blood of our Saviour Jesu Christ'.

- Two such orthodox statements of faith were counterbalanced with the claim that the primary function of the priesthood was to preach the Word, not the offering of Christ in the Mass.

- The administration of the sacraments took second place to preaching and the Mass was mentioned only twice in the whole book.

- No distinction was made between the office of bishop and that of priest, another deviation from orthodox Catholicism.

- Finally, the Ten Commandments were renumbered to highlight the mistaken practice of worshipping graven images.

A draft of the *Bishops' Book* was sent to Henry for approval, but he was preoccupied with the imminent birth of his son **Edward VI**, and had no time to read it. Later revisions appeared in the *King's Book* of 1543, suggesting that Henry was not entirely happy with what he read.

Cromwell and the English Bible

Both the Ten Articles and the *Bishops' Book* can be regarded as partial successes for the evangelical faction at court, and Cromwell in particular. Although neither offered a definitive statement of Protestant belief, neither towed the orthodox line. Indeed Cromwell was not foolish enough to believe that radical doctrinal change could be enacted overnight. He recognised that he could use his position of trust with Henry to further the evangelical position, but change had to happen quietly and slowly.

- Cromwell manipulated episcopal appointments to ensure that reformers were preferred to conservatives

- he organised preaching campaigns against Catholic practices such as the worshipping of images

- most importantly he promoted the circulation and use of a vernacular Bible.

There had been unofficial versions of the Bible in English before, but the first official translation appeared in 1537, when royal permission was given for the Matthew Bible to be sold. Henry saw the Bible in English as another propaganda tool, designed to further consolidate his imperial kingship, whereas his vice gerent viewed it as the most significant step towards placing the Word of God into the hands of the common man. Cromwell used £400 of his own money to begin the print run, which saw 3,000 Bibles printed in November 1539. One year previously, in 1538, Cromwell's second set of injunctions had required that all churches acquire a copy. By 1540 the suggested retail price of the English Bible had been cut, making it affordable to individuals.

Cromwell had thrown his political weight and a not inconsiderable amount of his personal wealth behind the English Bible, and for many its publication marks the high point of evangelical success in Henrician England. It did not matter that few rural parishes had purchased the Bible by 1540, nor that many conservatives disagreed with the translation. Cromwell had put the idea of a scripturally literate society into the public domain, and at the same time instigated positive and lasting evangelical reform.

Why were Anne Boleyn and Thomas Cromwell executed?

If the evangelical cause appeared to be making some headway in the years 1534–40, it was struck two mortal blows with the fall of both Anne Boleyn and then Thomas Cromwell.

Biography

Edward VI (1537–53)

King of England from 1547. Son of Henry VIII and his third wife, Jane Seymour. Edward was tutored in the Protestant faith and it was no surprise that his Regency Council was made up of those of that faith. Edward was only nine years old on his father's death in 1547 and his reign saw a struggle for power between the nobles.

Source A

Catholic hatred of Anne damned her for the break with Rome and for the entrance of heresy into England. It was right on both counts.

Eric Ives, *The Life and Death of Anne Boleyn*, 2004

The fall of Anne Boleyn 1536

Anne Boleyn had played a skilful and shrewd political game in the years leading up to her marriage. She had shown herself to be an ambitious and bright young lady, who was determined not to go the way of her sister Mary and become merely another notch on Henry's bedstead. Instead she withstood Henry's lustful advances until it was clear that the policy of separating the English Church from Rome was secure, and that Henry's first marriage to Catherine was going to be invalidated.

In many ways Anne was a pivotal figure in the Henrician Reformation not only because she was the object of Henry's affections but also because of her unquestionable adherence to 'reformed' religious ideas. Some might argue that there was a selfish aspect to Anne's evangelical sympathies in that a secure and permanent break with Rome strengthened her own position on the throne. Others dismiss this idea, as ultimately Henry had decided upon the new course and he could undo Cromwell's work in parliament if he so desired.

Anne's adherence to scriptural works and the idea of justification by faith were deeply personal, and possibly forged from her time in France. Before the authorised version of the English Bible appeared, Anne possessed many scriptural commentaries and translations in French. There is little doubt that she used her proximity to Henry to champion the evangelical cause, and the promotion of key figures in the reformed movement such as Cranmer stemmed from her influence over the King. Indeed, all ten bishops appointed during her reign as Queen between 1533–36 were of a reformed persuasion.

Anne's patronage of key evangelical figures such as Latimer, Shaxton and Skip would have long-term significance for the reformed cause in England. Her protégés usually emerged from Cambridge University, which held a reputation for turning out more radical thinkers than Oxford at this time. It was through Anne that Henry was introduced to the writings of William Tyndale and the anti-clerical lawyer Simon Fish. Henry's subsequent endorsement of an English Bible may well have been in part down to the influence of his second wife.

Yet Anne's future as Queen of England very much depended upon her ability to provide Henry with a son and heir. When Anne was delivered of a girl, Elizabeth, in September 1533, Henry did not hide his disappointment. In January 1536 another pregnancy ended in the miscarriage of a deformed foetus. As Warnicke has endeavoured to prove, Henry viewed this mishap as an evil omen, which boded ill for the future of his marriage. Anne's position was still safe as long as Catherine of Aragon was alive. Henry could not repudiate his second marriage without implicitly recognising the validity of his first marriage to Catherine of Aragon.

Catherine's death in the same month that Anne miscarried (January 1536) cleared the way for an attack on Boleyn. Anne had made many enemies during her rise to the top, especially among those who harboured secret sympathies for Catherine. Moreover, her reformed views did not sit easily with conservatives such as Gardiner and Norfolk. That said, **Thomas Howard**, as Anne's uncle, was in a difficult situation, as her fall would lessen his family's influence at court, but at the same time he hoped to undermine Cromwell's position through Anne's demise.

Source B

If the reports of the Queen be true, they are only to her dishonour not yours. I am clean amazed for I had never better opinion of any woman, but I think your Highness would not have gone so far if she had not been guilty. I was most bound to her of all creatures living and therefore beg that I may, with your Grace's favour, wish and pray that she may declare herself innocent. Yet, if she be found guilty, I consider him not a faithful subject who would not wish her punished without mercy. As I loved her not a little for the love which I judged her to bear towards God and His Gospel can ever favour her but must hate her above all others.

From a letter written by Thomas Cranmer to Henry VIII, 3 May 1536

In May 1536 Anne was accused of committing multiple adultery – one of her alleged lovers was her own brother. Anne was found guilty and executed along with Henry Norris (groom of the stool), Lord Rochford (Anne's brother), Sir Francis Weston, William Brereton and Mark Smeaton.

SKILLS BUILDER

1 Pick out the phrases in this letter which suggest that Cranmer was fond of Anne.

2 What was Cranmer's purpose in writing this letter to Henry?

3 What was it that made Anne and Cranmer so close?

Biography

Thomas Howard, 3rd Duke of Norfolk, Earl of Surrey (1473–1554)

Norfolk was an important member of the conservative faction at Henry's court. Anne Boleyn's uncle, as lord steward, had to preside over her trial for adultery in 1536. He introduced Henry to another of his nieces in 1540, Catherine Howard, as part of the plot to discredit Cromwell. Norfolk lost influence after Catherine's execution for adultery in 1542. He was disgraced in 1546 when his son, Henry, was arrested and executed for treason. Norfolk himself would have faced death had Henry not died first in January 1547, but he had to endure imprisonment under Edward VI and was only released on Mary's accession.

The conservative faction at court led by Gardiner and Norfolk had planned their assault carefully, and had set up Jane Seymour as the vehicle for their resurgence. Henry was smitten with Jane, and married her only eleven days after Anne's execution.

Cromwell survives

In some ways the conservatives hoped that they might be able to bring about Cromwell's fall through Anne's disgrace. That they failed was largely due to Cromwell's political skill and inherent ruthlessness. Cromwell foresaw Anne's demise and was able not only to distance himself from the whole affair but to control the events leading to her trial and execution. Cromwell brilliantly aligned himself with the anti-Boleyn faction in the early months of 1536 and then turned on them after her execution, accusing her enemies of seeking to restore Princess Mary to the succession. Ennobled as Lord Cromwell of Wimbledon and able to fill the Privy Chamber with his supporters, the future of the reformed cause in England was secure for the time being.

The fall of Thomas Cromwell, 1540

Question

What evidence here suggests that Cromwell was resigned to his fate in 1540?

Take it further

The French ambassador stated that Cromwell, on being arrested, asked whether *this was the reward for his services*. Research and plan out a brief biography of Cromwell. Find out about his background, rise to prominence and his key achievements between 1532–40. This should give you some idea of the enormity of Henry's decision to execute him in 1540.

Source C

Nothing else is spoken of here, except the arrest of Cromwell. In a week, at the latest, the said prisoner is expected to be executed and treated as he deserves. As soon as the Captain of the Guard declared his charge to make him a prisoner, Cromwell, in a rage, cast his bonnet on the ground, saying to the Duke of Norfolk and others of the Privy Council assembled there, that this was the reward for his services and that he appealed to their consciences as to whether he was a traitor. Since he was treated thus, he renounced all pardon, as he had never thought to have offended and only asked the King not to make him languish long.

From a letter written by the French Ambassador to the Duke of Montmorency, June 1540

Cromwell's reforming credentials

The two formularies of faith issued during Cromwell's vice gerency, alongside the two sets of injunctions that accompanied them, highlight his influence over spiritual affairs at this time. One might have expected Cranmer as Archbishop of Canterbury to be more active, but he was more of a scholar than a politician, and for the time being he stood aloof from the cut and thrust of court faction.

Cromwell drove the Reformation forward, as shown by the process by which the monasteries were dissolved. He was a ruthless achiever who carried out the King's wishes efficiently and effectively. Of course, in the process he created enemies; men who were waiting to strike should the vice gerent slip up and lose Henry's trust.

The foreign situation

Such an opportunity arose in the spring of 1540. By this time the international situation had changed:

- France and the Empire were now persecuting Protestants fiercely and both had agreed not to make an alliance with England;

- Henry felt isolated in Europe and vulnerable to attack, especially after the papacy repeatedly denounced Henry and called on Catholic Europe to join a crusade against England.

Henry's position

In the midst of such hostility Henry was eager to make an outward show of doctrinal conservatism, which in some ways explains the execution of **John Lambert** in 1538 and the Act of Six Articles in 1539. At the same time Cromwell was still intent on forging diplomatic relations with German Protestant princes, and to this end he had made overtures to the Duke of Cleves regarding a possible marriage between his daughter, Anne, and the King of England. Since the death of Jane Seymour in October 1537, after bearing the son that Henry so desperately wanted, namely Edward, Cromwell had seen a Protestant alliance as a means of ending English isolation in Europe.

Anne of Cleves

However, the proposed union of Henry and **Anne of Cleves** was a disaster for Cromwell and sealed his fate. To start with, Henry detested the sight of Anne, calling her the *Flanders mare* on account of her ordinary appearance. Henry's only sight of Anne before her arrival in January 1540 had been a portrait painted by **Holbein** on Cromwell's orders, which had rather flattered her appearance. Cromwell was out of favour the moment Henry resigned himself to *putting his head in the yoke* and marrying Anne of Cleves.

> ## Biography
>
> ### John Lambert (d.1538)
>
> Educated at Cambridge, a university with a reputation for turning out religious radicals in the sixteenth century. Lambert was an ordained priest, but was soon in trouble for reading forbidden books and for preaching. In 1532 Lambert was tried for refusing to recognise the real presence of Christ in the Eucharist. His sacramentarian outlook was close to that of Zwingli and far too extreme to have a place in Henry's England.

> ## Biography
>
> ### Hans Holbein the Younger (1497–1543)
>
> German painter and woodcut artist Court painter to Henry VIII from 1536, he was sent by Cromwell to produce a portrait of Anne of Cleves in 1539, which perhaps, in the end, flattered the sitter. Holbein's works remain the most recognisable portraits of the period, and a lasting testament to Henry's reign.

> ## Biography
>
> ### Anne of Cleves (1515–1557)
>
> Henry VIII's fourth wife, and daughter of John, Duke of Cleves. Anne was a victim of European diplomacy as England looked to Germany for an alliance. But by the time Anne arrived the fragile Franco-Spanish peace was already on the rocks, making the match unnecessary. Added to this was Henry's disgust with Anne's appearance. The marriage went ahead but remained unconsummated, and was declared null and void in July 1540. Anne accepted her fate with good grace and was given lands to the value of £3,000 and allowed to live out the rest of her life in England.

The foreign situation changes

Equally damaging for the vice gerent was the breakdown in Franco-Spanish relations, which rendered his Protestant union useless. An Anglo-French union was not out of the question, but Cromwell and the Protestant alliance stood in the way.

Enemies at Court

Finally, Cromwell's enemies led by Gardiner and Howard, but also including Bishop Tunstall, Lord Sandes and Sir Anthony Browne, had been gathering damaging information on him, which they now presented to the King. Among this material were allegations that:

- Cromwell had protected Protestants in Calais;
- he was unwilling to enforce the terms of the Act of Six Articles.

At around this time, the Duke of Norfolk introduced his pretty young niece to court, and Henry was immediately captivated by her charms. Cromwell faced a major dilemma, because if he were to accede to the King's demands and annul the Cleves marriage this would put Norfolk in a very strong position, but if he did not, then he would face the growing wrath of the King. Cromwell's final act was to provide the necessary evidence for the unconsummated Cleves marriage to be annulled.

Cromwell's execution

Cromwell's arrest in June 1540 was followed by his execution in July. The Norfolk–Gardiner faction had won. Henry had been persuaded to rid himself of the man who had secured three annulments of unwanted royal marriages, make the break with Rome and the Supremacy a reality, and double the King's annual income through the dissolution of the monasteries. For the evangelical cause, Cromwell's fall signalled the end of their immediate hopes and aspirations. Cranmer survived to carry on the fight, but for the meantime a conservative backlash was on the cards.

Source D

Thomas Cromwell, contrary to the trust and confidence that your Majesty had in him, caused many of your majesty's faithful subjects to be greatly influenced by heresies and other errors, contrary to the right laws and pleasure of Almighty God. And in the last day of March 1539 when certain new preachers, such as Robert Barnes, were committed to the Tower of London for preaching and teaching against your Highness's proclamations, Thomas Cromwell confirmed the preacher to be good. And moreover, the said Thomas Cromwell, being a man of very base and low degree, has held the nobles of your realm in great disdain, derision and detestation.

From the Parliament Roll of 1540, listing the charges made against Thomas Cromwell in the Act of Attainder, used to avoid the necessity of a trial

Source E

Cromwell accepted his defeat on religious policy and might have survived if his enemies at Court had not made good use of the collapse of the Cleves marriage. Henry's distaste for Anne was heightened by his growing desire for Catherine Howard, the pretty, young and flirtatious niece of the Duke of Norfolk – Cromwell's bitterest rival on the Privy Council. The Protestant alliance, Cromwell's religious preferences and the Cleves marriage created a suspicion in Henry's mind that his chief minister was pursuing his own interests rather than the king's. This was a suspicion that Cromwell's enemies were well placed to exploit, and on this occasion Henry's anger and desire seems to have clouded his judgement.

From A. Anderson and A. Imperato, *Tudor England 1485–1603*, 2001

SKILLS BUILDER

Do you agree with the view expressed in Source E that the fall of Thomas Cromwell in 1540 was primarily the work of his enemies at Court? Explain your answer using Sources D and E and your own knowledge. (40 marks)

Before you start to answer this question, remember:

- this is a (b) question and therefore requires you to use your own knowledge as well as the source material;
- leave yourself approximately 55 minutes to answer this question;
- use 5–10 minutes to plan your answer;
- fit the sources to your argument;
- unlike the last model answer we put together for a (b) question, this one only deals with two sources rather than three. Do not worry – there is still plenty of material to work with.

How far did 1539 mark a setback for the evangelical cause?

It is difficult to talk of a conservative reaction if we subscribe to the idea that Henry himself had never deviated from orthodox Catholic doctrine. That said, there is little doubt that the factional struggle swung the way of Norfolk and Gardiner in these years, and with Cromwell out of the way the path was clear for an English Church based on unambiguously conservative grounds.

The Act of Six Articles, 1539

Even in Cromwell's lifetime, that doctrinal shift had begun with the Act of Six Articles in 1539. This religious settlement was more to Henry's liking, as it endorsed the central tenets of traditional theology. More to the point Henry was very much behind their formulation, unlike the earlier formularies of 1536 and 1537.

The Act of Six Articles:

- confirmed transubstantiation, private Masses and auricular confession
- banned clerical marriage and the taking of **communion in both kinds** by the laity
- upheld vows of chastity, which deeply worried Archbishop Cranmer as his marriage was an open secret.

The Six Articles were a harsh penal Act of parliament, labelled *the whip with six strings* by its reformist opponents. Laws against heresy were to be strictly enforced, and failure to comply with the Six Articles could lead to imprisonment, confiscation of property and ultimately death if one denied transubstantiation.

Definition

Communion in both kinds

The Catholic Church stated that only the clergy received the bread and the wine at the Lord's Supper. The laity or ordinary people received only the bread as they were spiritually inferior. Protestant reformers disagreed and called for Communion in both kinds, that is the laity should receive both the bread and the wine as everyone was equal in the eyes of God.

Aside from restoring papal authority in England, the Act of Six Articles had reaffirmed Catholic worship. Latimer and Shaxton could see which way the wind was blowing, and resigned their sees the day after the passage of the Act through parliament.

Source F

I have delivered to the King a book concerning the misbehaviour and disobedience of many people in Calais. The parish priest of Our Lady church is a prisoner in the Fleet. I think that more will be sent for shortly, for an Act is passed which will set every true Christian in good quietness concerning the sacrament of the altar, and for calling in heretical books.

From a letter written to Lord Lisle, the Governor of Calais, 21 June 1539 (remember that Calais was an English territory at this time)

Source G

The impious Act of parliament which you saw has been enacted at the instance especially of the Bishops of London and Winchester, of whom one is dead and the other excluded from Court and public business. Bishops Latimer and Shaxton refused to sign and resigned their bishoprics but beyond this nothing is done for all execution is suspended. The King seems already displeased at the passing of the decree and little favourable to those who have astutely done this in order to remove Cromwell and the Archbishop of Canterbury and the Chancellor, excellent men and most friendly to the purer doctrine of the Gospel. I doubt not that the statute will shortly be abolished.

From a letter written to Philip Melanchthon, a leading German Lutheran, in October 1539

SKILLS BUILDER

Study Sources F and G. How far do these sources suggest that the Act of Six Articles made a significant impact?   (20 marks)

Exam tips

1 Clearly the sources are very different in their assessment of the impact of the Act of Six Articles. You need to think about why two authors can arrive at different interpretations of the same Act.
2 Look closely at the perspective of the authors and their situation in 1539.
3 Ask yourself how well informed the authors were on the matter, and whether religious/political loyalties might cloud their judgement.
4 Be sure to refer specifically to both sources in your answer and quote directly from the sources in order to reinforce your points of analysis.
5 Use your own knowledge to assess the accuracy and reliability of each statement.

Source H

Lambert was sent for by the archbishop, brought into open court and forced to defend his cause. For the archbishop had not yet favoured that doctrine of the sacrament which he was later to profess so ardently. The King commanded Cranmer to refute Lambert's assertion that the body of Christ was not present in the sacrament of the altar. Cranmer began his disputation very modestly saying *Doctor Lambert, let this matter be handled between us indifferently. If I convince you, by the Scriptures, that your argument is wrong, you will willingly refute the same. If you prove your argument true, by manifest testimonies of the Scriptures, I promise that I will embrace the same.*

When they had contended, Lambert answered so well that the King seemed to be greatly moved, and all the audience amazed. Then the Bishop of Winchester, who was appointed to speak in sixth place in the dispute, fearing that the argument would be lost, interrupted the archbishop.

Here it is much to be marvelled at that through the pestiforous counsel of this one Bishop of Winchester, Satan did here perform the condemnation of Lambert in the presence of the gospellers themselves, Taylor, Barnes, Cromwell and Cranmer.

From the *Book of Martyrs* by John Foxe

Source I

There is brought before me one Henry Totehill for provocative communication which he spoke concerning the bishop of Rome and Thomas Beckett, which matter I have examined, as your Lordship shall further see by a bill of the depositions which I enclose. Furthermore I have taken upon me your office in punishing of such trangressors as break the King's injunctions, for already I have committed two priests into the castle at Canterbury for permitting the Bishop of Rome's name in their books.

From a letter written by Cranmer to Thomas Cromwell, January 1539

SKILLS BUILDER

Read Sources H and I. How far do these sources suggest that Thomas Cranmer was an evangelical reformer?   (20 marks)

How important was Cranmer in the Henrician Reformation?

Cranmer was a divinity scholar at Cambridge who joined the White Horse group in the 1520s to discuss the new Lutheran ideas coming from continental Europe. He was probably a Protestant at heart but was wise enough to moderate his views and emerged as an evangelical reformer.

Cranmer was part of an ideological think tank on the Great Matter. In 1530 he helped draw up the *Collectanea satis copiosa*, which justified Henry's imperial kingship and served as the basis for the Royal Supremacy in 1534.

On the death of Archbishop Warham in 1532, he was given the top post in the English Church – Archbishop of Canterbury. Henry's intentions in asking the Pope to appoint Cranmer were twofold. First, Henry hoped to pressurise Rome into action on the divorce crisis by letting the Pope see that he was prepared to support the cause of a known evangelical. Second,

Henry knew that Cranmer would support a radical solution to the Great Matter if Rome did not deliver the goods.

Cranmer was a key figure in the evangelical cause:

- he helped draft the Ten Articles in 1536 and the Bishops' Book in 1537
- he supported Cromwell's campaign for a Bible in English and promoted reform in his diocese of Kent.

However, he was not as important in a political sense as Cromwell. Cranmer was very much the scholar in the background, supportive but not ruthless in the way that Cromwell was.

Cranmer was a survivor. When other evangelicals around him, including Cromwell, fell, Cranmer curbed his Protestant instincts and maintained a good relationship with Henry. When he did come under attack from conservative opponents for heresy in 1543, Henry stood by his loyal servant and protected him.

Cranmer continued to promote reform at a pace which was acceptable to Henry, resulting in the publication of an English **litany** in 1544. Cranmer was by this time politically astute and recognised that there was little point in pushing the boundaries of reform too far, too quickly.

What gains had Protestantism made by 1540?

Influence of the papacy removed

On the back of the Royal Supremacy there is little doubt that Protestantism made some gains in England. Much in the way of the traditional fabric of the Church came under attack during the reign of Henry VIII, and would not recover in future years. As we have already seen, most people simply acquiesced in the face of the suppression of Roman authority in England, suggesting that the masses held little loyalty or affection for the papacy.

Indeed, when Mary attempted to return England to the Roman fold she encountered some resistance from those who had grown accustomed to a national Church with the monarch at its head. Such a point just goes to show that the longer these reforms were in place the more difficult it became to overturn them.

Monasteries destroyed

Anther aspect of late-medieval spiritual life that was destroyed forever were the religious orders. Although nuns, monks and friars retained the respect of ordinary people on the eve of the Reformation, the dissolution of the monasteries stopped all lay contributions to such institutions. Of course, there was popular resistance to the dissolution in the north of England over the course of 1536–37, which suggests that there was popular opposition to the changes being enacted by Henry and Cromwell.

Definition

Litany

A form of prayer consisting of a series of petitions or biddings that are sung or said by the priest or minister, and to which the people make fixed responses.

On the other hand, laymen were first to seize any opportunity to strip monastic assets and plunder moveable goods from the friaries and abbeys. Moreover, there is evidence that lay respect for the secular clergy began to wane somewhat in the late 1530s and throughout the 1540s as a result of the anti-clerical legislation passed through parliament, and recruitment to the priesthood decreased significantly.

Popular enthusiasm for Catholicism diminished

Local communities seem to have been less willing to invest in their local parish churches after the Supremacy than before it. The annual income of churches in the south of England decreased markedly while contributions towards upkeep and rebuilding dropped also. At the same time, local religious guilds, which were established pillars of the local community, ceased to be so popular.

Traditional Catholic rites extinguished

It can be argued that Cromwell's orchestrated attacks on the traditional rites of the Catholic Church had some effect. Saints' Days were reduced in 1536. Pilgrimage, relic veneration and offering to images were prohibited by the royal injunctions of 1536–38. It could be argued that even if such actions did not have an immediate effect, they did erode local loyalties to the traditional Church in the long run.

Certainly the practice of saying prayers for the dead and associated intercessory institutions such as chantries suffered an irreversible decline in the years 1534–47. Therefore, it can be argued that on the ground there was a marked decline in the appeal of traditional Catholic worship, as formerly important features of traditional piety such as the veneration of saints, images, sites and relics came under attack from the government.

How far had Catholicism survived in 1540?

No positive Protestant reform

It is true to say, however, that although much was destroyed in the way of traditional Catholic rites and worship, little was introduced in the way of Protestantism. Little advance was made in reforming the standards and practice of the clergy, as bishop John Hooper found out in 1551 when he uncovered a number of pluralist and absentee clerics. Despite bouts of fierce anti-clericalism during the Henrician Reformation little was actively done to improve moral or educational standards among the English clergy. It is also important to note that any advance Protestantism did make during the reign of Henry VIII was patchy.

Catholicism remained popular?

Traditional religion still held on to a high level of popular support, especially in the north of England. The parish church remained the focal

Biography

John Frith (1503–33)

Frith was educated at Eton College and then Kings'. He fell in with Stephen Gardiner and Edward Fox. Frith was a fine scholar but his unorthodox religious views meant that he had to flee England in 1528 for Antwerp, where he met up with Tyndale. Frith returned in 1533 but his religious outlook was unchanged. He denounced transubstantiation, and was soon in the Tower.

Definition

Heterodox

Holding a religious opinion that altered from the one generally received.

Exam tip

It is useful to understand what happened in the period after 1540. But remember, in the exam you will only be required to focus on what happens between 1509 and 1540 and you will not receive any extra credit for referring to anything after 1540.

point of most local communities and many lives in England remained untouched by Henrician reform. In areas such as Lancashire and Yorkshire, the Henrician Reformation was met with resistance and unpopularity.

Yet, in other northern towns such as Hull and Leeds we can pinpoint important Protestant communities. Certainly in the southeast, in counties such as Essex and Kent, Protestantism made headway. Again, however, regional variation prevailed as Sussex and Hampshire were very conservative. It is therefore too simplistic to identify a north–south divide in assessing local responses to the Henrician Reformation. In embracing religious change, much often depended upon the leadership and influence of the local nobility as the common man frequently followed the lead of his social superiors.

Protestants were not tolerated

Ultimately, Protestantism made only slow headway during the reign of Henry VIII, and this should surprise no one given Henry's own distaste for Protestants. Just as papists were not tolerated during Henry's reign it was the same for those who denied the sanctity of the Mass or the seven sacraments. **John Frith** was burned at the stake in 1533 for his heretical beliefs, while Anne Askew went the same way in 1546. The message was clear – Henry would not tolerate **heterodox** opinion and in such an environment Protestant progress was always likely to be slow. By 1547 the Church had undergone reform and some of it such as the introduction of the English Bible would have a lasting effect. Yet despite the emergence of an influential political clique who were well-disposed towards Protestant ideas, the Reformation was far from secure in England.

1540–47

The King's Book 1543

In light of this conservative ascendancy the *Bishops' Book* was revised, emerging in 1543 as *A Necessary Doctrine and Erudition for any Christian Man* or the *King's Book*. Any traces of Lutheranism to be found in the *Bishops' Book* were removed as the *King's Book* outlined the traditional core of Catholic doctrine.

The Creed, seven sacraments, Ten Commandments and Lord's Prayer were all laid out according to the Act of Six Articles.

In the same year, 1543, an Act for the Advancement of the True Religion was passed that limited the right of reading the Bible to clerics, noblemen, merchants and gentlewomen. Essentially, only upper-class males were allowed access to the Word of God, and one of Cromwell's central achievements had been significantly curtailed.

It had been decided that it was simply too dangerous to place the Gospel in the hands of the common man and therefore Bible reading was restricted on the grounds of social status.

Henry takes the middle ground?

Yet conservatives did not have things all their own way in these years. Catherine Howard was accused of adultery in 1541 and executed in 1542, actions that discredited both Norfolk and the conservative cause. The same Act for the Advancement of the True Religion, which restricted Bible reading, also mitigated the penalties for violation of the Six Articles, by allowing offenders to recant on two occasions before they were condemned.

Here again we can perhaps see Henry's reluctance to allow one particular faction to gain ascendancy. Indeed, only days after Cromwell's execution in 1540 Henry condemned three reformers (Barnes, Jerome and Garrett) and three papists (Abell, Featherstone and Powell) simultaneously. This might be construed as a prime example of Henry taking the middle ground but in reality it should come as no surprise that he was unwilling to tolerate either those who harboured papal sympathies or those he regarded as heretics.

The English Church retained unique characteristics under Henry, in that the medium was that of the reformed but the doctrine was essentially orthodox, not forgetting the absence of the Pope. There is no doubt that having let the conservatives get their way over Cromwell, Henry was not going to let the same thing happen to Cranmer. In 1543 a concerted attack was made on the Archbishop of Canterbury by Gardiner, who aimed to undermine Cranmer's position by linking him to a number of known radicals in his diocese of Kent. It is certainly true that Cranmer had done much to further the Reformation in Kent through his promotion of radical preachers and chaplains, but Henry was unwilling to listen to Gardiner's claims of heretical wrongdoing and assured Cranmer of his support.

Catherine Parr

The reformed cause also received a boost when Henry married his sixth wife, **Catherine Parr**, in July 1543. Catherine unquestionably held evangelical sympathies, a point underlined by the fact that she had been patron to the English translation of Erasmus's *Paraphrases on the New Testament* and she edited a book entitled *Prayers Stirring the Mind unto Heavenly Meditation* in 1545.

Her influence would be crucial in the last years of Henry's life, not least because she ensured that the young Edward was educated by Protestant divines belonging to her circle, including John Cheke, Richard Cox and Anthony Cooke. The conservative faction was determined to break her

Biography

Catherine Parr (1512–48)

Henry VIII's sixth and last wife. Catherine quickly learned how to handle Henry, and she is recognised as having a calming influence over the King in his final years of ill health. It was probably she who persuaded him to restore Mary and Elizabeth to the succession. Catherine's religious views were probably reformist, and she saw to it that Edward was tutored by those of an evangelical persuasion. She narrowly escaped allegations of harbouring heretical views in 1546.

influence and in 1546 a Protestant cell was uncovered at Windsor Castle suggesting that courtly protection of heretics was preventing the strict enforcement of the Six Articles.

In July 1546 a Lincolnshire gentlewoman by the name of Anne Askew was interrogated, tortured and subsequently burned as a heretic. Catherine was implicated in her heresy but, again, Henry was reluctant to pursue the wishes of the conservatives, and his wife was saved on the grounds that she submitted to his way of thinking on religious matters.

It is clear that by 1545 Henry was tiring of the factional struggle at Court, and he openly condemned extremists on both sides of the religious argument. England was at war with Scotland from 1542–47 and with France from 1543–46, meaning that Henry could well do without disunity at home. Yet, as the King's health deteriorated and it became clear that his days were numbered, the stakes increased in the factional struggle. In the event of Henry's death, a regency council would rule the country, and it was likely that Henry would appoint the members to that council in his last will and testament. For evangelicals and conservatives alike the years 1546 and 1547 were crucial in determining their future influence over religious affairs.

Key speech: Henry's Christmas Eve address to parliament, 1545

Henry made the last major public statement of his lifetime on Christmas Eve 1545, in which he bemoaned the factional conflict at Court. Henry stated to parliament that *some be too stiff in their old mumpsimus, other be too busy and curious in their new sumpsimus*. Referring to the religious division among his courtiers, Henry addressed those that be too slow, and need the spur, as well as those who seem too quick, and need more of the bridle. This was Henry's final plea for unity and perhaps his final attempt to maintain religious concord.

What was the religious future of England likely to be after Henry's death?

Despite Henry's ongoing doctrinal conservatism, those closest to him were evangelicals.

- William Butts was Henry's long-serving doctor
- Sir Anthony Denny was the chief gentleman of the privy chamber
- heading the evangelical faction were Edward Seymour, Earl of Hertford, and John Dudley, Viscount Lisle.

Both Hertford and Lisle had served Henry well on the battlefield, and Hertford had the advantage of being Prince Edward's uncle. Hertford was a powerful politician in his own right, but his position was further bolstered in 1546 with the support of William Parr (brother of the Queen) and Sir William Herbert (brother-in-law of the Queen).

Gardiner and Norfolk self-destruct

In the face of such strong opposition, it is of little surprise that Gardiner and Norfolk were outmanoeuvred in the last months of Henry's life. Hertford's supporters held sway in the Privy Council, while reformers at Court surrounded the King. That said, the two ageing conservatives did little to better their chances, indeed they both self-destructed at exactly the wrong moment.

- First, Gardiner was excluded from the Privy Council for failing to exchange some of his lands with the King. The leading conservative cleric would not be around as the regency council was drawn up.

- Second, the Howards were disgraced when the Duke of Norfolk's son (the Earl of Surrey) openly paraded his descent from the medieval Kings of England on his coat of arms, an act that Henry interpreted as treason. In January 1547, Surrey was executed and his father would have gone the same way had the King not died first. The leading conservative nobleman was also out of the way, and the road was clear for Hertford to head the regency council when Henry died.

While he lived, Henry remained in control of affairs. A succession Act of 1543 had restored Mary and Elizabeth in line to the throne behind Edward. In his will Henry repeated the terms of this Act, and nominated a regency council of sixteen members to govern until Edward reached the age of eighteen. Henry died in the early hours of 28 January 1547, and suspicions remain that those at his bedside altered some of the terms of his will to further their own cause. Hertford and his supporters certainly came off best in terms of land and titles, with Edward Seymour himself adopting the title of Lord Protector. In factional terms, the evangelicals had won hands down. Gardiner and Norfolk were excluded from the regency council, and those now trusted with the well-being and good governance of the nine-year-old Edward VI were all reformers.

The grassroots reformation

The extent to which the Henrician Reformation was embraced by the masses has been the subject of heated academic debate among historians.

One school of thought, endorsed by historians such as Christopher Haigh and J.J. Scarisbrick, argues that the Henrician Reformation attacked a traditional Church that still held the devotion and loyalty of the people, and as a result reform was slow and unpopular.

Another school, to which historians such as A.G. Dickens would subscribe, puts forward the idea that the traditional Church was already in decline and that Henrician reform was greeted with enthusiasm by the masses and progress was therefore quick.

Both sets of historians have examined a variety of sources such as wills, court records and churchwardens' accounts in order to substantiate their ideas. Yet, as one can gather, these pieces of evidence have proved contradictory and inconclusive.

Key historian

Christopher Haigh

In his important work entitled *Reformation and Resistance in Tudor Lancashire*, published in 1975, Haigh presents a Henrician Reformation imposed from above that had only a slow impact on the Lancashire area.

Wills, for example, have been used extensively, but are problematic in that their content was often relayed by the testator to the priest whose job it was to write everything down. It has therefore been suggested that wills reflect the religious outlook of parish priests more than that of the common man. Further to this point, it has been argued that from 1530 onwards fewer people left money in wills for prayers to be said for the souls of the dead, and that the growing unpopularity of such a traditional Catholic practice shows the emerging strength of Protestantism in England. Others argue that these wills still retained the traditional preamble highlighting a continuing belief in the saints, and that Catholic rites largely withstood attempts by reformers such as Cromwell to outlaw them.

KNOWLEDGE FOCUS

- The break with Rome and the Royal Supremacy allowed more radical religious men to win favour at court because they were willing to support and endorse these ideas.

- On the back of the Supremacy, Cromwell and Cranmer were able to put forward moderately evangelical doctrines such as the Ten Articles and the *Bishops' Book*.

- Henry always remains Catholic, and Protestant ideas were not tolerated. Radical ideas such as reducing the number of sacraments were soon dropped.

- At the same time Roman Catholics were not tolerated as they symbolised the old regime.

- The key struggle at court takes place between the conservatives and the evangelicals.

- The publication of an English Bible is a major triumph for Cromwell and the evangelical faction.

- Henry remains paranoid that he is going to face a Catholic invasion of England that will overthrow his rule.

- There is something of a conservative backlash in the years 1539–45 when Henry predictably comes down on the side of the traditional, old religious doctrine as long as it does not teach the authority of the Pope over the Church.

- The Act of Six Articles, the fall of Cromwell and the *King's Book* are blows for the evangelical cause.

- Ultimately the conservative faction loses out as a result of the new men at court, such as Hertford and Lisle, the upbringing of Edward and the poor judgement of Norfolk and Gardiner.

SKILLS FOCUS

- In an (a) style question it is crucial to build up a sense of comparison.

- Make sure that you compare the context as well as the content of the sources.

- Ask yourself questions of the author and the date in all source related questions. Own knowledge is crucial in allowing you to evaluate the provenance of the sources.

- For a (b) question make sure you form an argument. That argument must revolve around the sources.

- Use the sources to structure your paragraphs and group them to maintain a sense of argument.

- Quote, explain and evaluate sources individually within their grouping.

- Use own knowledge to develop your argument.

- Arrive at a clear judgement on the question.

Thematic review: source-based debate and evaluation

It is important, especially when dealing with a topic that addresses change over time, to stand back and review the period you have been studying. You need to ask yourself not only what happened, but why it happened and why it happened then and not, say, 100 years earlier or twenty years later. What had driven change? Which factors were significant and which were not? Were there any events that were critical turning points? Thematic review questions, spanning the whole time period, will help to focus your thinking. These are the thematic review questions that relate to *Henry VIII: Authority, Nation and Religion 1509–40*. You can probably think of more, but for the moment these are the ones with which you will be working.

- How far did Henry VIII strengthen the monarchy in the first two decades of his reign?
- How far was Thomas Wolsey an '*Alter Rex*'?
- To what extent did the Henrician Reformation extend and increase royal power?

Choose one of these thematic review questions that you plan to answer. Working through this section will make much more sense if you have an actual question in mind.

Answering a thematic review question

There are two keys to answering a thematic review question: **select** and **deploy**.

Select	You need to select appropriate source material You need to select appropriate knowledge
Deploy	You need to deploy what you have selected so that you answer the question in as direct a way as possible

Unpacking 'select'

You will see that all the thematic review questions are asking for an evaluation. They ask 'How far . . .' 'To what extent . . .' 'How significant . . .' which means that you will have to weigh up the evidence given by the sources you have selected. You will, therefore, have to select sources that will give you a range of evidence. Six diary entries, for example, will not give you the range you want. You will also need to select sources that seem to provide evidence that pulls in different directions. Eight sources saying more or less the same thing but in different ways will not help you weigh up the significance of different sorts of evidence and reach a reasoned, supported conclusion.

So now go ahead.

(i) Look back through this book and select the sources, primary and secondary, that you think will give you the appropriate range, balance and evidence to answer this question.

(ii) Make notes of the knowledge you will need to use to contextualise the sources and create an argument.

You can not, of course, simply put some sources into an answer and hope that whoever is reading what you have written can sort things out for themselves. You need to evaluate the sources you have selected and use that evaluation to create the argument you will be making when you answer the question. Here is a reminder of some of the questions you will need to ask of a source before you can turn it into evidence:

- Is the **content** appropriate for the question I am answering?
- Can I supply the appropriate **context** for the source?
- How **reliable** is the source as evidence? Was the author or artist **in a position to know** what he or she was talking/painting about? What was the intended **audience** of the source? What was the **purpose** of the source?
- If it is a photograph, was it posed taken from a selected viewpoint?
- How **useful** is this source in developing an answer to the question? Remember that a source that is unreliable can still be useful.

Now you have your selection of source material, you need to think about it as a package. Does it do the job you want it to do? Does it supply you with enough evidence to argue your case, while at the same time providing you with enough evidence of different points of view so that you can show you have considered what weight the evidence will bear in reaching a reasoned, supported conclusion? In other words, can you effectively **cross-reference** between the sources, showing where they support and where they challenge each other?

Unpacking 'deploy'

The key to successful deployment of evidence and knowledge in answering a question such as the one you have selected is always to keep the question in the forefront of your mind: keep focused! Do not be tempted to go off into interesting by-ways. Make every paragraph count as you build your argument.

You have already had a lot of practice in essay planning and writing as you have worked through the book, so this is just a reminder of the main things you need to bear in mind.

Plan carefully how you are going to construct your answer and make out your case.

Structure your answer, and use this framework as a guide.

Introduction is where you 'set out your stall', briefly outlining your argument and approach.

Paragraphs should develop your argument using the evidence you have created by questioning the sources. As you create the case you are making, remember to cross-reference between the sources you are using so as to weigh the evidence, showing on which you place the greater weight.

Conclusion is where you should pull your case together, giving a supported summary of the arguments you have made and coming to a reasoned, supported judgement.

In other words, say what you are going to do, do it, and show that you have done it.

You do not, of course, have to respond to these thematic review questions by writing an essay all by yourself. You could work collaboratively in a small group, or you could use one or more of the questions to prepare for a class debate. In whatever way you are going to use these thematic review questions, the approach will be the same: select, deploy and keep to the point.

Good luck!

Exam zone

Getting started and about the exam

As part of your AS Level History course you are required to carry out an in-depth study of one period of British history, in this instance *Henry VIII: Authority, Nation and Religion 1509–40*. You will explore source material to develop an in-depth understanding of the attitudes, beliefs and structures of the societies studied.

At the end of your AS course you will take a written exam and you will need to answer two source-based questions. The sources will be supplied with the paper.

- In Question a) you will need to analyse, cross-reference and evaluate the source material to reach a judgement. This question will be worth 20 marks.

- In Question b) you will address a historical view or claim using two sources and your own knowledge. There will be a choice of two b) questions. This question will be worth 40 marks.

The exam will last 1 hour and 20 minutes. Make sure you plan your time carefully and allow enough time to answer both questions thoroughly.

> ### Exam tip
>
> Remember, the b) questions assess AO1 and AO2 and the marks are split between the two. You will be awarded 24 marks for AO1 and 16 marks for AO2.

Hot tips

What other students have said

FROM GCSE TO AS LEVEL

Many of the skills that I learned at GCSE were built on at AS level, especially in Unit 2 where the skills of source evaluation and analysis are very important.

I really enjoyed studying modern history at GCSE but I am glad that I had the chance to look at some sixteenth-century English history at AS level. It has been challenging but enjoyable to study a different period.

AS level History seems like a big step up at first with more demands made on independent reading and more complex source passages to cope with. However, by the end of the first term I felt as if my written work had improved considerably.

The more I practiced source-based questions, the more confident I became and quite quickly I picked up the necessary style and technique required for success.

I found it really helpful to look at the model answers in the textbook. It was reassuring to see what gained top marks.

WHAT I WISH I HAD KNOWN AT THE START OF THE YEAR

AS History is not just about learning the relevant material but also developing the skills to use it effectively. I wished that I had spent more time throughout the year practising source questions to improve my style and technique.

I used the textbook a lot during the revision period to learn the key facts. I really wished that I had used it from the beginning of the course in order to consolidate my class notes.

I wished that I had taken more time reading and noting other material such as the photocopied handouts issued by my teacher. Reading around the subject and undertaking independent research would have made my understanding more complete and made the whole topic more interesting.

I wish I had paid more attention to the advice and comments made by my teacher on the written work I had done. This would have helped me to improve my scores throughout the year.

HOW TO REVISE

I started my revision by buying a new folder and some dividers. I put all my revision work into this folder and used the dividers to separate the different topics. I really took pride in my revision notes and made them as thorough and effective as I could.

Before I started the revision process, I found it helpful to plan out my history revision. I used the Edexcel specification given to me by my teacher as a guideline of which topics to revise and I ticked off each one as I covered it.

I found it useful to revise in short, sharp bursts. I would set myself a target of revising one particular topic in an hour and a half. I would spend one hour taking revision notes and then half an hour testing myself with a short practice question or a facts test.

I found it useful to always include some practice work in my revision. If I could get that work to my teacher to mark all the better, but just attempting questions to time helped me improve my technique.

Sometimes I found it helpful to revise with a friend. We might spend 45 minutes revising by ourselves and then half an hour testing each other. Often we were able to sort out any problems between us and it was re assuring to see that someone else had the same worries and pressures at that time.

Refresh your memory: revision checklist

1 Cardinal Wolsey

- Reasons for Wolsey's rise to power
- Relationship between Wolsey and Henry
- Wolsey's domestic policy: justice, finance, administration, church and social
- Reasons for Wolsey's fall from power

2 Foreign policy

- First French War, 1512–14
- England's foreign policy objectives between 1515 and 1521
- Second French War, 1522–25
- How did foreign affairs affect Henry's attempts to annul his marriage to Catherine of Aragon?
- Who was in charge of foreign policy between 1514–29 – Henry or Wolsey?

3 Break with Rome

- Causes of the break with Rome
- Tudor dynasty and male heir

- Role of Anne Boleyn
- God's Law – Leviticus and Deuteronomy
- Henry's conscience
- Why was Clement VII unable to grant an annulment?

4 Royal supremacy

- Role of Thomas Cromwell and the Reformation Parliament
- *Collectanea satis copiosa*
- Pardon of the Clergy
- Submission of the Clergy
- Henry's marriage to Anne Boleyn
- Appointment of Cranmer as Archbishop of Canterbury
- Legislation – Act of Annates, Act in Restraint of Appeals, Act for the Submission of the Clergy, First Act of Succession, Act of Supremacy, Treason Act, Act for First Fruits and Tenths
- Opposition – Elizabeth Barton, Bishop Fisher and Thomas More

- How serious was opposition to the Royal Supremacy?

5 Dissolution of the monasteries

- Reasons for dissolution – financial, reform, political
- *Valor* Ecclesiasticus
- First Act for Dissolution – smaller monasteries
- Second Act for Dissolution – larger monasteries
- Methods and means of dissolution
- Opposition to dissolution – Pilgrimage of Grace
- How serious was the Pilgrimage of Grace?

6 Religious change

- Removal of the Pope as spiritual head of the Church

- Destruction of medieval Roman Catholicism
- Act of Ten Articles
- *Bishops' Book*
- Act of Six Articles
- *King's Book*
- English Bible
- Trial and execution of Thomas Cromwell.

7 Government

- The organs of Government – Court, Council and Privy Chamber
- Changes in Tudor government – Revolution?
- Role of Wolsey and Cromwell in Tudor Government
- Centralisation – Wales, the north and Ireland
- Faction – role of the nobility
- Government methods of suppressing opposition.

Putting it into practice: examining other students' work

Study Sources 1 to 8. Answer Question 1, parts (a) and (b). There is a choice of questions in part (b).

Part a) question

Source 1

When every man will rule, who shall obey? An order must be had and a way found where those who are the best rulers and Councillors should rule. It is most necessary for a commonwealth that those of the worser sort should be content that those who are wiser should govern them. They must realize that God has given to those who rule special virtues and good fortune and raised them to a high position in society so that they can promote love and friendship between high and low.

From a book entitled *A Remedy for Sedition* written by Richard Morrison and printed by the King's printer at the time of the rebellion

Source 2

The Cardinal du Bellay tells me that this great rebellion in England, though somewhat diminished, is not extinguished and that they can raise an even larger force when they please. It is widely believed that the people will, in the end, kill the king if he persists in his errors. For he was unable to disarm the rebels who had collected, at one time, more than 50,000 men and he has been forced to satisfy the people by arresting 3 or 4 Lutherans who went up and down the country. I see that they are ill disposed towards the King and in a future revolt they would beg the Pope to declare against him.

From a letter by the Bishop of Faenza to Monsignor Ambrogio, 4 December 1536

Source 3

It seems to me that the King should agree to our petition against the low born traitor Thomas Cromwell, his disciples and adherents and to exile them from the realm. Although it is argued that we should not take upon us to choose his Grace's Council, in fact it is necessary that virtuous men who love the commonwealth should be of his Council. Such virtuous men would regard the commonwealth above their prince's interests. It is argued that the King has the authority granted to him by parliament to suppress the abbeys. But I think that this parliament was of no authority or virtue as it was made up of Councillors appointed by the King. Parliaments ought to have knights of the shire and burgesses of the towns elected by their fellows, who could defend the wealth of the shire or town.

From an anonymous petition, October 1536

a) Study Sources 1, 2 and 3.

How far do these sources suggest that the Pilgrimage of Grace was a serious threat to the Crown? (20 marks)

What does the mark scheme say?

- Analyse and evaluate a range of appropriate source material with discrimination
- Show how the sources agree/disagree with the statement
- Reach a judgement in relation to the issue posed by the question
- Use the sources as evidence
- Look at the nature, origins, purpose and audience of the source

Model answer

All three sources largely agree that the Pilgrimage of Grace was a serious rebellion. Sources 2 and 3 in particular suggest that the rebellion was a real threat to Henry's Crown. Source 2 states that Henry 'was unable to disarm the rebels' showing us that royal authority was not strong enough to quash the rebellion. Source 3 does not actually comment on the rebellion directly but it does challenge Henry's right to make laws in parliament, stating that this parliament 'was of no authority or virtue as it was made up of Councillors appointed by the King'. This suggests that the rebellion was serious because Henry's government and kingship was being seriously undermined by such petitions as that in Source 3.

Indeed Source 1 may even have been written as a response to Source 2, because it emphasises the importance of 'order' in society and the need for 'those who are wiser' to govern over everyone else. Source 1 emphasises the idea that Henry's right to rule comes from God and therefore his rule must not be challenged. Therefore, while Sources 2 and 3 are written in favour of the rebellion, Source 1 was written in support of Henry and because of this we would expect their interpretations of the rebellion to be different.

What does the examiner say?

- Displays good, clear comprehension of the sources
- Cross-references the sources well
- Focuses on the question
- Address the issue of 'how far'
- Not enough consideration of the attributes of the sources i.e. origin, purpose and audience to reach level 4.

Level 3
Mark 11–15

What might have taken this answer into level 4?

- The answer above is perfectly adequate as a comprehension of the sources
- What it lacks is some specific evaluation
- Add these paragraphs to what is written above and we have a level 4 answer (16–20 marks)

While Source 1 is largely written to support Henry's rule, the very fact that such a justification had to be published in the first place shows the rebellion to be a serious one. It was published in October 1536 at the height of the Pilgrimage of Grace and phrases such as 'raised them to a high position in society so that they can promote love and friendship between high and low' suggest that the Crown was concerned that the social order had broken down.

Sources 2 and 3 are both written in support of the rebellion and therefore it is unsurprising that they undermine Henry's authority. That said, one might not consider the views in Source 3 to be entirely typical of views of the pilgrims in October 1536. The ideas in this source are very radical such as 'parliaments ought to have knights of the shire and burgesses of the towns elected by their fellows'. We know that not all rebels wanted to introduce such radical political ideas, and that many continued to show loyalty to Henry if not his councillors. Moreover, some lesser nobles such as Lord Darcy were involved in the rebellion, and they would not share these views. The fact that the petition was anonymous suggests that the rebellion lacked leadership and direction if not ideas.

Source 2 is written by a foreign bishop and gives us a slightly exaggerated opinion of the rebellion. The Bishop of Faenza was still loyal to Rome and likely to see Henry as a heretic. He states that the rebels collected over '50,000 men' which seems unlikely and that 'in a future revolt they would beg the Pope to declare against him'. Although displeased by the dissolution of the monasteries, there is *little evidence that the rebels would have turned back to Rome. The Bishop of Faenza seems uninformed and unreliable in his assessment of the mood in England in 1536, even suggesting that 'the people will, in the end, kill the king'.*

Part b) question

Source 4

Any thought that the political and doctrinal changes were simply and silently absorbed by the people must be forgotten . . . There was a real problem facing the King and his advisers, a real problem of disaffection, disobedience and disturbance. No doubt the problem can now in retrospect be seen to have been far from enormous, but at the time only its reality could be taken for granted, not its size.

From G R Elton, *Policy and Police: the Enforcement of the Reformation in the Age of Thomas Cromwell*, 1972

Source 5

I thank you for telling my son in law Roper that you wished to hear from me concerning my communications with the lewd nun of Canterbury. It is 8 or 9 years since I first heard of her, at which time the Archbishop of Canterbury sent to the King a letter containing certain words spoken during her trances. The King gave me the letter and asked my opinion. I told him there was nothing in it, since there was nothing there that a simple woman might not speak of her own wit.

From a letter written by Sir Thomas More to Thomas Cromwell in March 1534

Source 6

The holy Bishop of Rochester has been sent for. He is in great danger as he has spoken several times to the Nun of whom I wrote. More, the late Chancellor, has been examined by the Chancellor and Cromwell for a letter which he wrote to the Nun, which could not have been more prudent, as he exhorted her to attend to devotion and not to meddle in the affairs of princes. The persecution of these men is only because of their having taken the Queen's side.

From a letter written by Eustace Chapuys to the Emperor Charles V, March 1534

b) Do you agree with the suggestion in Source 4 that opposition to the Reformation was a real problem for Henry VIII in the years 1533–36? (40 marks)

Explain your answer, using Sources 4, 5 and 6 and your own knowledge.

Exam tip

Remember, you will have a choice of b) questions but you only have to answer one of these in the final exam.

What does the mark scheme say?

- Analyse how aspects of the past have been interpreted in different ways
- Integrate sources and your own knowledge
- Formulate a response that relates well to the focus of the question
- Support the analysis with accurate factual material, relevant to the question asked
- Demonstrate developed reasoning and weighing of evidence in order to create a judgement in relation to the stated claim.

Exam tips

1 A brief introduction showing how the sources fit the argument.

2 Group the two sources that seem to agree with the statement

3 Explain the message of these sources in your own words and how they relate to the question

4 Incorporate short quotations to reinforce your points.

5 Evaluate the origins, nature and purpose of the sources

6 Be prepared to challenge opinions on the grounds of reliability, completeness and typicality.

Build your answer

Sources 4 and 6 would agree that opposition to the Reformation was a real problem, although Source 4 is more general in its overview of opposition than Source 6 which discusses one particular opponent. Source 5 seems to disagree with the statement, in that Thomas More sees the Nun of Kent as only a simple woman, implying little threat to the Crown.

Sources 4 and 6 both see opposition to the Reformation in the years 1533–36 as a real problem. We know that in these years, the break with Rome and the Royal Supremacy were passed through parliament, and such revolutionary Acts were always going to provoke some opposition on the ground. G.R. Elton sees such opposition as a 'real problem' and makes the point that change was not just silently absorbed by the people. In saying this he may be referring to the Carthusian and Observant monks who made a stand against Henry's break with Rome or perhaps Bishop John Fisher, a key figure referred to in Source 6. Indeed it cannot be denied that there were some high profile opponents of the Reformation such as Fisher and Thomas More, who were real problems for Henry VIII as both of them had to be tried and executed for their opposition to the break with Rome and the Royal Supremacy.

Yet one might challenge Elton's claim in Source 4 that there was 'a real problem of disaffection, disobedience and disturbance'. While there may have been some high profile opponents of the Crown, the general populace acquiesced and did little to stand in Henry's way. Few people on the ground appeared to hold much loyalty to Rome, and those that did were probably too frightened to stand up to the King. Important men in London had to swear an oath to the Royal Supremacy in 1534, while a new treason law was introduced in 1535 to stop people from speaking out against the King's new marriage and the Supremacy. Along with the execution of opponents such as More, Fisher and Barton this kept the people quiet and Elton's claims of widespread opposition seem out of place. Perhaps, given the title of his book, he was trying to play up the role of Thomas Cromwell in suppressing the opposition. In Source 6 Chapuys is writing to defend More and Fisher, and in doing so he perhaps shows how important they were as opponents of the Crown. He refers to the 'holy Bishop' and the 'late Chancellor' emphasising the high status of these two figures. Chapuys also reveals that the cause of their opposition was allegiance to Catherine of Aragon as he writes, the persecution of these men is only because of their having taken the Queen's side. Chapuys was writing to his master, the Emperor Charles V, who was also the nephew of Catherine of Aragon, making this source somewhat unreliable. Chapuys was certainly writing in sympathy for Fisher and More, and he was perhaps trying to win support for their cause from Charles V.

Source 5 seems to disagree with the idea that opposition to the Reformation was a real problem. Thomas More suggests that the Elizabeth Barton was little threat to the Crown, and even describes her as 'lewd'. More writes that there was 'nothing' in her visions and that Henry should essentially ignore her as she was no more than 'a simple woman'. Yet Henry did take Barton's visions seriously, as her prophecies foretold of disaster for the Anne Boleyn marriage and the Tudor dynasty. Given the scale and pace of change in the years 1532-36, Henry could not allow any opposition to exist no matter how trivial. In April 1534 Barton was executed along with five of her followers suggesting that opposition was a real problem. Indeed one might question More's own motives in writing this letter, as he had been linked with the Nun of Kent and perhaps he was eager to distance himself from her in this letter. He is almost pleading his innocence to the man he knows will decide his fate. Eventually More would follow Barton to the scaffold in July 1535 for his opposition to the Royal Supremacy. It could be argued that More was Henry's most serious problem as he was a well known and respected figure across Europe. Moreover, he remained silent on the issue of the Royal Supremacy, refusing to swear the oath but not giving any reasons at the same time. His silence negated the recent Treason Law and ultimately More was convicted on dubious evidence supplied by Richard Rich. Opposition from More and Fisher was a problem for Henry but in different ways. Fisher had been in treasonable correspondence with Charles V and was openly opposed to the Reformation. More was silent and more implicit in his opposition making him more difficult to convict. Yet in the end both are executed, showing that if Henry had problems he dealt with them ruthlessly.

Still Henry had to face the most serious rebellion of his reign in 1536 with the Pilgrimage of Grace. By October 1536 Robert Aske had 30,000 men under arms in the north of England opposing the policies of the Crown. Many of the rebels were moved to take up arms as a consequence of religious change, particularly the recent dissolution of the smaller monasteries. This uprising was certainly a real problem for Henry and ultimately he had to give in to many of the rebel demands such as a free parliament in the north. The Pilgrimage of Grace perhaps shows that Henry faced more problems in the north than he did in the south. Eventually he was able to disband the rebels with promises of concessions and then crush them later in 1537.

Therefore, it is clear that opposition to the Supremacy was problematic for Henry, but his policies were still pushed through. No doubt the executions of More, Fisher and Barton frightened many people into submission whilst others seemed to owe more loyalty to the Tudors than they did to Rome. Opposition was a real problem but one that Henry dealt with successfully.

Exam tips

1 Pull in the source that appears to disagree
2 Explain how and why it disagrees
3 In order to do this one must look at the purpose and audience of the author
4 Develop the idea of opposition utilising own knowledge.

Exam tips

1 Develop the argument with relevant own knowledge
2 Make a clear judgement on the question.

169

Part b) question

Source 7

And where the great number of the king's subjects having little or no learning nor knowledge of letters have been put in opinion by divers laws and decrees made by the Bishop of Rome called the Pope that every man that in anything speaketh or doeth against the said pretended power or authority of the Bishop of Rome stands in danger of heresy. Wherefore be it enacted . . . that no manner of speaking or holding against the said Bishop of Rome, or his pretenced power or authority, which be repugnant or contrary to the laws and statutes of the realm or the king's prerogative royal, shall be deemed or taken to be heresy.

From an Act for the Punishment of Heresy, 1534

Source 8

And since you are in the habit of championing catholic truth most keenly in every discussion, you cannot better occupy your spare time than in publishing something in English which will reveal to simple and uneducated men the crafty wickedness of the heretics, and will better equip such folk against such impious supplanters of the Church. In so doing you have a very distinguished example, that of our most illustrious lord, King Henry VIII, who stood up for the sacraments of the Church against Luther, and thus won himself for all time the immortal title of Defender of the Church.

From a licence from the Bishop of London for Sir Thomas More to keep and read heretical books, 1528

Source 9

Henry had defied pope and emperor, brought into being in England and Ireland a national Church subject to his authority, wiped about a thousand religious houses off the face of his native land, and of those areas of Ireland under his influence, and bestowed on English kingship a profound new dignity. He who had broken the secular Church in England, hammered monks and friars, and recently, laid his hand on the chantries, had brought the Scriptures in the vernacular to his people, hesitantly and perhaps unwittingly, but nonetheless decisively allowed his country to be directed towards the Continental Reformation . . . and given to his people a new sense of unity-the unity of entire Englishmen.

From J.J. Scarisbrick, Henry VIIII, 1968

Exam tips

1 A brief introduction shows how the sources fit the argument.

2 Group the two sources that seem to agree with the statement.

3 Explain the message of these sources in your own words and how they relate to the question.

4 Incorporate short quotations to reinforce your points.

b) (ii) Use Sources 7, 8 and 9 and your own knowledge.

Do you accept the view expressed in Source 9 that England was directed towards the Continental Reformation under Henry VIII?

Explain your answer using Sources 7, 8 and 9 and your own knowledge. (40 marks)

Sources 7 and 9 agree that Henry moved England towards a Continental Reformation, but both sources suggest that he did so 'unwittingly', meaning that this was not his intention. Source 8 disagrees with the statement showing Henry to be loyal to Rome, but the date of this source is before the break with Rome making it unsurprising that he is critical of Luther.

Both Sources 7 and 9 make the point that Henry broke England's allegiance with Rome and in doing so created a national Church. Source 7 states that anyone continuing to profess loyalty to Rome 'stands in danger of heresy' while Source 9 asserts that Henry had 'defied both pope and emperor'. Therefore, both of these sources would agree that the character and loyalties of the Church in England had changed significantly in the reign of Henry VIII. Most importantly both sources agree that the Pope was no longer the spiritual head of the English Church, but whether this makes Henry's Reformation a continental one is debatable. Source 7 only makes the point that allegiance to Rome had been severed. Source 9 gives us more idea of change stating that 'a thousand religious houses' had been destroyed and 'scriptures in the vernacular' introduced. Both of these characteristics of the Henrician Reformation would have been applauded by Luther and other continental reformers but Scarisbrick himself is keen to point out that a radical reformation was not Henry's intention. It might be argued that the destruction of monasteries and chantries in Henry's reign paved the way for more radical reform in the future. Furthermore, both sources highlight the increased power of the King himself over the Church suggesting that Henry's intentions were perhaps not to move England towards a Continental Reformation but rather to enhance his own authority. We can see this in Source 7 when the Act refers to the King's 'prerogative royal' while in Source 9 Scarisbrick writes that Henry 'had bestowed on English kingship a profound new dignity'.

Both of the sources view the Henrician Reformation from Henry's perspective and neither source really looks at any change in the manner of worship among the people. Source 7 is an official royal document outlining Henry's Royal Supremacy, and therefore its purpose was merely to lay out the law of the land. It was a piece of legislation drafted by Thomas Cromwell and passed through the Reformation Parliament making it inevitable that it would state what Henry wanted, namely that papal power had been replaced by royal authority. The Act was not intended to state how people were now to worship nor to initiate a continental style Reformation, therefore it might be seen as of limited value. However, this important piece of legislation removed papal authority from England and in doing so gave more radical reformers such as Cromwell and Cranmer a chance to introduce other reforms such as the introduction of a Bible in English. Scarisbrick himself argues in Source 9 that the Henrician Reformation was hesitant and that Henry only allowed more radical reform to emerge unwittingly, but in time England did move towards a more continental style Reformation.

Source 8 disagrees with the statement, stating that Henry stood up for the sacraments of the Church and ruled England under the title of Defender of the Faith. Therefore, Source 8 is of the opinion that Henry was loyal to the Catholic Church and even defended it against

Exam tips

1 Evaluate the origins, nature and purpose of the sources.

2 Be prepared to challenge opinions on the grounds of reliability, completeness and typicality.

Exam tips

1 Pull in the source that appears to disagree.
2 Explain how and why it disagrees.
3 In order to do this, one must look at the purpose and audience of the author.

Exam tips

1 Develop the argument with relevant own knowledge.
2 Make a clear judgement on the question.

Luther's attack. The date of the source is key to our understanding of this view as it was written before the Great Matter and the Royal Supremacy when Henry had no reason to challenge the power of Rome. Furthermore, Source 8 was written by a Catholic bishop to one of the most Catholic laymen in England, namely Sir Thomas More who helped Henry write the Assertion of the Seven Sacraments against Luther and thus earn the King the title of Defender of the Faith from Rome. As such it was likely to be in praise of Roman Catholicism and flattering towards the King as we can see in phrases such as 'championing catholic truth' and 'our most illustrious lord'. Therefore, it is unsurprising that Source 8 makes no mention of a Reformation taking place in England, although this source could only have been written before 1534 as it implies loyalty to Rome.

It is clear that Henry did not intend for a continental style Reformation. Source 8 shows us the orthodoxy of his religious position before the Great Matter, and his personal loyalties towards Catholicism did not really waver. We can see this from the way in which Catholic doctrine did not really alter with the Act of Six Articles in 1539 making clear that there was only one faith in England. Moreover, those evangelicals who pushed reform too far towards the continent such as Barnes or Cromwell were still executed as heretics. Yet the destruction of so much associated with Roman Catholicism such as the monasteries and papal authority itself paved the way for more radical reform. The establishment of the Royal Supremacy in 1534 provided an opportunity for reformers to advance their cause, and by Henry's death in 1547 we might agree with Scarisbrick in Source 9 that England had been directed towards the Continental Reformation, albeit unwittingly by Henry.

Practice!

Now that you have seen how such questions might be answered here are two questions to test yourself with. Remember to stick to the guidelines that have been laid out in the previous model answers.

Question 1
(a) Study Sources 1, 2 and 3.

How far do these sources suggest that the monasteries were dissolved for financial profit?

Explain your answer, using the evidence of Sources 1, 2 and 3. (20 marks)

Source 1

I submit myself fully and wholly to your mastership, as all my refuge, help and succour is in you, glad of my voluntary mind to be bound in obligation of one hundred pounds to be paid to your mastership, so our House may be saved.

From a letter written by the Abbot of Rewley to Thomas Cromwell, 1536

Source 2

At Bruern, the abbot is not only virtuous and well learned in holy scripture but also hath very well repaired the ruin and decay of that house left by his predecessor's negligence and the convent now being brought to good order.

The prioress at Catesby is a very sad matron, the sisters also there, now being by the space of 20 years, hath been without suspicion of incontinent living.

Adapted from a letter written by John Tregonwell to Thomas Cromwell, 1535

Source 3

And where you allege that the service of God is much diminished, the truth thereof is contrary; for there be none Houses suppressed where God was well served, but where most vice, mischief and abomination of living was used: and that doth well appear by their own confession, subscribed by their own hands, in the time of our visitations.

From Henry VIII's answer to the Lincolnshire petition, 1536

(b) Use Sources 4, 5 and 6 and your own knowledge.

Do you agree with the suggestion in Source 6 that Henry treated Wolsey more as a partner than as a servant? (40 marks)

Source 4

He is set so hye
In his ierarchy
Of frantycke frenesy
And folysshe fantasy
That in the Chambre of Sterres
All maters there he marres
Clappying his rod on the borde.
No man dare speke a worde,
For he hath all the sayenge
Without any renayenge . . .
Set up a wretche on hye,
In a trone triumphantlye,
Make him a great astate,
And he wyll play checke mate
With ryall majeste
Count himself as good as he.

From John Skelton's Why come ye nat to courte? 1522

Source 5

He took upon him to disburden the king of so weighty a charge and troublesome business, putting the king in comfort that he shall not need to spare any time of his pleasure for any business that should necessary happen in the council as long as he being there, having the king's authority and commandment doubted not to see all things sufficiently furnished and perfected, the which would first make the king privy of all such matters before he would proceed to the finishing and determination of the same, whose mind and pleasure he would fulfil and follow to the uttermost wherewith the king was wonderfully pleased.

From A Life of Wolsey by George Cavendish, 1544

Source 6

It is true that Wolsey enjoyed exceptional favour and for a while he his position was different. Between 1515 and 1525 it can be argued that Henry treated him more as a partner than a servant. Wolsey enjoyed a uniquely privileged access to the king. They walked arm in arm together and were intimate confidantes to the exclusion of others.

(From Wolsey, Cromwell and the reform of government by John Guy, 1995)

References

Ackroyd, P. (1998) *The Life of Thomas More*, Chatto and Windus

Anderson, A. and Imperato, T. (2001) *Tudor England 1485–1603*, Hodder & Stoughton

Brigden, S. (1990) *London and the Reformation*, Clarendon Press

Brigden, S. (2000) *New Worlds, Lost Worlds: The Rule of the Tudors 1485–1603*, Allen Lane

Bush, M. (1996) *The Pilgrimage of Grace: A Study of the Rebel Armies of October 1536*, Manchester University Press

Cavendish, G. (1962) *Life and Death of Cardinal Wolsey* (edited by Roger Lockyer), Folio

Chambers, R.W. (1935) *Thomas More*, Jonathan Cape

Chrimes, S.B. (1972) *Henry VII*, Methuen

Coleman, C. (1986) 'Professor Elton's Revolution' in C. Coleman and D. Starkey, *Revolution Reassessed: Revisions in the History of Tudor Government and Administration*, Oxford University Press

Condon, M. (1979) 'Ruling Elites in the Reign of Henry VII' in C.D. Ross (ed.), *Patronage, Pedigree and Power in Later Medieval England*, Alan Sutton

Dickens, A.G. (1964) *The English Reformation*, Batsford

Duffy, Eamon (1992) *The Stripping of the Altars*, Yale University Press

Ellis, S.G. (1985) *Tudor Ireland: Crown, Community and the Conflict of Cultures 1470–1603*, Longman

Elton, G.R. (1953) *The Tudor Revolution in Government*, Cambridge University Press

Elton, G.R. (1955) *England Under the Tudors*, Methuen

Elton, G.R. (1973) *Reform and Renewal: Thomas Cromwell and the Common Weal*, Cambridge University Press

Fletcher, A. and MacCulloch, D. (1983) *Tudor Rebellions*, Longman

Graves, M.A.R. (1985) *The Tudor Parliaments, Crown, Lords and Commons, 1485–1603*, Longman

Grossell, D. (1998) *Henry VIII 1509–29*, London

Gunn, S.J. and Lindley, P.G. (eds) (1991) *Cardinal Wolsey – Church, State and Art*, Cambridge University Press

Guy, J. (1995) 'Henry VIII and His Ministers', *History Review*, No.23, December

Guy, J. (1988) *Tudor England*, Oxford University Press

Guy, J. (2000) Thomas More (Reputations Series), Hodder Arnold

Gwyn, P. (1990) *The King's Cardinal: The Rise and Fall of Thomas Wolsey*, Barrie & Jenkins

Haigh, C. (1975) *Reformation and Resistance in Tudor Lancashire*, Cambridge University Press

Haigh, C. (ed.) (1987) *The English Reformation Revised*, Cambridge University Press

Ives, E. (2004) *The Life and Death of Anne Boleyn*, WileyBlackwell

Lander, J.R. (1971) 'Bonds, Coercion and Fear; Henry VII and the Peerage' in J.G. Rowe and W.H. Stockdale, *Florilegium Historiale: Essays*, Toronto University Press

Loach, J. (1991) *Parliament Under the Tudors*, Clarendon Press

Lockyer, R. (1971) *Henry VII (Seminar Studies in History)*, Harper & Row

MacCulloch, D. (2003) *Reformation: Europe's House Divided*, Viking Books

Marius, R. (1984) *Thomas More: A Biography*, Dent

Randell, K. (1991) *Henry VIII and the Government of England*, Hodder & Stoughton

Randell, K. (2001) *Henry VIII and the Government of England* (2nd edn), Hodder & Stoughton

Ridley, J. (1982) *The Statesman and the Fanatic (Thomas Wolsey and Thomas More)*, Constable

Rogerson, D., Ellsmore, S. and Hudson, D. (2001) *The Early Tudors*, Hodder Murray

Scarisbrick, J.J. (1968) *Henry VIII*, Methuen

Scarisbrick, J.J. (1984) *The Reformation and the English People*, WileyBlackwell

Starkey, D. (1985) *The Reign of Henry VIII: Personalities and Politics*, Philip's

Starkey, D. (1986) 'After the Revolution' in C. Coleman and D.R. Starkey, *Revolution Reassessed: Revisions in the History of Tudor Government and Administration*, Oxford University Press

Whiting, R. (1989) *The Blind Devotion of the People: Popular Religion in the English Reformation*, Cambridge University Press

Glossary of key terms

The Act of Six Articles   Passed in 1539 the Act outlined the doctrinal position of Henry's Church in England and came down on the side of orthodox Catholicism

Agrarian society   A society and economy based on farming and working the land

Amicable Grant crisis   Wolsey's attempts to raise a non-parliamentary tax in 1525 in order to raise war funds for Henry VIII

Annates   The payments made to Rome by bishops when they took up their post for the first time

Anti-clericalism   Criticism of the practices and morality of the Catholic clergy

Appoint to benefices   Wolsey now had the authority, through Rome, to make clerical appointments in England

Attainder   An Act or Bill of Attainder is an Act of parliament which decrees that an accused person is guilty of treason with no requirement to prove it by precise points of law. The 'attainted' person is declared a traitor and is subject to the death penalty; his property is forfeited and his descendants disinherited

Attaint   To convict someone of treason

Benefice   A clerical position

Benefit of clergy   In English law, the benefit of clergy was originally a provision by which clergymen could claim that they were outside the jurisdiction of the secular courts and be tried instead under canon law

Bonds and recognisances   Contracts between the nobility and the Crown in which the aristocracy promised to remain loyal to the King

Caesaropapism   A political theory in which the head of state, notably the Emperor ('Caesar', by extension and 'equal' King), is also the supreme head of the Church ('papa', pope or analogous religious leader)

Chivalry   A medieval code relating to the forms and conventions of aristocratic warrior lifestyle

Clientele network   The ability of leading nobles to build a chain of connections with lesser nobles and gentry that served their own interests

Communion in both kinds   The Catholic Church stated that only the clergy received the bread and the wine at the Lord's Supper; the laity received only the bread as they were spiritually inferior. Protestant reformers disagreed and called for Communion in both kinds

Confraternities   Lay associations formed to pray for the souls of the dead

Consanguinity   The relationship between one person and another person's relatives by the sexual union of those two persons

Convocation   An assembly of clergy in the provinces of Canterbury (south) and York (north) to regulate the affairs of the Church

Council Learned in the Law   Established in 1495, the role of the council was to defend the King's position as a feudal landlord and make sure that he received all the financial dues owed to him

Court of Augmentations   Bureaucratic office set up by Cromwell to deal with the transfer of Church lands to the Crown

Court of Star Chamber   A royal law court that could be used by the King's subjects to get justice

Dispensation   An exemption, often given by the Pope, from an obligation of canon law

Ecclesiastical Council   A meeting of leading bishops to discuss the condition of the Church

Eltham Ordinances   A royal edict of 1526 that cut the number in the royal household

Enclosure   The process by which some commons (a piece of land owned by one person, but over which other people could exercise certain traditional rights, such as allowing their livestock to graze upon it), were fenced (*enclosed*) and *deeded* or *entitled* to one or more private owners, who would then enjoy the possession and profits of the land to the exclusion of all others

Episcopal see   A bishopric or the specific area over which a bishop has authority

Erastian kingship   A belief that the Church should be subordinate to the State

Evangelical   A term used to describe a reformer who believed in the authority of Scripture or God's Word

Excommunication   Exclusion from the communion of the Church

Fifteenths and tenths   The standard form of taxation in England paid by towns and boroughs to the Crown

First Fruits and Tenths   Any new benefice holder (e.g. a bishop) originally paid one years' income to the papacy, then after the 1534 Act of Supremacy, to the Crown. They also paid an annual levy of one-tenth the annual value of that benefice thereafter

Gentlemen of the Bedchamber   Henry's personal attendants and advisors

Great matter, the   refers to Henry's divorce crisis over his first marriage to Catherine of Aragon

Heterodox   Holding a religious opinion that altered from the one generally received

Holy League   Formed by Pope Julius II in 1511, the Holy League consisted of Spain, Venice and England

Humanism   An intellectual movement based on the study of the classical world

Indulgences   Pieces of paper signed by the Pope that could be purchased by the laity. The recipient of an indulgence was cleansed of sin

Justices of the peace   local commissioners entrusted with maintaining law and order in the localities

Legate a latere   A personal representative of the Pope, deputed for important diplomatic missions on the papacy's behalf

Leviticus   A book of the Old Testament from which Henry VIII found scriptural justification for his divorce from Catherine of Aragon

Lord Chancellor   One of the top political offices in sixteenth century England

Magnates   Magnates were leading nobles who possessed large amounts of land and political power

Mass   The Mass is the Eucharistic celebration in the Latin liturgical rites of the Roman Catholic Church

Papal bulls   Legal pronouncements from the Pope in Rome concerning the Church

Papal dispensation   An exemption from an obligation of canon law given by the papacy

Papal infallibility   The Pope was the sole authority on matters of doctrine – he could not be wrong

Papal primacy   The Pope was the spiritual head of the Catholic Church

Particularism   The concentration of power away from the centre of government and the pursuit of local interests at the expense of national ones

Penance   To reinforce repentance for sin through prayer, confession, fasting and good works

Praemunire   the judicial charge of acknowledging a foreign authority (Rome) over the Crown

Princes   The German princes were those leading nobles who ruled over the 400 or so semi-autonomous states in the Holy Roman Empire

Privy chamber   The King's private chamber at Court where he was waited on by the gentlemen of the privy chamber. It was here that political decisions were increasingly made

Privy Council   Inner cabinet consisting of the King's leading ministers

Probate courts   Ecclesiastical courts dealing with wills left by the laity that often included monetary donations to the Church

Purgatory   A place of punishment where those who have died with some sins unforgiven must go until they have done sufficient penance

Radicals v conservatives   The key factional battle at court during the lengthy and winding road towards divorce

Real presence   The Real Presence is the term various Christian traditions use to express their belief that, in the Eucharist, Jesus Christ is *really* (and not merely symbolically, figuratively or by his power) present in what was previously just bread and wine. Radical reformers rejected the Real Presence

Reformation   An ideological and doctrinal challenge to the Catholic Church

Reformation Parliament   The name given to the seven sessions of parliament that met on and off 1529–36. The legislation began as an attack on the clergy and a warning to Rome, but it increasingly served to sever links with the Papacy and assert Henry's control over the Church in England

Regency government   A government that rules a country on behalf of someone else

Renaissance   The revival of classical literature and artistic styles over the course of the fourteenth to sixteenth centuries

Retaining   When a noble keeps a private army that owes loyalty first to him and then to the King

Revisionist historian   One who challenges accepted historical lines of argument and puts forward new ideas

Royal Almoner   A royal official whose task it is to distribute the king's alms (charity)

Royal Council   The king's main advisory body, made up of the most important political figures in the land

Royal Supremacy   the assertion of royal authority over Church and state

Sacrament   A sacrament is a holy rite instituted by Christ which assists individuals in their spiritual progress. The Catholic Church recognizes seven sacraments

Salvation   God's act of saving man from sin and conferring eternal happiness upon him through admission to Heaven

Statute of Uses   Law that changed the way in which property could be left in wills which highlighted the King's feudal right to claim property on the death of a tenant and was thus resented by the gentry

Subsidy   A tax granted to the Crown by parliament which assesses the amount to be paid on the graded wealth of individual taxpayers

Tithes   One tenth of the produce of land and livestock payable to the Church

Transubstantiation   The change of the substance of bread and wine into the Body and Blood of Christ occurring in the Eucharist according to the teaching of the Roman Catholic Church

***Valor* Ecclesiasticus**   The *Valor* was the result of Cromwell's ecclesiastical census and visitation of 1535. It gave the Crown a financial assessment of the wealth and condition of the Church

Vice gerent in spirituals   Title given by Henry VIII to Thomas Cromwell allowing Cromwell to make policy on religious as well as secular matters

Visitation   Inspection of a church or religious house by Crown commissioners

Vulgate   The Latin version of the Bible

Wars of the Roses   A series of civil wars in England, which started mid-fourteenth century during the weak monarchy of Henry VI

White Rose Party   Relatives of the Yorkist line replaced by Henry VII in 1485

Zwinglians   Followers of the Swiss reformer Zwingli, who were more radical than Lutherans in that they believed that the Eucharist was a purely symbolic ritual

Index

Page references in italics indicate illustrations.